Victorious Jesus!

Supreme Teacher &
Non-Violent Rebel With a Cause!

Mya Chavis
Enterprise™

Intrigue, Attract, Inspire

Mya A Chavis

All inquiries should be sent to support@myachavis.com

All author Inquiries should be sent to mya@myachavis.com

Written by Mya A Chavis

Mya Chavis Enterprise LLC

www.myachavis.com

TABLE OF CONTENTS

Matthew 4:19

DEDICATION

"I Dedicate this devotional to my resilient mother *Sharon W Chavis*.". The Strongest woman I know. She fought many fights. She won some fights. She lost some fights but she never backed down from a battle. Her highest depths of faith, were times she's has yet to realize.

Mya A Chavis

But thanks be unto God! He gives us the victory through our Lord Jesus Christ.

1 Corinthians 15:57

Luke 2:1-7

BIBLICAL CAUTIONING

" Fight the good fight of the faith. Take hold of the eternal life to which you were called when you made your good confession in the presence of many witnesses. In the sight of God, who gives life to everything, and of Christ Jesus ... From the days of John, the Baptist until now the kingdom of heaven suffered violence, and the violent take it by force. ...Thanks be unto God! He gives us the victory through our Lord Jesus Christ.

Ephesians 4 17-18, Matthew 11:12, 1
Corinthians 15:57

The Lamb of God, Promised Messiah

John 3:16

INTRODUCTION

Who was Jesus Christ? God who came forth as flesh. The man from Galilee. The one who departed His heavenly tenancy for the lost sheep(you & me) perishing to sin. Many have described him as, the *Lamb of God, The promised Messiah, Lion of Judah, Son of God, Lily of the Valley, The Great Physician, Teacher, Rabbi, Friend, King of the Jews, Healer, Provider, Protector, Lord* and *Savior, Immanuel, Mighty Counselor, Redeemer, Defender and Lover of My Soul, Bread of Life, Advocate, Wonderful, Son of God, Ruler of heaven and earth,* and *Nonviolent Rebel, A revolutionary with a very imperative cause.* There are many titles to describe His unique being. From his birth. Matthew 1:18-25, Matthew 2:1-12, Luke 1:26-38, Luke 2:1-7, Isaiah 7:14, Micah 5:2, John 1:1-14, The reign of his ministry Luke 4:14-30: Hebrews 5:1-10, Until his death, persecution and burial. Mark 15:22-47, Matthew 27:32-56, Luke 23:32-49, John 19:17-30, Matthew 26:57-68, Mark 14:43-65, Luke 22:47-53, John 18:1-27. Matthew 27:57-66, Notwithstanding His resurrection. Matthew 28:1-10, Matthew 28:16-20, Mark

16:1-8, Mark 16:9-14, Luke 24:1-12, Luke 24:13-35, Luke 24:36-49, John 20:1-18, John 20:19-29, John 21:1-23, 1 Corinthians 15:1-8, Acts 1:1-11. Undeniably "He Paid it All" His Love, the ransom for many. An "eternal liability" higher than the "*Global debt market*" which estimates to be about 305 trillion dollars. A debt that we could never afford to pay and no amount of worldly riches could satisfy. For the price was too steep and the stakes too high. Although He laid His life on the line allowing us to enter into eternal everlasting life it's important to recognize many are lovers of and confess God but far fewer that confess Jesus Christ as Lord

Matthew 24:10-20 NIV " *At that time many will turn away from the faith and will betray and hate each other, and many false prophets will appear and deceive many people. Because of the increase of wickedness, the love of most will grow cold, but the one who stands firm to the end will be saved.*"

Matthew 15:8-9 " *These people draw near to Me with their mouth, And honor Me with their lips, But their heart is far from Me. And in vain they worship Me, Teaching as doctrines the commandments of men.*"

As for me and mine. we will serve the Lord. By the time this "devotional study" is complete, you will Irrefutably understand why "Falling in Love with Jesus was the best thing I ever did". While we will intricately explore the focal point of "why" He is still very relevant today our main focus will be, Jesus the Supreme Teacher, His victories, the cost of discipleship, appropriate kingdom combat, and the greatest commandment. We are also going to dive into tussling with the demon of distraction, the great commission, ransom for sinners, His Kingdom's Ultimate Authority, and him being a Non-Violent Rebel with a very serious cause.

It is important to note that the connotation of the word "rebel" can vary depending on the situation and circumstance. It can be realized as courageous and admirable, particularly when challenging unjust, corrupt and convoluted authority. We use the term "Rebel" to explicitly elaborate on how Jesus challenged the status quo, and boldly rose in opposition employing "unarmed", and "nonviolent resistance", against misguided established religious leaders, rulers and chief priests of that day. Matthew 6:1-18, Matthew 23, Luke 6:41-42, 1 John 4:1-6, Proverbs 6:16-19, 2 Peter 2:20-22, Galatians 1:6-9, The connotation of the word "rebel" can vary depending on the perplexity of the situation and circumstance. It can be realized as courageous and admirable, particularly when challenging unjust, corrupt and convoluted authority. We use the term "Rebel" to explicitly elaborate on how Christ through His life & ministry challenged the "Status-Quo", and boldly rose in opposition employing an "unarmed", and "nonviolent resistance", against the established religious leaders, rulers and chief priests of His day. Matthew 6:1-18, Matthew 23, Luke 6:41-42, 1 John 4:1-6, Proverbs 6:16-19, 2 Peter 2:20-22, Galatians 1:6-9.

We in an elaborate way, analyze the courageous, bold, unorthodox, yet admirable actions that Jesus appropriated throughout His life and ministry to Spread the "Good News of the Gospel" to those who were lost, sick ostracized and severely demon-possessed, especially when it came to challenging a dishonorable, debauched, convoluted religious leadership, to the extent of what some might say, abused their power, to glorify "themselves" opposed to glorifying God. He defied the Pharisees and the Sadducees' authority because He was "The Infinite Authority" and all authority belonged to Him on Heaven and Earth. He spiritually challenged in a superior authoritative manner with sound doctrine and unmatched wisdom. On many occasions, this left the "Status Quo" awestruck and baffled. His bold authoritative actions could very well be interpreted as courageous and admirable, devoted at best. Especially, as He without thought stood up to what He deemed to be unjust, unethical, unfruitful religious officials, using its power in reckless and irresponsible ways that did not nurture or lead God's sheep towards the appropriate path in achieving salvation. In the same manner that the church of Thyatira false prophetess was leading it people astray. (Revelation 2:20). He boldly took an authoritative stance against the fruitless deeds of the societal, political, and religious legalistics of His era.

He authoritatively brought forth "kingdom resistance" to their "traditional established norms" by means of correcting, rebuking and dismissing many of their erroneous "self-glorified claims". Jesus openly resisted and renounced publicly, their false political narratives, that openly glorified man, as opposed to glorifying God.

What makes Him stand out above all? is that his "Holy Insurrection" never included "violent" or "hateful tactics". He publicly took a stance against them. In the most elegant tactful and precise manner, He rebelled against the societal, political, and religious influencers of His day with divine wisdom bestowed upon Him from the heavens. Heavenly Wisdom was His main weapon of defense. As much as He witnessed and which grieved Him within his heart," Violence and Hatred" were two tactics He never condoned.

Henceforth Jesus was indeed a Non-Violent Rebel with a very imperative cause. A cause that revolutionized new hope for sinners. That cause was the "Gift of Life" otherwise known as salvation. All the same, we live in a society where Jesus Christ is involuntarily being removed from nearly all aspects of societal life as we know it. Most of that having to do with the same politics that ruled the Sanhedrin over 3000 years ago. Today in many circumstances most military personnel are prohibited from openly praying while on active duty. It is against church and state to refer to Jesus in public places of business and most state-run college institutions (except for areas of approved allowed academic study). He's been taken out of the classroom. Removed from the courtroom. It's not even politically correct to say His name at an (AA) alcoholic anonymous meeting. Most modern-day gospel artists receiving mainstream music contracts are now no longer allowed to mention Jesus Christ name publicly in music songs or excerpts, if they do, His name is muffled and distorted to the point of non-recognition. That's more than likely so that they can cross-breed this socially correct form of "Modern Day Gospel Music" to anybody's god or anybody's religious gospel. By casually referring to the Son of God as "He" or "Him" all the time it opens the door to satan and his "Evasive Spiritual Cyanide Poisoning", a culture of worshipers slowly being converted into conformist. It is indeed a bittersweet money-making scheme the believers have to be mindful of. Jesus warned in His word "If you deny me before man, I will deny you before my Father in Heaven" Matthew 10:33. Little by little satan and this intrinsic Army are making bold moves to ensure that the King of kings, the one we call Jesus! he who is the "Christ", is permanently etched out of everyday current life and permanently blotted out of history. There have even been rumors of AI artificial intelligence programmers planning to re-write the Bible to make it more politically correct in efforts to appease such groups as LGBT, agnostics, scientologist as well as atheist communities. The world ruler of wickedness and his co army mean serious business. They are working overtime diligently; they are not letting up. It is up to us the believers to stay awake, prayed up, worded up that your gift of eternal life, your inheritance of salvation is not robbed from you. 2 Corinthians 2:11 so that we would not be outwitted by Satan; for we are not ignorant of his devices. This my friends, is only the beginning but be not dismayed because it is written that when heaven and earth pass away Gods word will never pass away. There is nothing that they can do to make Jesus Christ go away. There is nothing in their limited power that could deny his existence, who He was and inevitably what he stood for. Therefor we will also intricately focus on the "WHY Factor", Why Jesus Christ was relevant then and why he remains relevant now.

Jesus Christ Relevancies'

1. *He is the Son of God He sits at the Right hand of Yahweh:* "But from now on the Son of Man will be seated at the right hand of the power of God" (*Luke 22:69*).

2. *No one gets to the Father except by the son and no one gets to the Son except the Father*: "All things have been committed to me by my Father. No one knows the Son except the Father, and no one knows the Father except the Son and those to whom the Son chooses to reveal him" (*Matthew 11:27*).

3. *He came for the lost and the sick:* "Jesus answered them, 'It is not the healthy who need a doctor, but the sick. I have not come to call the righteous but sinners to repentance'" (*Luke 5:31-32*).

4. ***His sacrificial death made an appropriate atonement for the remission of sins***: "God presented Him as the atoning sacrifice through faith in His blood, in order to demonstrate His righteousness, because in His forbearance He had passed over the sins committed beforehand" (***Romans 3:25***).

5. ***All Authority on Heaven and Earth belongs to Him***: "Then Jesus came to them and said, 'All authority in heaven and on earth has been given to me" (***Matthew 28:18***).

6. ***He loves you as you are but he wants and expects you to keep his Law and Commandments***: "If you love me, keep my commandments" (***John 14:15***).

7. ***Every Word he Spoke is True and coming to Pass***: ""Every word of God proves true; he is a shield to those who take refuge in him. Do not add to his words, lest he rebuke you and you be found a liar." (**Proverbs 30:5-6**).

8. ***He holds the key to internal Life: "I am the living one***! I was dead, but now I am alive forever and ever. I have authority over death and the world of the dead" (***Revelation 1:18***).

9. ***There is power in Jesus Name to break every chain***: "In the name of Jesus Christ of Nazareth, rise up and walk!" (***Acts 3:6***).

10. *Any man be in Christ Jesus is a New Creation*: "Therefore if any man be in Christ, he is a new creature: old things are passed away; behold, all things are become new" (*2 Corinthians 5:17*).

11. *He who endures to the end and doesn't abandon their faith shall receive a "Crown of Life"*: "Blessed is the man that endureth temptation: for when he is tried, he shall receive the crown of life, which the Lord hath promised to them that love him" (*James 1:12*).

12. *Nothing "they" say, do or write can deny His existence*: "In the beginning was the Word, and the Word was with God, and the Word was God" (*John 1:1*).

13. *He reigned, was persecuted, then rose again just like he said He would*: "He is not here: for he is risen, as he said. Come, see the place where the Lord lay" (*Matthew 28:6*).

14. *No one gets to the Father except through the Son*: "Jesus saith unto him, I am the way, the truth, and the life: no man cometh unto the Father, but by me" (*John 14:6*).

The Lamb of God, Promised Messiah

Matthew 28:1

FAITHFUL LORD TO
THE FAITHLESS

The Word of God vividly explores Jesus' "Faithfulness to the Faithless" in several ways, outlining multiple aspects of His unwavering love and commitment to the lost and the faithless. In **Hebrews 3:2,** it is written that "*He was faithful to the One who appointed Him, just as Moses was faithful in all God's house*". Emphasizing Jesus' faithfulness to God His Father, who appointed and trusted Him to do his important work. Furthermore, He was just as faithful to lost sinners who were at risk of jeopardizing the opportunity to enter into eternal life due to their sinful nature and being born into sin, **2 Timothy 2:13** states that "*If we are faithless, he remains faithful [true to his word and his righteous character], for he cannot deny himself*". Highlighting Jesus' unwavering faithfulness to those who are His, even when they are faithless. God is married to the backslider. The word of God offers many aspects of Jesus' faithfulness to sinners even when (we) the sinners are not completely faithful to Him.

Nonetheless, Jesus continually dealt with sinners in a compassionate and merciful way indicative of non-violent fostering. He did not judge them with a harsh hand, but rather a "stern rebuke He showed them love and forgiveness. Jesus dealt with sinners with compassion, mercy, and love. He showed them forgiveness and grace, urging repentance of sin as a pre-requisite to eternal salvation. Urging them to choose salvation He welcomed them into His kingdom. (we) the sinners are not completely faithful to Him. Nonetheless, Jesus continually dealt with sinners in a compassionate and merciful way indicative of non-violent fostering. He did not judge them with a harsh hand, but rather a "stern rebuke He showed them love and forgiveness. Jesus dealt with sinners with compassion, mercy, and love. He showed them forgiveness and grace, urging repentance of sin as a pre-requisite to eternal salvation. Urging them to choose salvation He welcomed them into His kingdom.

1. ***The Parable of the Lost Sheep***: In *Luke 15:1-7,* Jesus compares himself to a shepherd who tirelessly searched for one lost sheep, leaving the ninety-nine safely behind. Symbolizing His determined love and pursuit of even those who stray from faith.

2. ***The Parable of the Prodigal Son***: *Luke 15:11-32* vividly illustrated a sequence of events, telling of a son who first demanded and squandered his inheritance, then returns home in a state of dyer

destitution. Despite the son's mistakes and disregard for order and authority, the Father welcomes him back home, unreservedly without thought or questions but with open arms and a thankful heart, demonstrating God's unconditional love and forgiveness towards those homesick, lost sheep who return and repent.

3. ***Jesus' Ministry to Outcasts and Sinners:*** Throughout His ministry, Jesus reached out to the marginalized, disregarded and ostracized, including tax collectors, prostitutes, demon possessed and the sick. He outright and boldly challenged *"extreme religious authorities"* who condemned and ostracized these groups, emphasizing God's mercy and desire for all whom confesses with their mouth and believe with their heart to experience His love.

4. ***The Crucifixion:*** The ultimate act of Jesus' faithfulness was His sacrifice on the cross. He willingly died in order for sinners to have everlasting life. Only *"His sacrificial shed blood"* would atone for the remission of sin. Although many rejected him and his teachings. This unprecedented act of devotion embodies God's boundless love and commitment to reconcile lost sinners to eternal life, despite their faithlessness.

5. ***The Promise of Redemption:*** Even in the face of widespread disbelief, hatred and rejection, Jesus remained faithful in His promises of ultimate reconciliation and redemption. He assures His followers that God's faithfulness will ultimately prevail, and all who repent of their sin and turn to Him will find forgiveness and eternal life.

6. ***Unwavering Love and Compassion:*** Jesus consistently extends love and compassion to those who doubt, even those who did not know Him and others who actively opposed Him. He engaged with the Samaritan woman at the well despite customary traditions and societal prejudices. He healed the daughter of a Canaanite woman who begged for His help, and countless times forgave His disciples for their moments of uncertainty.

7. ***Persistence and patience:*** Jesus doesn't give up on those who struggle with faith. Rather He forgives trespasses as he urges us to forgive one another's trespasses. He patiently explains complex concepts, answers their questions, and offers parables to illustrate His diverse Heavenly Wisdom. He understands that faith is a journey, not a destination, and encourages continued seeking, learning, praying, studying , meditating and growth.

8. ***Emphasis on action over words:*** Jesus emphasizes the importance of actions over mere belief. He teaches that true faith manifests in deeds, the overt actions of love, compassion, and service. He critiques those who claim to believe but lack corresponding actions, calling them "hypocrites." Calling all believers to be doers, not observers and spectators.

9. ***Parables of grace and forgiveness:*** Jesus illustrated parables such as, the Lost Sheep and the Prodigal Son to showcase God's unwavering love and forgiveness, even to those who stray. These scenarios emphasize God's willingness to welcome back the lost and celebrate their return. Along with Christ unmerited devotion to not see sinners perish.

10. ***Call to faith through repentance:*** While Jesus offers unconditional love, it is important to note that He also calls people to faith by way of ***"Repentance"***. He urges them to open their hearts to the word and instructions of God. Yet also to His teachings, commandments and warnings in order to embrace a destiny driven life transformed by God's grace.

11. ***Unwavering love:*** The Gospel of John emphasizes Jesus' unwavering love for the lost, even when faced with rejection and betrayal.

John 3:16 famously declares, "For God so loved the world that he gave his one and only Son, that whoever believes in him shall not perish but have eternal life." This verse exemplifies Jesus' unmerited love for the sinner who is called to repentance that he/she will not miss out on eternal life. Irregardless to circumstance sin is sin in the eyes of our Lord. Which is why all should seek the Lord while He may be found.

12. ***Parables of God's grace:*** Jesus often used parables to illustrate God's abundant grace and forgiveness. The parable of the lost sheep (*Luke 15:3-7)* portrays Jesus as the shepherd who relentlessly searches for a single lost sheep, representing God's unwavering pursuit of even those who stray from faith. Similarly, the parable of the prodigal son *(Luke 15:11-32)* showcases God's unconditional acceptance and love for those who repent and return to him.

Faithfulness to the faithless. A father to the fatherless, a doctor to the sick in the need of healing. Friend to the friendless. A Supreme teacher for those hungry for "Heavenly Wisdom". Even in the midst of His own suffering being absent from his treasured Kingdom in Heaven. Jesus, "Lord, in the flesh" suffered as we suffered, tempted as we were tempted, felt as we felt, even wept as we wept. Yet He stayed the course of His mission on earth to save the lost heal the sick and call sinners to repentance. Jesus' own life and ministry demonstrate His faithfulness amidst a faithlessness and ungrateful generation. He endured rejection, persecution, and ultimately, crucifixion, yet remained committed to His unyielding task of "love and redemption of sin". His sacrifice on the cross serves as the ultimate expression of God's faithfulness and love to his children, offering forgiveness and reconciliation even for even the greatest transgressions.

"Love" and "Faithfulness ='s Devotion". Ultimately devotion serves as two sides of the same coin, each contributing uniquely to the richness and complexity of a heartfelt bond and connection fundamentally and uniquely connected, creating an unmistakable unyielding tapestry of devoutness, commitment and dedication to an imperative cost. Jesus devoted His Life and ministry to the Lost Sheep of Israel.

Devotion: A core element of love is devotion, a steadfast commitment to another. Faithfulness embodies this devotion, translating it into consistent action and unwavering, sometimes unexplainable presence. It is the act of choosing someone *[sinners of the world]* repeatedly over again, not just in moments of passion, but throughout the mysteries and constant rotation of life.

Sacrifice: Love often demands sacrifice, prioritizing the well-being of another above personal desires. Faithfulness puts these sacrifices into action, demonstrating a willingness to make difficult choices even when it's most challenging and difficult [*persecution for atonement of sin*]

Jesus love for sinners, the lost and the sick led to an unexplainable and undeniable devotion even unto His death. The price he paid with His own life. A price that no other was willing to pay especially, to sinners, outcast, demon possessed and the sick. Jesus calls His believers to demonstrate a life of faith through love, obedience, compassion, forgiveness and trust in God's promises. **Romans 10:9** states, "If you declare with your mouth, 'Jesus is Lord,' and believe in your heart that God raised him from the dead, *you will be saved*." This verse highlights the reciprocal nature of Jesus Christ faithfulness to the redemption of sin – God's faithfulness should inspire and motivate an unshakable faith, leading to salvation and eternal life.

2 Timothy 2:13 states that "*If we are faithless, he remains faithful [true to his word and his righteous character], for he cannot deny himself*" . *Isaiah 53 3 -12* "*He is despised and rejected by men, A Man of sorrows and acquainted with grief. And we hid, as it were, our faces from Him; He was despised, and we did not esteem Him. Surely He has borne our griefs And carried our sorrows; Yet we esteemed Him stricken, Smitten by God, and afflicted. But He was wounded for our transgressions, He was bruised for our iniquities; The chastisement for our peace was upon Him, And by His stripes we are healed. All we like sheep have gone astray; We have turned, every one, to his own way; And the Lord has laid on Him the iniquity of us all. He was oppressed and He was afflicted,*

Yet He opened not His mouth; He was led as a lamb to the slaughter, And as a sheep before its shearers is silent, So He opened not His mouth. He was taken from prison and from judgment, And who will declare His generation? For He was cut off from the land of the living; For the transgressions of My people He was stricken. And they made His grave with the wicked — But with the rich at His death, Because He had done no violence, Nor was any deceit in His mouth. Yet it pleased the Lord to bruise Him; He has put Him to grief. When You make His soul an offering for sin, He shall see His seed, He shall prolong His days, And the pleasure of the Lord shall prosper in His hand. He shall see the labor of His soul, and be satisfied. By His knowledge My righteous Servant shall justify many, For He shall bear their iniquities. Therefore I will divide Him a portion with the great, And He shall divide the spoil with the strong, Because He poured out His soul unto death, And He was numbered with the transgressors, And He bore the sin of many, And made intercession for the transgressors".

Isaiah 53 the Old Testament of the Bible intricately prophesied the portrayal of the suffering "Servant Messiah" paying the ultimate cost for the Redemption of sin. It vividly defines how the Messiah was ***despised*** and ***rejected*** by men yet remained faithful to the very end, He was indeed the root of David, the tender plant, and the right arm of the LORD. It also declares that He will be a light, savior and restorer for many nations. The one true Promised Risen Messiah a savior for His people. Jesus showed his faithfulness to people in many ways during his earthly ministry. Here are some examples:

1. *He healed the sick:* Jesus had compassion for those who were sick and suffering, and he healed many people of their illnesses .

2. *He raised the dead*: Jesus raised Lazarus and others from the dead after Lazarus had been in the grave for three days, demonstrating his love and power .

3. *He fed the hungry:* Jesus fed a crowd of over 5,000 people with just five loaves of bread and two fish, showing his love and compassion for those who were hungry .

4. *He preached the kingdom:* Jesus taught people about the kingdom of God and how they could be a part of it, showing his love for all people .

5. *He forgave sins:* Jesus forgave sins and showed mercy to those who had sinned, demonstrating his love and grace .

6. *He welcomed children:* Jesus welcomed children and blessed them, showing his love for the little ones .

7. *He died for us:* Jesus showed his ultimate love for us by dying on the cross for our sins, so that we could be reconciled to God .

Reflecting on the prophecies fulfilled at the cross will deepen our understanding of Jesus' message and ministerial purpose here on earth. The fact that Jesus remained faithful to God even in the face of unmeasurable suffering should serve as a source of strength and inspiration for believers facing their own spiritual challenges. It demonstrates the power of faith and conviction to overcome adversity. Jesus' actions on the cross epitomizes as an ultimate display of love and compassion. He endured suffering and humiliation, even praying for His tormentors, despite His own agony. Jesus' prayer for his enemies on the cross embodies the ultimate act of forgiveness. The cross by its own recognizance is a symbol of victory over sin and death. Jesus' sacrifice paid the penalty for our sins, offering us the hope of eternal life and forgiveness. Jesus' example of selflessness and sacrifice should very well inspire us to live a life that prioritizes love and service to others. The prophecies fulfilled at the cross demonstrates God's incredible love for us. He was willing to send His own Son to suffer and die for our sins, showing the depth of His compassion and commitment to our redemption. This can bring us comfort, hope, and a sense of security in God's presence. Seeing these prophecies unfold centuries beforehand, confirms Jesus's claim to be the Promised Messiah and validates His assignment of redemption. This strengthens the believer's faith and provides validity in his teachings.

Prophecies Fulfilled at the Cross

➢ *He was forsaken* (Zech.13:7, Matt. 26:56)

➢ *He was crucified* (Matt. 27:24, John 20:25)

➢ *His garments were divided* (Ps. 22:18 Matt 27:35)

➢ *He was ridiculed and taunted* (Ps. 22:18, Matt. 27:39-41

➢ *He was looked upon with sneering* (PS. 69 21: Luke 23:35)

➢ *He was given sour wine with gall* (Ps. 69:21, Matt. 27:34, 48)

➢ *He cried from the cross* (Ps. 22:1 Mark 15:34)

➢ *He Prayed for His enemies* (Is. 53:12, Luke 23:34)

➢ *He had no bones broken* (Ps. 34.20, John 19:33)

➢ *He had his side pierced* (Zech. 12:10, John19:34)

➢ *He was in darkness* (Amos 8:9, Matt 27:45)

➢ *He was buried in a rich man's tomb* (Is.53-9, Matt. 27:50-60)

NON-VIOLENT REBEL

J*obn 1 17:* "For the law was given through Moses, but "*grace*" and "*truth*" came through Jesus Christ. Jesus was inaugurated by God His Father in the most authentic charismatic ways imaginable, ways Moses could not, showcasing Him most merciful and loving as no other god presented before Him. Jesus, as the Word of God, made flesh, represents the ultimate truth about God and His people. Jesus', life, purpose and ministry embodied the truest "purpose" and "meaning" of the Law in-and-of-itself, surpassing legalistic rules, traditions and callous rituals. We will examine the law as it relates to Mosaic customs, grace and truth along with the unconventional way He communicated, corrected and related it to elders, Leaders and chief priest making Him in addition to Lord & Savior; one of the boldest "Non-Violent Rebels of all time". To further this context, we will also examine the Emotions of Jesus. *With Him being God in the flesh having "Carnal Emotions" which out rightly gave Him the ability to feel ,*

the same joy, sorrows and love that we are able to feel. Essentially revolutionizing faith as we know it.

➢ **Law** in terms of "Biblical Chronology" refers to ancient Mosaic Law, given to the Israelites through Moses. It served as religious standards and strict code of conduct, enforcing God's requirements and regulations pertaining to human sinfulness. (Genesis 4:13) (Leviticus 26:41) (Job 19:29) (Psalm 149:7) (Lamentations 4:22) (Ezekiel 14:10).

Types of punishment the Law encompassed as penalties for sin was

1. **Death:** This was the maximum penalty for crimes such as murder, adultery, blasphemy, idolatry, homosexuality, witchcraft, and rebellion against parents. The methods of execution included stoning, burning, beheading, and hanging. (Exodus 19:13,32:27) (Numbers 25:7) (1 Kings 2:25,34; 19:1) (2 Chronicles 21:4)

2. **Stripes:** This was a merciless form of corporal punishment that involved whipping or flogging the offender with a rod or a lash. The number of stripes was limited to forty, but usually reduced to thirty-nine to avoid exceeding the limit 34.(Deuteronomy 25 1-4)

3. ***Imprisonment:*** This was a rare punishment in ancient Israel, as there were no official formal prisons or jails. Offenders were usually confined in a house, a pit, or a cage, often without food or water . (Revelation 2:10) (Luke 12:58) (Matthew 5:25-26) (2 Corinthians 6:5)

4. ***Payment of money:*** This was a way of compensating the injured party or the community for the damage or loss caused by the offender. The amount of money was either fixed by the law or determined by the victim. Sometimes, the offender could also offer an animal or a crop as a substitute for money . (Exodus 21:18-36) (Leviticus 24:18-21; 19:21)

5. ***Stoning :*** The Mosaic Law established stoning as a form of extreme force of "Mob-Justice" utilized as a severe form of capital punishment for several crimes, including adultery, blasphemy, child sacrifice, and bestiality. (Exodus 17:4) (Luke 20:6)(John 10:31) (Acts 14:5).

6. ***Burning :*** The Mosaic Law boldly provided the heartless utensil of "burning" as a method of executing the death penalty to be inflicted upon those persons convicted of the following offenses: adultery (for a married woman and her lover), bestiality, blasphemy, child sacrifice, idolatry, incest, rebellion against parents,

sodomy, and witchcraft. (Genesis 38:24) (Leviticus 21:9).

7. **_Strangulation:_** The Mosaic Law provided for the "death by strangulation" as an executable death penalty to be inflicted upon those persons convicted of the following offenses: adultery (for a married woman and her lover), bestiality, blasphemy, child sacrifice, idolatry, incest, rebellion against parents, sodomy, and witchcraft.

8. **_Beheading:_** A cruel and heinous form of Mosaic Law that provided for the death by the severing of one's head. This abrasive death sentence was to be inflicted upon those persons convicted of the following offenses: adultery (for a married woman and her lover), bestiality, blasphemy, child sacrifice, idolatry, incest, rebellion against parents, sodomy, and witchcraft. (Exodus 19:13; 32:27) (Numbers 25:7)

➢ **_By Contrast "Grace"_** represents God's unmerited love, forgiveness and favor freely bestowed upon those who **_believe_** and **_repent_** through Jesus Christ. It's not earned and can't be bought but is offered as Gods personal gift, rendering forgiveness and reconciliation despite our sinful shortcomings and carnal nature.

1. ***Ephesians 2:8-9*** "For it is by grace you have been saved, through faith and this *is not from yourselves, it is the gift of* God not by works, so that no one can boast."

2. ***John 3:16*** "For God so loved the world that he gave His only begotten Son, that whoever believes in him shall not perish but have eternal life."

3. ***James 2:17,*** "In the same way, faith by itself, if it is not accompanied by action, is dead."

4. ***Romans 5:8,*** "While we were still sinners, Christ died for us."

5. ***Romans 5:2,*** "Through him we have obtained access by faith into this grace in which we stand,".

6. ***Romans 6:23,*** "the wages of sin is death, but the gift of God is eternal life in Christ Jesus our Lord."

"Mosaic Law" and "Grace" offer opposing approaches in achieving righteousness that "appropriately" atones for sin, satisfying the will of God: redeeming the sinner from the life sentence of eternal death. Mosaic Law emphasizes external behavior relating to adherence of rules, rituals and traditions, while Grace focuses on an "Inward Spiritual Transformation" based on repentance and faith in Jesus Christ. Mosaic Law aims to set apart

God's chosen people, while Grace seeks to reconcile all sinners who repent to Gods everlasting salvation. Salvation under Mosaic Law is only achieved through perfect obedience of rules, practices and rituals, while Grace offers forgiveness and redemption as a gift from God. The relationship with God under Mosaic Law is based on obedience through fear and perfect adherence to the established guidelines , while Grace emphasizes love and mercy, forgiveness and redemption through Christ. Ultimately, Mosaic Law serves as a preliminary step to achieving Grace, which must fulfill its principles at a deeper level that frees believers from the Law's affliction and liability. Only the shedding of Christ Blood could achieve this purpose.

As a result of achieving this purpose, the nonviolent, revolutionary non-conformist way Jesus dealt with blind guides, hypocrites and false teachers who perverted the law; is what in fact made Him one of the boldest "*Non-Violent rebels* with a vital cause" of all time! His way of conducting "Kingdom Business" on earth during his active ministry "revolutionized" faith, salvation and redemption as we know it. As they knew it and as the world came to know it. Many weren't ready than and most are ready now. Nonetheless his Spiritual Legacy will live on to the believers until the second coming of Christ.

He showed Mercey and compassion to the Woman caught in the act of adultery

"Let him without sin cast the first stone at her". J*obn 8:7.*

He called out Hypocrisy

And why do you look at the speck in your brother's eye, but do not consider the plank in your own eye? **Matthew 7:3**

He healed on the Sabbath,

" Then He said to them, "What man is there among you who has one sheep, and if it falls into a pit on the Sabbath, will not lay hold of it and lift it out? Of how much more value then is a man than a sheep? Therefore it is lawful to do good on the Sabbath." Then He said to the man, "Stretch out your hand." And he stretched it out, and it was restored as whole as the other. Then the Pharisees went out and plotted against Him, how they might destroy Him". **Matthew 12 11-14**

He justified his disciples who plucked the grain from the fields on the Sabbath

Jesus Is Lord of the Sabbath

" Now it happened that He was passing through some grainfields on a Sabbath; and His disciples were picking the heads of grain, rubbing them in their hands, and eating the grain. But some of the Pharisees said, "Why do you do what is not lawful on the Sabbath?" And Jesus answering them said, "Have you not even

read what David did when he was hungry, he and those who were with him, how he entered the house of God, and took and ate the consecrated bread which is not lawful for any to eat except the priests alone, and gave it to his companions?" And He was saying to them, "The Son of Man is Lord of the Sabbath."

On another Sabbath He entered the synagogue and was teaching; and there was a man there whose right hand was withered. The scribes and the Pharisees were watching Him closely to see if He healed on the Sabbath, so that they might find reason to accuse Him. But He knew what they were thinking, and He said to the man with the withered hand, "Get up and come forward!" And he got up and came forward. And Jesus said to them, "I ask you, is it lawful to do good or to do harm on the Sabbath, to save a life or to destroy it?" After looking around at them all, He said to him, "Stretch out you" **Luke 6:1**

He cleared the temple and called out false teachers.

Jesus Cleanses the Temple

" Now the Passover of the Jews was at hand, and Jesus went up to Jerusalem. And He found in the temple those who sold oxen and sheep and doves, and the money changers doing business. When He had made a whip of cords, He drove them all out of the temple, with the sheep and the oxen, and poured out the changers' money and overturned the tables. And He said to those who sold doves, "Take these things away! Do not make My Father's house a house of merchandise!" Then His disciples remembered that it was written,

"Zeal for Your house has eaten Me up." So the Jews answered and said to Him, *"What sign do You show to us, since You do these things?"* Jesus answered and said to them, *"Destroy this temple, and in three days I will raise it up. "*Then the Jews said, *"It has taken forty-six years to build this temple, and will You raise it up in three days?"* But He was speaking of the temple of His body. Therefore, when He had risen from the dead, His disciples remembered that He had said this to them; and they believed the Scripture and the word which Jesus had said *John 2:13-25*

He ate with, tax collectors and sinners.

" As he walked along, he saw Levi son of Alphaeus sitting at the tax collector's booth. "Follow me," Jesus told him, and Levi got up and followed him. While Jesus was having dinner at Levi's house, many tax collectors and sinners were eating with him and his disciples" Mark 2:13-1

He hung out with prostitutes

"And certain women, which had been healed of evil spirits and infirmities, Mary called Magdalene, out of whom went seven devils, Luke 8:2

The Samaritan Women at the well meets her Messiah

" Then the woman of Samaria said to Him, "How is it that You, being a Jew, ask a drink from me, a Samaritan woman?" For Jews have no dealings with Samaritans. Jesus answered and said to her,

"If you knew the gift of God, and who it is who says to you, 'Give Me a drink,' you would have asked Him, and He would have given you living water." The woman said to Him, "Sir, You have nothing to draw with, and the well is deep. Where then do You get that living water? Are You greater than our father Jacob, who gave us the well, and drank from it himself, as well as his sons and his livestock?"

Jesus answered and said to her, "Whoever drinks of this water will thirst again, but whoever drinks of the water that I shall give him will never thirst. But the water that I shall give him will become in him a fountain of water springing up into everlasting life." The woman said to Him, "Sir, give me this water, that I may not thirst, nor come here to draw." Jesus said to her, "Go, call your husband, and come here." The woman answered and said, "I have no husband." Jesus said to her, "You have well said, 'I have no husband,' for you have had five husbands, and the one whom you now have is not your husband; in that you spoke truly." The woman said to Him, "Sir, I perceive that You are a prophet. Our fathers worshiped on this mountain, and you Jews say that in Jerusalem is the place where one ought to worship." Jesus said to her, "Woman, believe Me, the hour is coming when you will neither on this mountain, nor in Jerusalem, worship the Father. You worship what you do not know; we know what we worship, for salvation is of the Jews. But the hour is coming, and now is, when the true worshipers will worship the Father in spirit and truth; for the Father is seeking such to worship Him. God is Spirit, and those who worship Him must worship in spirit and truth." The woman said to Him, "I know that Messiah is coming" (who is called Christ). "When He comes, He will tell us all things." Jesus said to her, "I who speak to you am He." *John 4:1-42,*

He rebukes the chief priest along with their distorted misconceptions and did it without fear.

Woe to the Scribes and Pharisees

Then Jesus spoke to the multitudes and to His disciples, saying: "The scribes and the Pharisees sit in Moses' seat. Therefore whatever they tell you to observe, that observe and do, but do not do according to their works; for they say, and do not do. For they bind heavy burdens, hard to bear, and lay them on men's shoulders; but they themselves will not move them with one of their fingers. But all their works they do to be seen by men. They make their phylacteries broad and enlarge the borders of their garments. They love the best places at feasts, the best seats in the synagogues, greetings in the marketplaces, and to be called by men, 'Rabbi, Rabbi.' But you, do not be called 'Rabbi'; for One is your Teacher, the Christ, and you are all brethren. Do not call anyone on earth your father; for One is your Father, He who is in heaven. And do not be called teachers; for One is your Teacher, the Christ. But he who is greatest among you shall be your servant. And whoever exalts himself will be humbled, and he who humbles himself will be exalted.

"But woe to you, scribes and Pharisees, hypocrites! For you shut up the kingdom of heaven against men; for you neither go in yourselves, nor do you allow those who are entering to go in. Woe to you, scribes and Pharisees, hypocrites! For you devour widows' houses, and for a pretense make long prayers. Therefore you will receive greater condemnation.

"Woe to you, scribes and Pharisees, hypocrites! For you travel land and sea to win one proselyte, and when he is won, you make him twice as much a son of hell as yourselves.

"Woe to you, blind guides, who say, 'Whoever swears by the temple, it is nothing; but whoever swears by the gold of the temple, he is obliged to perform it.' Fools and blind! For which is greater, the gold or the temple that sanctifies the gold? And, 'Whoever swears by the altar, it is nothing; but whoever swears by the gift that is on it, he is obliged to perform it.' Fools and blind! For which is greater, the gift or the altar that sanctifies the gift? Therefore he who swears by the altar, swears by it and by all things on it. He who swears by the temple, swears by it and by Him who dwells in it. And he who swears by heaven, swears by the throne of God and by Him who sits on it.

"Woe to you, scribes and Pharisees, hypocrites! For you pay tithe of mint and anise and cummin, and have neglected the weightier matters of the law: justice and mercy and faith. These you ought to have done, without leaving the others undone. Blind guides, who strain out a gnat and swallow a camel!

"Woe to you, scribes and Pharisees, hypocrites! For you cleanse the outside of the cup and dish, but inside they are full of extortion and self-indulgence. Blind Pharisee, first cleanse the inside of the cup and dish, that the outside of them may be clean also.

"Woe to you, scribes and Pharisees, hypocrites! For you are like whitewashed tombs which indeed appear beautiful outwardly, but inside are full of dead men's bones and all uncleanness. Even so you also outwardly appear righteous to men, but inside you are full of hypocrisy and lawlessness.

"Woe to you, scribes and Pharisees, hypocrites! Because you build the tombs of the prophets and adorn the monuments of the righteous, and say, 'If we had lived in the days of our fathers, we would not have been partakers with them in the blood of the prophets.'

"Therefore you are witnesses against yourselves that you are sons of those who murdered the prophets. Fill up, then, the measure of your fathers' guilt. Serpents, brood of vipers! How can you escape the condemnation of hell? Therefore, indeed, I send you prophets, wise men, and scribes: some of them you will kill and crucify, and some of them you will scourge in your synagogues and persecute from city to city, that on you may come all the righteous blood shed on the earth, from the blood of righteous Abel to the blood of Zechariah, son of Berechiah, whom you murdered between the temple and the altar. Assuredly, I say to you, all these things will come upon this generation. *Mathew 23*

He never "copped-out" to vain repetitious traditions

"He said to them, 'Isaiah was right when he prophesied about you hypocrites: "This people honor me with their lips, but their hearts are far from me. They worship me in vain, teaching human traditions as doctrines." And you have neglected the commandment of God and hold on to human traditions Mark 7:6-8... "Not everyone who says to me, 'Lord, Lord,' will enter the kingdom of heaven, but only the one who does the will of my Father in heaven.

Many will say to me on that day, 'Lord, Lord, did we not prophesy in your name and cast out demons in your name and do many great things in your name?' Then I will declare to them, 'I never knew you. Depart from me, you who practice lawlessness **Matthew 7:21-23:**

He took the brutality of persecution like no one else could.

"Then Pilate took Jesus and flogged him. And the soldiers twisted thorns into a crown and put it on his head, and they arrayed him in a purple robe. They came up to him and said, 'Hail, King of the Jews!' And they struck him on the face with their hands." John 19:1-3 ... "So Pilate, wanting to gratify the crowd, released Barabbas to them and handed Jesus over after he had him flogged. Then the soldiers led him away into the palace (that is, the governor's headquarters) and called together the whole battalion. They dressed him in a purple robe and put a crown of woven thorns on his head, and began to greet him, 'Hail, King of the Jews!' And they struck his head with a reed and spat on him and knelt down and worshiped him." **Mark 15:15-19:**

He showed women the utmost adoration, love and respect irregardless to their past

When she heard about Jesus, she came up behind him in the crowd and touched his cloak, because she thought, "If I just touch his clothes, I will be healed." Immediately her bleeding stopped and she felt in her body that she was freed from her suffering. At once Jesus realized that power had gone out from him. He turned around in

41

the crowd and asked, "Who touched my clothes?" "You see the people crowding against you," his disciples answered, "and yet you can ask, 'Who touched me?'" "But Jesus kept looking around to see who had done it. Then the woman, knowing what had happened to her, came and fell at his feet and, trembling with fear, told him the whole truth. He said to her, "Daughter, your faith has healed you. Go in peace and be freed from your suffering." *Mark 5 28-34*

He stood up for the children proclaiming them to be the greatest.

The Greatest in the Kingdom of Heaven

At that time the disciples came to Jesus and asked, "Who, then, is the greatest in the kingdom of heaven?" He called a little child to him, and placed the child among them. And he said: "Truly I tell you, unless you change and become like little children, you will never enter the kingdom of heaven. Therefore, whoever takes the lowly position of this child is the greatest in the kingdom of heaven. And whoever welcomes one such child in my name welcomes me. *Matthew 18 2-5*

On the mount he gave hope to the hopeless as issued the beatitudes.

Now when Jesus saw the crowds, he went up on a mountainside and sat down. His disciples came to him, and he began to teach them.

The Beatitudes He said:

"*Blessed are the poor in spirit, for theirs is the kingdom of heaven.*

Blessed are those who mourn, for they will be comforted.

Blessed are the meek, for they will inherit the earth. Blessed are those who hunger and thirst for righteousness, for they will be filled. Blessed are the merciful, for they will be shown mercy. Blessed are the pure in heart, for they will see God. Blessed are the peacemakers,

for they will be called children of God. Blessed are those who are persecuted because of righteousness, for theirs is the kingdom of heaven. "Blessed are you when people insult you, persecute you and falsely say all kinds of evil against you because of me. Rejoice and be glad, because great is your reward in heaven, for in the same way they persecuted the prophets who were before you. Mathew 5

He washed the disciples' feet.

It was just before the Passover Festival. Jesus knew that the hour had come for him to leave this world and go to the Father. Having loved his own who were in the world, he loved them to the end. The evening meal was in progress, and the devil had already prompted Judas, the son of Simon Iscariot, to betray Jesus. Jesus knew that the Father had put all things under his power, and that he had come from God and was returning to God; so he got up from the meal, took off his outer clothing, and wrapped a towel around his waist. After that, he poured water into a basin and began to wash his disciples' feet, drying them with the towel that was wrapped around him. He came to Simon Peter, who said to him, "Lord, are you

going to wash my feet?" Jesus replied, "You do not realize now what I am doing, but later you will understand." "No," said Peter, "you shall never wash my feet." Jesus answered, "Unless I wash you, you have no part with me." "Then, Lord," Simon Peter replied, "not just my feet but my hands and my head as well!" Jesus answered, "Those who have had a bath need only to wash their feet; their whole body is clean. And you are clean, though not every one of you." For he knew who was going to betray him, and that was why he said not everyone was clean. When he had finished washing their feet, he put on his clothes and returned to his place. "Do you understand what I have done for you?" he asked them. "You call me 'Teacher' and 'Lord,' and rightly so, for that is what I am. Now that I, your Lord and Teacher, have washed your feet, you also should wash one another's feet. I have set you an example that you should do as I have done for you. Very truly I tell you, no servant is greater than his master, nor is a messenger greater than the one who sent him. Now that you know these things, you will be blessed if you do them.
John 13:1-1

Though He was rich at home here, He had nowhere to lay His head. The son of Man was Homeless

And Jesus said to him, "Foxes have holes and birds of the air have nests, but the Son of Man has nowhere to lay His head. "
Matthew 8:20

He healed the ear of the soldier who peter cut off.

When Jesus' followers saw what was going to happen, they said, "Lord, should we strike with our swords?" And one of them struck the servant of the high priest, cutting off his right ear. But Jesus answered, "No more of this!" And he touched the man's ear and healed him. **Luke 22:49-51**

Jesus teaches to the Pharisee Nicodemus (His Opposition)

Now there was a Pharisee, a man named Nicodemus who was a member of the Jewish ruling council. He came to Jesus at night and said, "Rabbi, we know that you are a teacher who has come from God. For no one could perform the signs you are doing if God were not with him." Jesus replied, "Very truly I tell you, no one can see the kingdom of God unless they are born again."

"How can someone be born when they are old?" Nicodemus asked. "Surely they cannot enter a second time into their mother's womb to be born!" Jesus answered, "Very truly I tell you, no one can enter the kingdom of God unless they are born of water and the Spirit. Flesh gives birth to flesh, but the Spirit gives birth to spirit. You should not be surprised at my saying, 'You must be born again.' The wind blows wherever it pleases. You hear its sound, but you cannot tell where it comes from or where it is going. So it is with everyone born of the Spirit." "How can this be?" Nicodemus asked. "You are Israel's teacher," said Jesus, "and do you not understand these things? Very truly I tell you, we speak of what we know, and we testify to what we have seen, but still you people do not accept our testimony. I have spoken to you of earthly things and you do not

believe; how then will you believe if I speak of heavenly things? No one has ever gone into heaven except the one who came from heaven—the Son of Man. Just as Moses lifted up the snake in the wilderness, so the Son of Man must be lifted up, that everyone who believes may have eternal life in him." For God so loved the world that he gave his one and only Son, that whoever believes in him shall not perish but have eternal life. For God did not send his Son into the world to condemn the world, but to save the world through him. *Whoever believes in him is not condemned, but whoever does not believe stands condemned already because they have not believed in the name of God's one and only Son.* This is the verdict: Light has come into the world, but people loved darkness instead of light because their deeds were evil. Everyone who does evil hates the light, and will not come into the light for fear that their deeds will be exposed. But whoever lives by the truth comes into the light, so that it may be seen plainly that what they have done has been done in the sight of God. ***John 3:1-21***

His father was rich in houses and land, the creator of all, yet He remained humble

"They make their phylacteries wide and the tassels on their garments long. They love the place of honor at feasts and the best seats in the synagogues. They love to be greeted in the marketplaces and to be called 'Rabbi' by men." *Matthew 23:5*: ... " No one can serve two masters. Either you will hate the one and love the other, or you will be devoted to the one and despise the other. You cannot serve both God and money." ***Matthew 6:24:***

Women with the issue of Blood

*"But Jesus turned around, and when He saw her He said, "Be of good cheer, daughter; your faith has made you well." And the woman was made well from that hour **Matthew 9:22**".*

He chilled with His homies Moses & Elijah

Jesus Transfigured on the Mount

*" Now after six days Jesus took Peter, James, and John his brother, led them up on a high mountain by themselves; and He was transfigured before them. His face shone like the sun, and His clothes became as white as the light. And behold, Moses and Elijah appeared to them, talking with Him. Then Peter answered and said to Jesus, "Lord, it is good for us to be here; if You wish, let us make here three tabernacles: one for You, one for Moses, and one for Elijah." While he was still speaking, behold, a bright cloud overshadowed them; and suddenly a voice came out of the cloud, saying, "This is My beloved Son, in whom I am well pleased. Hear Him!" **Matthew 17:1-13***

In this context we recognize the use of the word "rebel" representing Jesus Christ as an honorable, faithful, fearless, heroic Lord and Savior. Unapologetically challenging and calling out an unjust, corrupt and convoluted authority that did not line up with God "his Fathers" Word nor Ideals. He challenged the "powers that be", the Chief Priest, Elders, Sadducees and Pharisees. Boldly He rose in opposition resisting their untruths. Employing an "unarmed", "nonviolent resistance", against the established religious, rulers and chief priest of that day. He stood His ground on "love" "Non-violence" and forgiveness. Wisdom, a Stern Rebuke and Heavenly Authority were his selected weapons of choice. There is no other god alive that exercised His authority in this manner. He made clear to his disciples that they ought not be afraid of their faces. *Matthew 10:28* "*And do not fear those who kill the body but cannot kill the soul. But rather fear Him who is able to destroy both soul and body in hell*". He rebuked his disciple Peter after he struck the soldier with a sword cutting of his ear. *Matthew 26:51-53* "*Put your sword back in its place," Jesus said to him, "for all who draw the sword will die by the sword. Do you think I cannot call on my Father, and he will at once put at my disposal more than twelve legions of angels?* Although he openly practiced the non-violent form of resistance that did not make Him in any way "soft" or "weak". When analyzing Jesus, as "God in the Flesh" He exemplified many human emotions most of which were that of love , compassion, and grief. There were only a few documented recordings of him being angry. Clearly without a shadow of a doubt the cleansing of the Temple was one that clearly made Him angry. Once again, we will focus on the possibilities of the "*why factor*".

- ✓ The disrespect, disregard and what a discourteous offense it was to the "Holiness of Gods' Sacred Temple".

- ✓ Their market practices and rituals served no relevant place for serving Gods' people Spiritually or Morally

- ✓ The Synagogue was originally purposed as a place of prayer and worship but where money is there greed is also

- ✓ Perhaps Jesus was looking for an intimate place to pray and commune with His Father instead he got a "religious circus"

- ✓ The Hygiene Factor with all the livestock and cage doves couldn't have pronounced a sweet pleasant aroma to God

- ✓ The Money Changers, you had all types of hustlers, fast talkers, loan sharks and tax collectors...They midst well had been playing craps on a cardboard for dollars.

- ✓ All in all, it was obvious that Jesus felt as if these thoughtless actions were the Ultimate disrespect to God his Father, the temple and what it was designed for

- ✓ God declared that "His Fathers House" shall be a House of Prayer and not a den of thieves.

The possibilities as to why Jesus angered to this degree are endless. One can only imagine the thoughts that ran rampant through His immortal mind. One thing was for certain two things, for sure, He didn't play about his church at all. When He saw unsatisfactory, corrupt and immoral things operating in the House of the Lord, it angered Him, just as it angered God. Assuredly it should anger us as well. Anger us to make a move that will either shed light or eradicate the outward source of "Spiritual Poison".

Jesus arrived as a "Spiritual Transformative Kingdom Shift". He dismantled the rigid framework of profitless external performances, replacing it with a transforming emphasis on inner faith, repentance and divine grace. Prior to Jesus, religious practice was a rigorous factory line of rituals, legalistic demands, and the ever-present spectator of divine judgment. Jesus broke the glass ceiling, shattering the old system, redefining faith, salvation and redemption with unconventional revolutionary acts of grace, healing, unmerited wisdom and unconditional love. This revolutionary approach Jesus Christ took for the lost, sick and demon possessed to be reconciled to God not only reshaped the practice by which faith itself was examined, but also redefined the very relationship between sinners, His chosen as well as the redeemed of God. Freed from the gruesome chains of repetitive tedious, ritualistic obligations; instead, faith was sovereignly repainted as a trust based, spiritual, connection, empowered by unmeasured gratitude and powered by grace. Through it all Jesus never gave up on us. He never threw us away although he had the power to. In this profound transformation, sinners, the lost, outcast and the ostracized found a new path to salvation through Jesus Christ the true "Promised Risen Messiah", but also an emancipation from the burden of satisfying the Law. Freed from the limitations of fruitless rituals and customary traditions, we became free from the law. Whom the son sets free is free indeed. Nobody in recorded history did it like Jesus. He was a "Non-Violent Rebel" for a very imperative cause. His ways, His Ministry, His teachings, His call, His purpose, His life, Death and Resurrection _revolutionized_ the grace we have obtained and how salvation is reached. There is nothing that the devil or the powers that be can do about it. He reins today and forevermore.

THE EMOTIONS OF JESUS CHRIST			
Incident Emotion Cause Jesus Reaction			
He meant a leaper (Mark 1:4)	Compassion	Leper begged for healing	He touched and healed them
Rich ruler came to him (Mark 10:21)	Love	Ministered to the young man	He told him what he lacked
5,000 followed Him (Matt 14:14)	Compassion	They had no Shephard	He fed and taught them
Pharisees demand a sign (Mark 8:11)	Distress	They wanted to entrap Him	Spoke the truth and left them
He healed on the Sabbath(Luke 7:9)	Greif, Anger	The hardness of their hearts	He challenged the Pharisees and left
He Cleared out the Temple (John 2:13)	Anger	Converted the Temple into a market place	Cleared the temple & chased away the money changers
4,000 followed Him (Mark 8;2)	Compassion	They were hungry	He fed them
A funeral passed (Luke 7:13-15)	Compassion	Widow lost her only son	He raised her son to Life
Crucified for the sins of the world (Ishia 53)	Love	Redemption of Sin	He died on the cross
He approached Lazarus tomb (John 11:38)	Greif	He comforted Mary & Martha	He raised Lazarus from the dead
The Last Supper (John 13:21)	Love	He knew he was leaving soon	He washed their feet
Entered Jerusalem (Matt 23:27)	Sorrow	Jerusalem coming destruction	He wept over the city

The Lamb of God, Promised Messiah

John 3:16

THE ATONEMENT OF SIN

Atonement for sin establishes a mandatory reconciliation between the sinful carnal nature of mankind and the Holy Sinless God, Yahweh. This acceptable reconciliation is only possible through the "atoning sacrifice" of Jesus Christ, as expressed in **Romans 3:25**, **Romans 5:11**, and **Romans 5:19**

A New Covenant

"*For this is the covenant that I will make with the house of Israel after those days, says the Lord: I will put My laws in their mind and write them on their hearts; and I will be their God, and they shall be My people. None of them shall teach his neighbor, and none his brother, saying, 'Know the Lord,' for all shall know Me, from the least of them to the greatest of them. For I will be merciful to their unrighteousness, and their sins and their lawless deeds I will remember no more." In that He says, "A new covenant," He has made the first obsolete. Now what is becoming obsolete and growing old is ready to vanish away.* **Hebrew 8 10-12**

The Fundamental Cruciality of Blood The Mediator's Death Necessary

For where there is a **testament,** there must also of necessity be the **death of the testator**. <u>For a testament is in force after men are dead, since it has no power at all while the testator lives</u>. Therefore, not even the first covenant was dedicated without blood. For when Moses had spoken every precept to all the people according to the law, he took the blood of calves and goats, with water, scarlet wool, and hyssop, and sprinkled both the book itself and all the people, saying, "This is the blood of the covenant which God has commanded you." Then likewise he sprinkled with blood both the tabernacle and all the vessels of the ministry. **<u>And according to the law almost all things are purified with blood, and without shedding of blood there is no remission. Hebrews 9 16-22</u>**

Christ by the shedding of "His Own Blood" is the Mediator of the "New Covenant" Hebrews 9 15:

But Christ came as High Priest of the good things to come, with the greater and more perfect tabernacle not made with hands, that is, not of this creation <u>Not with the blood of goats and calves, but with His own blood He entered the Most Holy Place once for all, having obtained eternal redemption</u>. For if the blood of bulls and goats and the ashes of a heifer, sprinkling the unclean, sanctifies for the purifying of the flesh, <u>how much more shall the blood of Christ, who through the eternal Spirit offered Himself without spot to God, cleanse your conscience from dead works to serve the living God?</u> And for this reason, He is the Mediator of the new covenant,

<u>*by means of death, for the redemption of the transgressions under the first covenant, that those who are called may receive the promise of the eternal inheritance.*</u> ***Hebrews 9 15:***

"Christ , as "High Priest" [over heaven] and of good things to come entered the "greater and more perfect tabernacle" in heaven. In the presence of God, the most holy place, <u>He offered his own blood.</u> What Jesus accomplished by this act was"...

- ➤ Eternal Redemption of sins
- ➤ Cleansing of the conscience of those saved from "*dead works*" and "*useless rituals*"

In contrast, the Levitical sacrifice could only cleanse "the flesh".

Why Christ death was necessary

This emphasizes the finality and irrevocable nature of Jesus Christ death as sacrifice. The testament (metaphorically operating as a living will) requires the death of the testator (the one making the covenant) in order for it to be valid. Reflecting the "early legal" understanding that a will only took effect after the person who made it died. While alive, the testator can always change or revoke the testament.

This symbolically emphasizes the finality and irrevocable nature of Jesus Christ sacrifice compared to the temporary offerings of the Old Covenant. Emphasizing the Necessity of "*Jesus Christ Death*", "*The*

Power of His Death" as well as the *"Uniqueness of A Brand-New Covenant".* It essentially jump started the new covenant into effect. The first covenant (the Old Covenant) wasn't truly effective or legally binding to God because it didn't involve any relevance to a "permanent sacrifice". The primitive death of animals, the temporary nature of the offerings, couldn't provide the ***lasting forgiveness*** , ***reconciliation with God*** and ***redemption of sins*** that the death of Jesus Christ on the cross achieved.

> ➤ It made it possible for redemption of transgressions
> ➤ Set forth an eternal inheritance
> ➤ Satisfied the debt for forgiveness for sins
> ➤ It purified heavenly things

Christ bore the sins of many

"He has appeared to put away sin by the sacrifice of Himself. And as it is appointed for men to die once, but after this the judgment, so Christ was offered once to bear the sins of many. To those who eagerly wait for Him He will appear a second time, apart from sin, for salvation." ***Hebrews 9 26:28***

Only Jesus Christ Death could Fulfill God's Will

"Therefore, when He came into the world, He said:

*"Sacrifice and offering You did not desire, But a body You have prepared for Me. In burnt offerings and sacrifices for sin You had no pleasure. **Then I said, 'Behold, I have come In the volume of the book it is written of Me To do Your***

will, O God.' " Previously saying, "Sacrifice and offering, burnt offerings, and offerings for sin You did not desire, nor had pleasure in them" (which are offered according to the law), then He said, "**Behold, I have come to do Your will, O God.**" He takes away the first that He may establish the second. By that will we have been sanctified through the offering of the body of Jesus Christ once for all. Hebrews 10 5:10."

Christ's Death Perfects the Sanctified

And every priest stands ministering daily and offering repeatedly the same sacrifices, which can never take away sins. But this Man, after He had offered one sacrifice for sins forever, sat down at the right hand of God, from that time waiting till His enemies are made His footstool. For by one offering He has perfected forever those who are being]sanctified. But the Holy Spirit also witnesses to us; for after He had said before, "This is the covenant that I will make with them after those days, says the Lord: I will put My laws into their hearts, and in their minds I will write them," then He adds, "Their sins and their lawless deeds I will remember no more." Now where there is remission of these, there is no longer an offering for sin.

By the shedding of Christ Blood there is "Redemption of sins"

"Behold! The Lamb of God who takes away the sin of the world! *John 1 29* . For all have sinned and fallen short of the glory of God, being justified freely by His grace through the redemption that is in Christ Jesus, whom

God set forth as a propitiation by His blood, through faith, to demonstrate His righteousness, because in His forbearance God had passed over the sins that were previously committed, *Romans 3:23-25* In Him we have redemption through His blood, the forgiveness of sins, according to the riches of His grace which He made to abound toward us in all wisdom and prudence, *Ephesians 1:7-8.*

Never Forget what Christ sacrificed for you!

Therefore, brethren, having boldness to enter the Holiest by the blood of Jesus, by a new and living way which He consecrated for us, through the veil, that is, His flesh, and having a High Priest over the house of God, let us draw near with a true heart in full assurance of faith, having our hearts sprinkled from an evil conscience and our bodies washed with pure water. *Let us hold fast the confession of our hope without wavering, for He who promised is faithful.*

He Graced us to be Gracious to one another never taking advantage of His Grace

Remind them to be subject to rulers and authorities, to obey, to be ready for every good work, to speak evil of no one, to be peaceable, gentle, showing all humility to all men. For we ourselves were also once foolish, disobedient, deceived, serving various lusts and pleasures, living in malice and envy, hateful and hating one another.

But when the kindness and the love of God our Savior toward man appeared, not by works of righteousness which we have done, but according to His mercy He saved us, through the washing of regeneration and renewing of the Holy Spirit, whom He poured out on us abundantly through Jesus Christ our Savior, that having been justified by His grace we should become heirs according to the hope of eternal life. *TITUS 3*

Beware of Antichrist Deceivers

For many deceivers have gone out into the world who <u>do not confess Jesus Christ as coming in the flesh</u>. This is a deceiver and an antichrist. Look to yourselves, that we do not lose those things we worked for, but that we may receive a full reward. *Whoever transgresses and does not abide in the doctrine of Christ does not have God. He who abides in the doctrine of Christ has both the Father and the Son. If anyone comes to you and does not bring this doctrine, do not receive him into your house nor greet him; for he who greets him shares in his evil deed 2 John 1 7:11*

The word "atone" is defined as amends or reparation, for an offense, sin, or a crime. God commanded Israel to set aside one day each year, the tenth day of the seventh month, which He called "the day of atonement" (Leviticus 16:29-30; 23:27-28). He specifically informed the children of Israel in the offering, an innocent animal sacrifice "whose blood was brought in to make atonement" (Leviticus 16:27). God had said, "For the life of the flesh is in the blood: and I have given it to you upon the altar to make an atonement for your souls: for it is the blood that maketh an atonement for the soul" (Leviticus 17:11) ". . . and without shedding of blood is no remission" (Hebrews 9:22). Consequently, the offering of animal's blood for an atonement would no longer due. Only the priceless "Blood of the Lamb" would suffice. For the first covenant was no longer acceptable to provide the lasting forgiveness, reconciliation with God and redemption of sin, that would atone for man's sin. Christ death as a sacrifice for sinners for man's sin was necessary because only Jesus' blood serves as the atoning sacrifice that satisfied God's Prerequisites.

The word "atone" is defined as amends or reparation, for an offense, sin or a crime. In the time of ancient Israel God commanded the state of Israel to set aside one day each year, the tenth day of the seventh month, which He called "the day of atonement" *(Leviticus 16:29-30; 23:27-28)*. He specifically informed the children of Israel in offering, an innocent animal sacrifice "whose blood was brought in to make atonement" *(Leviticus 16:27)*. God had said, "For the life of the flesh is in the blood: and I have given it to you upon the altar to make an atonement for your souls: for it is the blood that maketh an atonement for the soul" *(Leviticus 17:11)* ". . . and without shedding of blood is no remission" *(Hebrews 9:22)*. Consequently, the offering of animal's blood for an atonement would no longer due. Only the priceless "Blood of the Lamb" would be suffice. For the first covenant was no longer acceptable to provide the, lasting forgiveness , reconciliation with God and redemption of sin, that would atone for man's sin. Christ death as a sacrifice for sinners for man's sin was necessary because

- ➢ It made it possible for the redemption of transgressions
- ➢ Set forth an eternal inheritance
- ➢ Satisfied the debt of forgiveness for sins
- ➢ It purified heavenly things
- ➢ And Gave Birth to a New Covenant

Through the "atonement of sin" by way of Jesus shedding blood on the cross "Gods' redeemed" have been reconciled to Christ through the redemption of sin. Christ bore the sins of many even though he didn't have to. Only Jesus Christ Death could Fulfill God's Will. Jesus Christ's Death Perfected the Sanctified. By the shedding of Christ Blood (And only His Blood) there is" Redemption of sins. Never Forget what Christ sacrificed for you! He Graced us to be Gracious to one another, never taking advantage of His Grace. Beware of Antichrist Deceivers. By grace and mercy, He is with us always, even to the end of the age.

Jesus Christ's victory over sin through the Atonement is significant and shouldn't be taken for granted:

Immensity of Sin: Sin's burden weighs heavily on individuals and can cost the believer "eternal life". It severs connections and relationships with God, oneself, and others, leading to suffering and isolation. The Bible teaches us that sin has a profound impact on the life of a believer. It can rob them of their ability to understand spiritual truth and quench the teaching ministry of the Holy Spirit. Sin can also cause a believer to lose the joy of their salvation and seek worldly pleasures to fill the void. The immensity of sin can negatively impact the eternal life of a believer in several ways. For instance, it can cause a believer to lose their spiritual sensitivity and become desensitized to sin. It can also lead to a hardening of the heart and a loss of spiritual discernment.

Cost of Victory: Jesus' sacrifice wasn't effortless. He willingly endured immense physical and spiritual pain to bridge the gap created by sin. The price of redemption is the precious blood of Christ, as of a lamb without blemish and without spot. The Father gave His all by giving His beloved Son to redeem sinners. The blood of Jesus Christ is both the price God paid to purchase a people for Himself and the means of liberating those He purchased. The significance of the price God paid in order to provide redemption for people like us is immense. The Bible says, "For if the blood of bulls and goats and the ashes of a heifer, sprinkling the unclean, sanctifies for the purifying of the flesh, how much more shall the blood of Christ, who through the eternal Spirit offered Himself without spot to God, cleanse your conscience from dead works to serve the living God?" (Hebrews 9:13-14, ESV) "Through faith in His sacrifice, we receive forgiveness of sin and come into a right relationship with God. Because His life was worth more than all human life combined, His sacrifice paid the price for all sin. He redeemed us from the penalty that the breaking of God's law imposes and freed us to live righteously. This act of ultimate love demonstrates the gravity of sin and the lengths God went to for reconciliation".

Priceless Gift of Grace: Salvation through the Atonement isn't earned but freely given. The gift of grace is a priceless gift that God has given to us. It is a gift that we do not deserve, but one that God has given to us out of His love and mercy. We should never take this gift for granted because it is the only way to be saved from our sins and have eternal life. The Word of God explains that we are saved by grace through faith in Jesus Christ. This means that we cannot earn our salvation by our own works or good deeds. It is only through faith in Jesus Christ that we can receive the gift of salvation. Taking the gift of grace for granted can lead to complacency and a lack of spiritual growth. It can also lead to a lack of gratitude and a failure to recognize the magnitude of what God has done for us. We should always remember that the gift of grace is a precious gift that we should never take for granted. As the Bible says, "For by grace you have been saved through faith. And this is not your own doing; it is the gift of God, not a result of works, so that no one may boast" (Ephesians 2:8-9, ESV) Recognizing this undeserved gift fosters humility and gratitude, motivating us to live lives that honor the sacrifice made.

Continuous Self-Renovation: The Atonement isn't a one-time event but a continuous process. Continuous self-renovation is an important aspect of the Christian faith. It involves a daily commitment to grow in our relationship with God and become more like Christ in heart and in spirit. The Bible teaches that we are to "put off your old self, which belongs to your former manner of life and is corrupt through deceitful desires, and to be renewed in the spirit of your minds, and to put on the new self, created after the likeness of God in true righteousness and holiness" (Ephesians 4:22-24, ESV). The atonement of Jesus Christ is central to the process of continuous self-renovation. Through His sacrifice, we are forgiven of our sins and given the power to overcome sin and live a life that is pleasing to God. The Word of God proclaims, "Therefore, if anyone is in Christ, he is a new creation. The old has passed away; behold, the new has come" (2 Corinthians 5:17, ESV). As we grow in our relationship with God, we become more aware of our sinfulness and our need for a Savior. We begin to see the depth of our need for the atonement of Jesus Christ and the power that it has to transform our lives. Accepting its power requires ongoing repentance, striving to align ourselves with Christ's teachings, and extending that grace to others.

Eternal Implications: The Atonement's impact transcends earthly carnal life completely. Taking the atonement of Jesus Christ for granted can have eternal implications. The Bible teaches that salvation is a gift of God's grace, which we receive through faith in Jesus Christ. However, if we take this gift for granted and fail to live a life that is pleasing to God, we risk losing our salvation. The Bible warns us against taking the grace of God for granted. In ***(Hebrews 10:26-27***), it says, "*For if we go on sinning deliberately after receiving the knowledge of the truth, there no longer remains a sacrifice for sins, but a fearful expectation of judgment, and a fury of fire that will consume the adversaries*". In other words, if we continue to sin deliberately after receiving the knowledge of the truth, we risk losing our salvation and facing eternal judgment. Therefore, it is important that we do not take the atonement of Jesus Christ for granted. We should strive to live a life that is pleasing to God and seek to grow in our relationship with Him. As the Bible says, "*Therefore, my beloved, as you have always obeyed, so now, not only as in my presence but much more in my absence, work out your own salvation with fear and trembling, for it is God who works in you, both to will and to work for his good pleasure*" ***(Philippians 2:12-13, ESV).*** Through repentance, faith, and striving to live a Christ-like life, we can be cleansed and empowered to overcome sin's hold on our lives. This ongoing process requires our active participation and gratitude.

Unconceivable Sacrifice: Jesus, the sinless Son of God, willingly endured unimaginable suffering and death on the cross, taking on the burden of humanity's sins. The Bible teaches that the sacrifice of Jesus Christ is an incomprehensible act of love, mercy and devotion that must never be taken for granted. The book of Hebrews explains that the Old Testament sacrifices were only a shadow of the good things to come and that the blood of bulls and goats could never take away sins . However, Jesus Christ, the unblemished sacrifice, offered Himself once for all time to take away the sins of the world .The significance of Jesus Christ's sacrifice is immeasurable. Through His death and resurrection, we are given the opportunity to receive forgiveness of sins and eternal life. The Bible says, "For God so loved the world, that he gave his only Son, that whoever believes in him should not perish but have eternal life" (John 3:16, ESV). However, taking the sacrifice of Jesus Christ for granted can have eternal implications. *__The Bible warns us against sinning deliberately after receiving the knowledge of the truth because there no longer remains a sacrifice for sins.__* In other words, if we take the sacrifice of Jesus Christ for granted and continue to live in sin, we risk losing our salvation, and facing eternal judgment.

Reconciliation Impact: The Atonement's consequences reach far beyond individual lives. It opens the door to reconciliation with God, and eternal salvation. Reconciliation is a vital aspect of the Christian faith. It involves the restoration of a broken relationship between God and humanity. The Bible teaches that sin has separated us from God and that we are in need of reconciliation. Through the atonement of Jesus Christ, we are reconciled to God and given the opportunity to have a right relationship with Him. The impact of reconciliation through the atonement of Jesus Christ is immeasurable. It provides us with the opportunity to receive forgiveness of sins and eternal life. The Bible says, "Therefore, if anyone is in Christ, he is a new creation. The old has passed away; behold, the new has come" (2 Corinthians 5:17, ESV). The impact of reconciliation through the atonement of Jesus Christ is infinite. It provides us with the opportunity to receive forgiveness of sins and eternal life.

A Constant Reminder: Taking the Atonement for granted can lead to complacency in our spiritual journey. The atonement of Jesus Christ serves as a constant reminder of God's incredible love and mercy for sinners. It provides us with the opportunity to receive forgiveness of sins and eternal life. As we grow in our understanding of the atonement of Jesus Christ, we begin to see the depth of our need for a Savior and the magnitude of what God has done for us. We begin to see the ways in which sin has affected our lives and the lives of those around us. We also begin to see how God is effectively working in our lives to bring about change and transformation. Regularly remembering and appreciating this sacrifice motivates us to live with purpose, extend compassion to others, and continually seek to refine ourselves.

More Than Just Forgiveness: The Atonement transcends mere pardon. It's a life-altering transformational act, washing away not just the guilt but the very stain of sin. The atonement of Jesus Christ was more than just forgiveness. It was a powerful act of love and mercy that provided a way for humanity to be reconciled to God. Through His sacrifice, we are given the opportunity to receive forgiveness of sins and eternal life. The atonement of Jesus Christ also dealt with the root cause of sin and prepared us for transformation into new creatures. The Bible teaches that through faith in Jesus Christ, we become new creations and are given the power to overcome sin and live a life that is pleasing to God. The atonement of Jesus Christ also provides us with the opportunity to be reconciled to one another. Through His sacrifice, we are able to overcome our differences and work together for the common good Through Christ's sacrifice, we're not simply declared "not guilty," but made truly clean, and empowered to live with a renewed heart and purpose.

A Path to Change: The victory over sin isn't a passive event; it's an invitation to active participation in exercising our faith in every way possible. The atonement of Jesus Christ is a powerful reminder of God's incredible love and mercy for mankind. It is proof that God is willing to go to great lengths to reconcile us to Himself and restore our relationship with Him. As we grow in our understanding of the atonement of Jesus Christ, we begin to see the depth of our need for a Savior and the magnitude of what God has done for us. We begin to see the ways in which sin has affected our lives and the lives of those around us. We also begin to see the ways in which God is working in our lives to bring about change and transformation. Christ's sacrifice paves the way for us to embrace righteousness, to choose God's will over our own will, and to become change agents of God's word, and His commandments in fulfilling the Great Commission.

A Gift to be Cherished Should Never be Taken for Granted: Because redemption was so freely given, it's easy to forget the immense price Jesus paid for our salvation. To take the Atonement for granted is to diminish the act of power and the responsibility it carries. Recognizing the depth of Christ's sacrifice should constantly ignite our gratitude, inspire our actions, and keeps us forever connected to the rock of our salvation who is able to keep us from stumbling. The atonement of Jesus Christ is a gift to be cherished and should never be taken for granted. It is proof of God's incredible love and mercy for humanity. Through His sacrifice, we are given the opportunity to receive forgiveness of sins and eternal life. The Bible teaches that salvation is a gift of God's grace, which we receive through faith in Jesus Christ. This means that we cannot earn our salvation by our own works or good deeds. It is only through faith in Jesus Christ that we can receive the gift of salvation. Taking the atonement of Jesus Christ for granted can have eternal implications. The Bible warns us against sinning deliberately after receiving the knowledge of the truth because there no longer remains a sacrifice for sins. In other words, if we take the sacrifice of Jesus Christ for granted and continue to live in sin, we risk losing our salvation and facing eternal judgment. Therefore, it is important that we cherish the gift of atonement of Jesus Christ and never take it for granted. We should strive to live a life that is pleasing to God and seek to grow in our relationship with Him. As the Bible says, "For by grace you have been saved through faith. And this is not your own doing; it is the gift of God, not a result of works, so that no one may boast" *(Ephesians 2:8-9, ESV).*

Jesus Christ's Atonement is like that of a gift of unimaginable magnitude, freely given to conquer the seemingly insurmountable power of sin.

The Lamb of God, Promised Messiah

1 Samuel 15:23

JESUS VICTORIES

By offering himself as a sacrifice on the cross, Jesus paid the penalty for humanity's sin, offering forgiveness and reconciliation with God (John 3:16, Romans 3:23-24). Jesus's death and subsequent resurrection conquered death and opened the door to eternal life for all who believe in him being victorious over death (1 Corinthians 15:54-57, John 11:25-26). Victorious over satan. Temptation in the wilderness Jesus resisted all of Satan's temptations, demonstrating His perfect obedience to God and his power over evil (Matthew 4:1-11, Luke 4:1-13). Victorious Over sickness and disease Jesus healed countless individuals, demonstrating His power over illness and suffering (Mark 2:1-12, John 4:46-54). Over nature victoriously, Jesus calmed the storm and walked on water, showcasing his dominion over the natural world (Matthew 14:22-33, Mark 4:35-41). Over injustice and oppression, Jesus did not conform to fruitless mediocracy, and challenged the religious and political authorities of His day, offering hope and liberation to those who were marginalized and oppressed (Luke 4:18-19, John 8:3-11). Triumphantly Overcoming the World offering himself as a sacrifice on the cross, Jesus paid the penalty for humanity's sin, offering forgiveness and reconciliation with God (John 3:16, Romans 3:23-24). Jesus's death and subsequent resurrection conquered death and opened the door to eternal life for all who believe in him being victorious over death (1 Corinthians 15:54-57, John 11:25-26). Victorious over satan. Temptation in the wilderness Jesus resisted all of Satan's temptations, demonstrating his perfect obedience to God and his power over evil (Matthew 4:1-11, Luke 4:1-13). Victorious Over sickness and disease Jesus healed countless individuals, demonstrating His power over illness and suffering (Mark 2:1-12, John 4:46-54). Over nature victoriously, Jesus calmed the storm and walked on water, showcasing his dominion over the natural world (Matthew 14:22-33, Mark 4:35-41). Over injustice and oppression, Jesus did not conform to fruitless mediocrity, and challenged the religious and political authorities of His day, offering hope and liberation to those who were marginalized and oppressed (Luke 4:18-19, John 8:3-11). Triumphantly Overcoming the world and its temptations and distractions Jesus warned his disciples about the dangers of the world and its temptations. He taught them to rely on God and his teachings to overcome worldly desires and temptations (John 16:33). Boldly Triumphing over persecution and opposition Jesus faced constant opposition from religious leaders and authorities during his ministry. He was ridiculed, rejected, and ultimately crucified. However, he remained steadfast in his faith and ultimately triumphed over his enemies (John 18:37). Reconciling the Redeemed of God. Through His life, death, and resurrection, Jesus bridged the gap between humanity and God. He offered a path to forgiveness and reconciliation, making it possible for people to experience God's love and grace (Romans 5:1). Spiritually Empowering and inspiring His believers, Jesus empowered His disciples to carry on his mission and spread the gospel message to the world. He instilled in them repentance, compassion, faith, and love, enabling them to face challenges and overcome obstacles (Matthew 28:18-20). Offering hope and salvation to all through His sacrifice, Jesus offered hope and salvation to all people in need of a shepherd irregardless of, race, class or creed. He opened the door to eternal life and provided a way for the human race to be restored to a relationship with God (John 3:16). Authoritatively establishing His Kingdom Jesus came to earth to establish God's kingdom, a realm of compassion, repentance, and love. Although not yet fully realized, His teachings and actions laid the foundation for this kingdom to come (Matthew 6:10).

JESUS VICTORIOUS OVER SIN

Matthew 4:1-11: Then Jesus was led up by the Spirit into the wilderness to be tempted by the devil. And when He had fasted forty days and forty nights, afterward He was hungry. Now when the tempter came to Him, he said, "If You are the Son of God, command that these stones become bread." But He answered and said, "It is written, 'Man shall not live by bread alone, but by every word that proceeds from the mouth of God.' "Then the devil took Him up into the holy city, set Him on the pinnacle of the temple, 6 and said to Him, "If You are the Son of God, throw Yourself down. For it is written: 'He shall give His angels charge over you,' and, 'In their hands they shall bear you up, Lest you dash your foot against a stone.' "Jesus said to him, "It is written again, 'You shall not tempt the Lord your God.' "Again, the devil took Him up on an exceedingly high mountain and showed Him all the kingdoms of the world and their glory. 9 And he said to Him, "All these things I will give You if You will fall down and worship me." Then Jesus said to him, "Away with you, Satan! For it is written, 'You shall worship the Lord your God, and Him only you shall serve.' "Then the devil left Him, and behold, angels came and ministered to Him.. _This shows Jesus' unwavering commitment to righteousness and his power over temptation._

Hebrews 4:15: "For we do not have a high priest who cannot sympathize with our weaknesses, but one who in every respect has been tempted as we are, yet without sin." _This verse emphasizes Jesus' sinless nature and his ability to understand and help those who struggle with sin._

Romans 8:3-4: "For God has done what the law, weakened by the flesh, could not do. By sending his own Son in the likeness of sinful flesh and for sin, he condemned sin in the flesh, in order that the righteous requirement of the law might be fulfilled in us, who walk not according to the flesh but according to the Spirit." *This passage explains how Jesus, through his sacrifice on the cross, defeated the power of sin and made it possible for us to live righteous lives.*

1 John 3:5: "You know that he appeared to take away sins, and in him there is no sin." *This verse reaffirms Jesus' sinlessness and his purpose in coming to earth: to redeem humanity from the bondage of sin.*

1 Corinthians 15:57: "But thanks be to God, who gives us the victory through our Lord Jesus Christ." *This verse expresses gratitude to God for giving us victory over sin through Christ's sacrifice and resurrection.*

Hebrews 2:14-15: "Since therefore the children share in flesh and blood, he himself likewise partook of the same things, that through death he might destroy the one who has the power of death, that is, the devil, and deliver all those who through fear of death were subject to lifelong slavery." *This passage highlights how Jesus' death on the cross defeated the power of sin and death, bringing freedom and hope to humanity.*

The Bible offers a rich embroidery of enriched scripture passages that speak to His sinless nature, His power over temptation, and his ultimate triumph over sin and death. Understanding and reflecting on these scriptures will deepen our faith providing us hope renewed in our own struggles against sin.

JESUS IS VICTORIOUS OVER DEATH

Old Testament:

Isaiah 25:8: "He will swallow up death forever, and the Lord God will wipe away tears from all faces, and the reproach of his people he will take away from all the earth, for the Lord has spoken." *This passage prophesies about the future abolition of death and the wiping away of tears through God's intervention.*

Hosea 13:14: "I shall ransom them from the power of Sheol; I shall redeem them from Death. O Death, where are your stings? O Sheol, where is your victory?" *This verse expresses a triumphant hope over death and its ultimate defeat.*

Job 19:25-27: "For I know that my Redeemer lives, and at last he will stand upon the earth. And after my skin has been thus destroyed, yet in my flesh I shall see God. I myself shall see him, my eyes shall behold him, and not another. My heart faints within me!" *This passage, though written in the context of personal suffering, expresses a strong belief in God's ultimate triumph over death and the hope of resurrection.*

New Testament:

Matthew 28:5-7: "And the angel said to the women, 'Do not be afraid, for I know that you seek Jesus who was crucified. <u>He is not here, for he has risen</u>, as he said. Come, see the place where he lay. Then go quickly and tell his disciples that he has risen from the dead, and behold, he is going before you to Galilee. There you will see him. See, I have told you.'" *<u>This passage describes the empty tomb and announces Jesus' resurrection, marking the beginning of his victory over death.</u>*

John 11:25-26: "Jesus said to her, 'I am the resurrection and the life. Whoever believes in me, though he die, yet shall he live, and everyone who lives and believes in me shall never die. Do you believe this?'" *<u>This statement by Jesus explicitly claims his power over death and offers the promise of eternal life to those who believe in him.</u>*

1 Corinthians 15:54-57: "When the perishable puts on the imperishable, and the mortal puts on immortality, then shall come to pass the saying that is written: '<u>Death is swallowed up in victory</u>.' 'O Death, where is your sting? O Sheol, where is your victory?' The sting of death is sin, and the power of sin is the law. But thanks be to God, who gives us the victory through our Lord Jesus Christ." *<u>This passage celebrates Jesus' victory over death and its sting, which is sin. Through his sacrifice, he offers believers the gift of eternal life.</u>*

Revelation 1:18: "I died, and behold I am alive forevermore, and I have the keys of Death and Hades." *<u>This statement by the resurrected Jesus affirms his authority over death and the afterlife{Hell}.</u>*

Revelation 21:4: "He will wipe away every tear from their eyes, and death shall be no more, neither shall there be mourning, nor crying, nor pain anymore, for the former things have passed away." *This passage describes the future state of heaven, where death and suffering are abolished, and believers experience eternal joy and peace.*

These scriptures provide a prevailing message of Blessed Assurance, hope & confidence, assuring believers that Jesus **has conquered death like no other before or after Him.** They are fruit for the soul. They highlight the promise of eternal life to those who follow His commands, repent, and accept His Plan for salvation. They provide a glimpse into the ultimate victory over death and the establishment of God's reign of love and righteousness.

JESUS IS VICTORIOUS OVER SATAN

Old Testament

Genesis 3:15: "And I will put enmity between you and the woman, and between your offspring and her offspring; he shall bruise your head, and you shall bruise his heel." *This deep-seated fundamental verse, prophesy's the ultimate victory of Christ (the woman's offspring) over the serpent (representing Satan).*

Isaiah 53:5: "But he was pierced for our transgressions; he was crushed for our iniquities; upon him was the chastisement that brought us peace, and with his wounds we are healed." *This verse, while primarily focusing on Jesus' sacrifice for sin, can also be seen as a representation of his triumph over the forces of evil and darkness.*

New Testament:

Matthew 4:1-11: "Then Jesus was led up by the Spirit into the wilderness to be tempted by the devil. And when He had fasted forty days and forty nights, afterward He was hungry. Now when the tempter came to Him, he said, "If You are the Son of God, command that these stones become bread." But He answered and said, "It is written, 'Man shall not live by bread alone, but by every word that proceeds from the mouth of God." Then the devil took Him up into the holy city, set Him on the pinnacle of the temple, and said to Him, "If You are the Son of God, throw Yourself down. For it is written:

'He shall give His angels charge over you,' and, 'In their hands they shall bear you up, Lest you dash your foot against a stone." Jesus said to him, "It is written again, 'You shall not tempt the Lord your God.' " Again, the devil took Him up on an exceedingly high mountain, and showed Him all the kingdoms of the world and their glory. And he said to Him, "All these things I will give You if You will fall down and worship me." Then Jesus said to him, "Away with you, Satan! For it is written, 'You shall worship the Lord your God, and Him only you shall serve.' "Then the devil left Him, and behold, angels came and ministered to Him. *This passage describes Jesus' temptation in the wilderness, where he successfully resists the devil's attempts to* _lead him astray. This demonstrates Jesus' power over temptation and his unwavering commitment to righteousness._

Mark 1:21-28: "Now there was a man in their synagogue with an unclean spirit. And he cried out, saying, "Let us alone! What have we to do with You, Jesus of Nazareth? Did You come to destroy us? I know who You are the Holy One of God!" But Jesus rebuked him, saying, "Be quiet, and come out of him!" And when the unclean spirit had convulsed him and cried out with a loud voice, he came out of him. Then they were all amazed, so that they questioned among themselves, saying, What is this? What new doctrine is this? For with authority, He commands even the unclean spirits, and they obey Him." Jesus encounters a demon-possessed man in the synagogue and commands the demon to come out of him. _The demon acknowledges Jesus' authority and obeys. This illustrates Jesus' power over demons and evil spirits._

Luke 10:17-20: "And the seventy returned again with joy, saying, Lord, even the devils are subject unto us through thy name. And he said unto them, I beheld Satan as lightning fall from heaven. Behold, I give unto you power to tread on serpents and scorpions, and over all the power of the enemy: and nothing shall by any means hurt you. Notwithstanding in this rejoice not, that the spirits are subject unto you; but rather rejoice, because your names are written in heaven". _This passage describes how Jesus' disciples rejoiced after successfully casting out demons in his name. Jesus confirms their victory and emphasizes his authority over evil forces._

John 12:31-33: Jesus declares that " Now is the judgment of this world: now shall the prince of this world be cast out. And I, if I be lifted up from the earth, will draw all men unto me." *This statement implies Jesus' ultimate victory over Satan and his dominion over the world.*

Colossians 2:15: "He disarmed the rulers and authorities and put them to open shame, by triumphing over them in him." *This verse explicitly declares Jesus' victory over the rulers and authorities of darkness, which are often interpreted as demons or evil forces.*

Hebrews 2:14-15: "Since therefore the children share in flesh and blood, he himself likewise partook of the same things, that through death he might destroy the one who has the power of death, that is, the devil, and deliver all those who through fear of death were subject to lifelong slavery." *This passage explains how Jesus' death on the cross defeated the power of death (ultimately controlled by Satan) and liberated humanity from its enslavement.*

Old Testament:

Job 1:6-12: "Now there was a day when the sons of God came to present themselves before the Lord, and Satan also came among them. And the Lord said to Satan, "From where do you come?" So Satan answered the Lord and said, "From going to and from on the earth, and from walking back and forth on it." Then the Lord said to Satan, "Have you considered My servant Job, that there is none like him on the earth, a blameless and upright man, one who fears God and shuns evil?" So Satan answered the Lord and said, "Does Job fear God for nothing? Have You not made a hedge around him, around his household, and around all that he has on every side? You have blessed the work of his hands, and his possessions have increased in the land. But now, stretch out Your hand and touch all that he has, and he will surely curse You to Your face!" And the Lord said to Satan, "Behold, all that he has is in your power; only do not lay a hand on his person." So Satan went out from the presence of the Lord." _This passage describes how Satan challenges God's claim that Job is righteous and seeks permission to test him. This scenario portrays Satan as a powerful adversary, but ultimately subject to God's authority and purpose._

Zechariah 3:1-2: "And he shewed me Joshua the high priest standing before the angel of the Lord, and Satan standing at his right hand to resist him. And the Lord said unto Satan, The Lord rebuke thee, O Satan; even the Lord that hath chosen Jerusalem rebuke thee: is not this a brand plucked out of the fire?" _This passage depicts Satan accusing the high priest Joshua but is ultimately rebuked by the Lord. This incident reinforces the notion of Satan as an accuser and attacker, but one who is ultimately defeated by God's intervention._

New Testament:

Matthew 12:22-29: " Then one was brought to Him who was demon-possessed, blind and mute; and He healed him, so that the blind and mute man both spoke and saw. And all the multitudes were amazed and said, "Could this be the Son of David?"

Now when the Pharisees heard it they said, "This fellow does not cast out demons except by Beelzebub, the ruler of the demons." But Jesus knew their thoughts, and said to them: "Every kingdom divided against itself is brought to desolation, and every city or house divided against itself will not stand. If Satan casts out Satan, he is divided against himself. How then will his kingdom stand? And if I cast out demons by Beelzebub, by whom do your sons cast them out? Therefore they shall be your judges. But if I cast out demons by the Spirit of God, surely the kingdom of God has come upon you. Or how can one enter a strong man's house and plunder his goods, unless he first binds the strong man? And then he will plunder his house". *Jesus confronts the Pharisees' accusation of casting out demons by the power of Beelzebul (another name for Satan). He explains that such an act is only possible by the power of the Holy Spirit, highlighting his authority over demons and their source.*

Luke 11:14-26:" And He was casting out a demon, and it was mute. So it was, when the demon had gone out, that the mute spoke; and the multitudes marveled. But some of them said, "He casts out demons by Beelzebub, the ruler of the demons. Others, testing Him, sought from Him a sign from heaven. But He, knowing their thoughts, said to them: "Every kingdom divided against itself is brought to desolation, and a house divided against a house falls. If Satan also is divided against himself, how will his kingdom stand? Because you say I cast out demons by Beelzebub. And if I cast out demons by Beelzebub, by whom do your sons cast them out? Therefore they will be your judges. But if I cast out demons with the finger of God, surely the kingdom of God has come upon you. When a strong man, fully armed, guards his own palace, his goods are in peace. But when a stronger than he comes upon him and overcomes him, he takes from him all his armor in which he trusted, and divides his spoils. He who is not with Me is against Me, and he who does not gather with Me scatters". *This passage echoes Matthew's account of Jesus casting out a demon and emphasizes the weakening of Satan's kingdom as a consequence of Jesus' ministry.*

Acts 10:38: Peter describes Jesus as "anointed with the Holy Spirit and with power, who went about doing good and healing all who were oppressed by the devil, for God was with him." *This statement further confirms the connection between Jesus' power over evil and the presence of the Holy Spirit.*

1 John 3:8:"He who sins is of the devil, for the devil has sinned from the beginning. For this purpose, the Son of God was manifested, that He might destroy the works of the devil". *This verse declares that "the reason the Son of God appeared was to destroy the works of the devil." This explicitly connects Jesus' mission to overcoming the power and influence of evil.*

Revelation 20:1-3: "Then I saw an angel coming down from heaven, having the key to the bottomless pit and a great chain in his hand. He laid hold of the dragon, that serpent of old, who is the Devil and Satan, and bound him for a thousand years; and he cast him into the bottomless pit, and shut him up, and set a seal on him, so that he should deceive the nations no more till the thousand years were finished. But after these things he must be released for a little while" *This passage describes the future Arrest of Satan for a thousand years, symbolizing the ultimate triumph of God and his kingdom over the forces of evil.*

Jesus' victory over Satan and the forces of evil. These passages offer Christians hope and assurance that Jesus ultimately holds authority over evil and has paved the way for our own victory through faith in him ... *These scriptures provide further related evidence and context for Jesus' wide-ranging victory over Satan. They describe Him as the ultimate conqueror of evil, authoritatively exercising power over demons, challenging Satan's accusations, and ultimately achieving His mission of dismantling the works of the devil. These passages offer hope and assurance to Christians that evil will not ultimately prevail, and God's kingdom will reign victorious in the end throughout the ages.*

JESUS IS VICTORIOUS OVER SICKNESS AND DISEASE

New Testament

Matthew: 8:2-3: " And behold, a leper came and worshiped Him, saying, "Lord, if You are willing, You can make me clean." Then Jesus put out His hand and touched him, saying, "I am willing; be cleansed." Immediately his leprosy was cleansed. *Jesus heals a leper who kneels before him and begs for healing, demonstrating Jesus' willingness to touch and heal even those considered unclean.*

Matthew: 8:5-13: " Now when Jesus had entered Capernaum, a centurion came to Him, pleading with Him, saying, "Lord, my servant is lying at home paralyzed, dreadfully tormented." And Jesus said to him, "I will come and heal him." The centurion answered and said, "Lord, I am not worthy that You should come under my roof. But only speak a word, and my servant will be healed. For I also am a man under authority, having soldiers under me. And I say to this one, 'Go,' and he goes; and to another, 'Come,' and he comes; and to my servant, 'Do this,' and he does it." When Jesus heard it, He marveled, and said to those who followed, "Assuredly, I say to you, I have not found such great faith, not even in Israel! And I say to you that many will come from east and west, and sit down with Abraham, Isaac, and Jacob in the kingdom of heaven. But the sons of the kingdom will be cast out into outer darkness. There will be weeping and gnashing of teeth." Then Jesus said to the centurion, "Go your way; and as you have believed, so let it be done for you." And his servant was healed that same hour." *Jesus heals the Centurion's servant who is lying in bed paralyzed, highlighting Jesus' ability to heal even at a distance.*

Matthew: 8:14-15:" Now when Jesus had come into Peter's house, He saw his wife's mother lying sick with a fever. So He touched her hand, and the fever left her. And she arose and served them". _Jesus heals Peter's mother-in-law who is sick with a fever, showcasing his power to heal within the home and family._

Matthew: 9:2-8: " Then behold, they brought to Him a paralytic lying on a bed. When Jesus saw their faith, He said to the paralytic, "Son, be of good cheer; your sins are forgiven you." And at once some of the scribes said within themselves, "This Man blasphemes!" But Jesus, knowing their thoughts, said, "Why do you think evil in your hearts? For which is easier, to say, 'Your sins are forgiven you,' or to say, 'Arise and walk'? But that you may know that the Son of Man has power on earth to forgive sins" then He said to the paralytic, "Arise, take up your bed, and go to your house." And he arose and departed to his house. Now when the multitudes saw it, they marveled and glorified God, who had given such power to men. "_Jesus heals a paralytic man lowered through the roof, demonstrating his forgiveness of sins and power over physical ailments._

Matthew: 9:20-22:" And suddenly, a woman who had a flow of blood for twelve years came from behind and touched the hem of His garment. For she said to herself, "If only I may touch His garment, I shall be made well." But Jesus turned around, and when He saw her He said,

"Be of good cheer, daughter; your faith has made you well." And the woman was made well from that hour." *Jesus heals a woman suffering from bleeding for twelve years, emphasizing his compassion for women and marginalized individuals.*

Matthew: 12:10-13: " And behold, there was a man who had a withered hand. And they asked Him, saying, "Is it lawful to heal on the Sabbath?" that they might accuse Him.11 Then He said to them, "What man is there among you who has one sheep, and if it falls into a pit on the Sabbath, will not lay hold of it and lift it out? Of how much more value than is a man than a sheep? Therefore it is lawful to do good on the Sabbath." Then He said to the man, "Stretch out your hand." And he stretched it out, and it was restored as whole as the other. *Jesus heals a man with a withered hand on the Sabbath, challenging religious restrictions and prioritizing compassion over legalistic interpretations.*

Matthew: 14:35-36: "And when the men of that place recognized Him, they sent out into all that surrounding region, brought to Him all who were sick, and begged Him that they might only touch the hem of His garment. And as many as touched *it* were made perfectly well." *Jesus heals many sick people who touch him, showcasing the power flowing from him and the healing available through faith.*

Matthew: 20:30-34: "And behold, two blind men sitting by the road, when they heard that Jesus was passing by, cried out, saying, "Have mercy on us, O Lord, Son of

David!" Then the multitude warned them that they should be quiet; but they cried out all the more, saying, "Have mercy on us, O Lord, Son of David!"

So Jesus stood still and called them, and said, "What do you want Me to do for you?" They said to Him, "Lord, that our eyes may be opened." So Jesus had compassion and touched their eyes. And immediately their eyes received sight, and they followed Him." *Jesus heals two blind men on his way to Jerusalem, demonstrating his power to restore sight and fulfill prophecies.*

Mark:

Mark: 1:29-31:" Now as soon as they had come out of the synagogue, they entered the house of Simon and Andrew, with James and John. But Simon's wife's mother lay sick with a fever, and they told Him about her at once. So He came and took her by the hand and lifted her up, and immediately the fever left her. And she served them." *Jesus heals Simon Peter's mother-in-law who is sick with a fever, demonstrating his power to heal within the home and family.*

Mark: 1:40-42: "Now a leper came to Him, imploring Him, kneeling down to Him and saying to Him, "If You are willing, You can make me clean." Then Jesus, moved with compassion, stretched out His hand and touched him, and said to him, "I am willing; be cleansed." As soon as He had spoken, immediately the leprosy left him, and he was cleansed." *Jesus heals a leper, highlighting his willingness to touch and heal even those considered unclean.*

Mark: 2:5-12:" When Jesus saw their faith, He said to the paralytic, "Son, your sins are forgiven you." And some of the scribes were sitting there and reasoning in their hearts, "Why does this Man speak blasphemies like this? Who can forgive sins but God alone?" But immediately, when Jesus perceived in His spirit that they reasoned thus within themselves, He said to them, "Why do you reason about these things in your hearts? Which is easier, to say to the paralytic, 'Your sins are forgiven you,' or to say, 'Arise, take up your bed and walk'? But that you may know that the Son of Man has power on earth to forgive sins" He said to the paralytic, "I say to you, arise, take up your bed, and go to your house." Immediately he arose, took up the bed, and went out in the presence of them all, so that all were amazed and glorified God, saying, "We never saw anything like this!" *Jesus heals a paralytic man lowered through the roof, demonstrating his forgiveness of sins and power over physical ailments.*

Mark: 5:25-34: "Now a certain woman had a flow of blood for twelve years, and had suffered many things from many physicians. She had spent all that she had and was no better, but rather grew worse. When she heard about Jesus, she came behind Him in the crowd and touched His garment. For she said, "If only I may touch His clothes, I shall be made well." Immediately the fountain of her blood was dried up, and she felt in her body that she was healed of the affliction. And Jesus, immediately knowing in Himself that power had gone out of Him, turned around in the crowd and said, "Who touched My clothes?" But His disciples said to Him, "You see the multitude thronging You, and You say, 'Who touched Me?' "And He looked around to see her who had done this thing. But the woman, fearing and trembling, knowing what had happened to her, came and fell down before Him and told Him the whole truth. And He said to her, "Daughter, your faith has made you well. Go in peace, and be healed of your affliction." *Jesus heals a woman suffering from bleeding for twelve years, emphasizing his compassion for women and marginalized individuals.*

Mark: 7:31-37: "Again, departing from the region of Tyre and Sidon, He came through the midst of the region of Decapolis to the Sea of Galilee. Then they brought to Him one who was deaf and had an impediment in his speech, and they begged Him to put His hand on him. And He took him aside from the multitude, and put His fingers in his ears, and He spat and touched his tongue. Then, looking up to heaven, He sighed, and said to him, "Ephphatha," that is, "Be opened." Immediately his ears were opened, and the impediment of his tongue was loosed, and he spoke plainly. Then He commanded them that they should tell no one; but the more He commanded them, the more widely they proclaimed it. And they were astonished beyond measure, saying, "He has done all things well. He makes both the deaf to hear and the mute to speak." *Jesus heals a deaf and mute man, showcasing his power to restore senses and communication.*

Mark: 10:46-52: "Now they came to Jericho. As He went out of Jericho with His disciples and a great multitude, blind Bartimaeus, the son of Timaeus, sat by the road begging. And when he heard that it was Jesus of Nazareth, he began to cry out and say, "Jesus, Son of David, have mercy on me!" Then many warned him to be quiet; but he cried out all the more, "Son of David, have mercy on me!" So Jesus stood still and commanded him to be called. Then they called the blind man, saying to him, "Be of good cheer. Rise, He is calling you." And throwing aside his garment, he rose and came to Jesus.

So Jesus answered and said to him, "What do you want Me to do for you?" The blind man said to Him, "Rabboni, that I may receive my sight." Then Jesus said to him, "Go your way; your faith has made you well." And immediately he received his sight and followed Jesus on the road. *Jesus heals Bartimaeus, a blind beggar who calls out to him for mercy, demonstrating his response to faith and perseverance.*

Luke:

Luke: 4:38-39:" Now He arose from the synagogue and entered Simon's house. But Simon's wife's mother was sick with a high fever, and they made request of Him concerning her. So He stood over her and rebuked the fever, and it left her. And immediately she arose and served them". *Jesus heals Simon Peter's mother-in-law who is sick with a fever, demonstrating his power to heal within the home and family.*

Luke: 5:12-14:" And it happened when He was in a certain city, that behold, a man who was full of leprosy saw Jesus; and he fell on his face and implored Him, saying, "Lord, if You are willing, You can make me clean." Then He put out His hand and touched him, saying, "I am willing; be cleansed." Immediately the leprosy left him. And He charged him to tell no one, "But go and show yourself to the priest, and make an offering for your cleansing, as a testimony to them, just as Moses commanded." *Jesus heals a leper, highlighting his willingness to touch and heal even those considered unclean.*

Luke: 5:18-26: "Then behold, men brought on a bed a man who was paralyzed, whom they sought to bring in and lay before Him. And when they could not find how they might bring him in, because of the crowd, they went up on the housetop and let him down with his bed through the tiling into the midst before Jesus. When He saw their faith, He said to him, "Man, your sins are forgiven you." And the scribes and the Pharisees began to reason, saying, "Who is this who speaks blasphemies? Who can forgive sins but God alone?" But when Jesus perceived their thoughts, He answered and said to them, "Why are you reasoning in your hearts? Which is easier, to say, 'Your sins are forgiven you,' or to say, 'Rise up and walk'? But that you may know that the Son of Man has power on earth to forgive sins" He said to the man who was paralyzed, "I say to you, arise, take up your bed, and go to your house." Immediately he rose up before them, took up what he had been lying on, and departed to his own house, glorifying God. And they were all amazed, and they glorified God and were filled with fear, saying, "We have seen strange things today!" *Jesus heals a paralytic man lowered through the roof, demonstrating his forgiveness of sins and power over physical ailments.*

Luke: 7:11-15: " Now it happened, the day after, that He went into a city called Nain; and many of His disciples went with Him, and a large crowd. And when He came near the gate of the city, behold, a dead man was being carried out, the only son of his mother; and she was a widow. And a large crowd from the city was with her. When the Lord saw her, He had compassion on her and said to her, "Do not weep." Then He came and touched the open coffin, and those who carried him stood still. And He said, "Young man, I say to you, arise." So he who was dead sat up and began to speak. And He presented him to his mother. *Jesus raises the son of the widow of Nain from the dead, showcasing his power over death and offering hope and comfort.*

Luke: 8:43-48: "Now a woman, having a flow of blood for twelve years, who had spent all her livelihood on physicians and could not be healed by any, came from behind and touched the border of His garment. And immediately her flow of blood stopped. And Jesus said, "Who touched Me?" When all denied it, Peter and those with him said, "Master, the multitudes throng and press You, and You say, 'Who touched Me?' "But Jesus said, "Somebody touched Me, for I perceived power going out from Me." Now when the woman saw that she was not hidden, she came trembling; and falling down before Him, she declared to Him in the presence of all the people the reason she had touched Him and how she was healed immediately. And He said to her, "Daughter, be of good cheer; your faith has made you well. Go in peace." *Jesus heals a woman suffering from bleeding for twelve years, emphasizing his compassion for women and disregarded marginalized cast out individuals.*

Luke: 14:1-4: "Now it happened, as He went into the house of one of the rulers of the Pharisees to eat bread on the Sabbath, that they watched Him closely. And behold, there was a certain man before Him who had dropsy. And Jesus, answering, spoke to the lawyers and Pharisees, saying, "Is it lawful to heal on the Sabbath?"

But they kept silent. And He took him and healed him, and let him go. *Jesus heals a man suffering from dropsy on the Sabbath, highlighting the importance of compassion over legalistic interpretations.*

Luke: 17:11-19: "Now it happened as He went to Jerusalem that He passed through the midst of Samaria and Galilee. Then as He entered a certain village, there met Him ten men who were lepers, who stood afar off.

And they lifted up their voices and said, "Jesus, Master, have mercy on us!" So when He saw them, He said to them, "Go, show yourselves to the priests." And so it was that as they went, they were cleansed. And one of them, when he saw that he was healed, returned, and with a loud voice glorified God, and fell down on his face at His feet, giving Him thanks. And he was a Samaritan. So Jesus answered and said, "Were there not ten cleansed? But where are the nine? Were there not any found who returned to give glory to God except this foreigner?" And He said to him, "Arise, go your way. Your faith has made you well." *Jesus heals ten lepers, emphasizing the power of faith and the need for gratitude.*

Luke: 22:49-51: "When those around Him saw what was going to happen, they said to Him, "Lord, shall we strike with the sword?" And one of them struck the servant of the high priest and cut off his right ear. But Jesus answered and said, "Permit even this." And He touched his ear and healed him" *Jesus heals the ear of the high priest's servant who is cut off by Peter, demonstrating his power to heal and his commitment to peace.*

John:

John: 4:46-54: "So Jesus came again to Cana of Galilee where He had made the water into wine. And there was a certain nobleman whose son was sick at Capernaum. When he heard that Jesus had come out of Judea into Galilee, he went to Him and implored Him to come down and heal his son, for he was at the point of death. Then Jesus said to him, "Unless you people see signs and wonders, you will by no means believe." The nobleman said to Him, "Sir, come down before my child dies!" Jesus said to him, "Go your way; your son lives." So the man believed the word that Jesus spoke to him, and he went his way. And as he was now going down, his servants met him and told him, saying, "Your son lives!" Then he inquired of them the hour when he got better. And they said to him, "Yesterday at the seventh hour the fever left him." So the father knew that it was at the same hour in which Jesus said to him, "Your son lives." And he himself believed, and his whole household. This again is the second sign Jesus did when He had come out of Judea into Galilee. *Jesus heals the son of a royal official who is sick in Cana, showcasing his power to heal at a distance and his responsiveness to faith.*

John: 5:1-9: "After this there was a feast of the Jews, and Jesus went up to Jerusalem. Now there is in Jerusalem by the Sheep Gate a pool, which is called in Hebrew, Bethesda, having five porches. In these lay a great multitude of sick people, blind, lame, paralyzed, waiting for the moving of the water. For an angel went down at a certain time into the pool and stirred up the water; then whoever stepped in first, after the stirring of the water, was made well of whatever disease he had. Now a certain man was there who had an infirmity thirty-eight years.

When Jesus saw him lying there, and knew that he already had been in that condition a long time, He said to him, "Do you want to be made well?" The sick man answered Him, "Sir, I have no man to put me into the pool when the water is stirred up; but while I am coming, another steps down before me." Jesus said to him, "Rise, take up your bed and walk." And immediately the man was made well, took up his bed, and walked. And that day was the Sabbath". *Jesus heals a man who has been paralyzed for thirty-eight years at the pool of Bethesda, demonstrating his power to heal on the Sabbath and His authority over physical limitations.*

John: 9:1-7: "Now as Jesus passed by, He saw a man who was blind from birth. And His disciples asked Him, saying, "Rabbi, who sinned, this man or his parents, that he was born blind?" Jesus answered, "Neither this man nor his parents sinned, but that the works of God should be revealed in him. I must work the works of Him who sent Me while it is day; the night is coming when no one can work. As long as I am in the world, I am the light of the world." When He had said these things, He spat on the ground and made clay with the saliva; and He anointed the eyes of the blind man with the clay. And He said to him, "Go, wash in the pool of Siloam" (which is translated, Sent). So he went and washed, and came back seeing *Jesus heals a man born blind, showcasing his power to restore sight and overturn religious beliefs about sin and suffering.*

John: 11:1-44: "Now a certain man was sick, Lazarus of Bethany, the town of Mary and her sister Martha. It was that Mary who anointed the Lord with fragrant oil and wiped His feet with her hair, whose brother Lazarus was sick. Therefore the sisters sent to Him, saying, "Lord, behold, he whom You love is sick." When Jesus heard that, He said, "This sickness is not unto death, but for the glory of God, that the Son of God may be glorified through it." Now Jesus loved Martha and her sister and Lazarus. So, when He heard that he was sick, He stayed two more days in the place where He was. Then after this He said to the disciples, "Let us go to Judea again." The disciples said to Him, "Rabbi, lately the Jews sought to stone You, and are You going there again?" Jesus answered, "Are there not twelve hours in the day? If anyone walks in the day, he does not stumble, because he sees the light of this world. But if one walks in the night, he stumbles, because the light is not in him." These things He said, and after that He said to them, "Our friend Lazarus sleeps, but I go that I may wake him up." Then His disciples said, "Lord, if he sleeps he will get well." However, Jesus spoke of his death, but they thought that He was speaking about taking rest in sleep.

Then Jesus said to them plainly, "Lazarus is dead. And I am glad for your sakes that I was not there, that you may believe. Nevertheless let us go to him." Then Thomas, who is called the Twin, said to his fellow disciples, "Let us also go, that we may die with Him."

The Resurrection and the Life

So when Jesus came, He found that he had already been in the tomb four days. Now Bethany was near Jerusalem, about two miles away. And many of the Jews had joined the women around Martha and Mary, to comfort them concerning their brother. Then Martha, as soon as she heard that Jesus was coming, went and met Him, but Mary was sitting in the house. Now Martha said to Jesus, "Lord, if You had been here, my brother would not have died. But even now I know that whatever You ask of God, God will give You." Jesus said to her, "Your brother will rise again." Martha said to Him, "I know that he will rise again in the resurrection at the last day." Jesus said to her, "I am the resurrection and the life. He who believes in Me, though he may die, he shall live. And whoever lives and believes in Me shall never die. Do you believe this?" She said to Him, "Yes, Lord, I believe that You are the Christ, the Son of God, who is to come into the world."

Jesus and Death, the Last Enemy

"And when she had said these things, she went her way and secretly called Mary her sister, saying, "The Teacher has come and is calling for you." As soon as she heard that, she arose quickly and came to Him. Now Jesus had not yet come into the town, but was in the place where Martha met Him. Then the Jews who were with her in the house, and comforting her, when they saw that Mary rose up quickly and went out, followed her, saying, "She is going to the tomb to weep there." Then, when Mary came where Jesus was, and saw Him, she fell down at His feet, saying to Him, "Lord, if You had been here, my brother would not have died." Therefore, when Jesus saw her weeping, and the Jews who came with her weeping, He groaned in the spirit and was troubled. And He said, "Where have you laid him?" They said to Him, "Lord, come and see." Jesus wept. Then the Jews said, "See how He loved him!" And some of them said, "Could not this Man, who opened the eyes of the blind, also have kept this man from dying?"

Lazarus Raised from the Dead

Then Jesus, again groaning in Himself, came to the tomb. It was a cave, and a stone lay against it. Jesus said, "Take away the stone." Martha, the sister of him who was dead, said to Him, "Lord, by this time there is a stench, for he has been dead four days." Jesus said to her, "Did I not say to you that if you would believe you would see the glory of God?" Then they took away the stone from the place where the dead man was lying. And Jesus lifted up His eyes and said, "Father, I thank You that You have heard Me. And I know that You always hear Me, but because of the people who are standing by I said this, that they may believe that You sent Me." Now when He had said these things, He cried with a loud voice, "Lazarus, come forth!" And he who had died came out bound hand and foot with graveclothes, and his face was wrapped with a cloth. Jesus said to them, "Loose him, and let him go." _Jesus raises Lazarus from the dead, demonstrating His power over death and offering a glimpse into future resurrection._

These scriptures vividly demonstrate Jesus' healing various illnesses and diseases among many different individuals. These accounts exemplify the power thar Jesus Christ held in His Psalm. They tell a powerful message of love, hope, redemption and restoration. Compassion through healing, demonstrating Jesus' concern for suffering individuals and His undeniable power over sickness and disease. They remind us that Jesus came to not only preach the good news but also to bring healing and wholeness to those in need, especially to those who believe.

ADDITIONAL SCRIPTURES OF JESUS HEALING SICKNESS AND DISEASE:

Matthew:

Matthew: 15:21-28: "Then Jesus went out from there and departed to the region of Tyre and Sidon. And behold, a woman of Canaan came from that region and cried out to Him, saying, "Have mercy on me, O Lord, Son of David! My daughter is severely demon-possessed." But He answered her not a word. And His disciples came and urged Him, saying, "Send her away, for she cries out after us." But He answered and said, "I was not sent except to the lost sheep of the house of Israel." Then she came and worshiped Him, saying, "Lord, help me!" But He answered and said, "It is not good to take the children's bread and throw it to the little dogs." And she said, "Yes, Lord, yet even the little dogs eat the crumbs which fall from their masters' table."

Then Jesus answered and said to her, "O woman, great is your faith! Let it be to you as you desire." And her daughter was healed from that very hour." *Jesus heals the daughter of a Canaanite woman, demonstrating his willingness to reach out to people of different backgrounds.*

Matthew: 21:14: "Then the blind and the lame came to Him in the temple, and He healed them." *Jesus heals the sick in the temple, revealing his mission to bring healing and restoration to everyone.*

Mark:

Mark: 2:23-28: "Now it happened that He went through the grainfields on the Sabbath; and as they went His disciples began to pluck the heads of grain. And the Pharisees said to Him, "Look, why do they do what is not lawful on the Sabbath?" But He said to them, "Have you never read what David did when he was in need and hungry, he and those with him, how he went into the house of God in the days of Abiathar the high priest, and ate the showbread, which is not lawful to eat except for the priests, and also gave some to those who were with him? "And He said to them, "The Sabbath was made for man, and not man for the Sabbath. Therefore the Son of Man is also Lord of the Sabbath." *Jesus heals a man with a*

withered hand while walking through grain fields, highlighting his
freedom from legalistic restrictions.

Mark: 5:2-20: "And when He had come out of the boat,
immediately there met Him out of the tombs a man with
an unclean spirit, who had his dwelling among the tombs;
and no one could bind him, not even with chains, because
he had often been bound with shackles and chains. And
the chains had been pulled apart by him, and the shackles
broken in pieces; neither could anyone tame him. And
always, night and day, he was in the mountains and in the
tombs, crying out and cutting himself with stones. When
he saw Jesus from afar, he ran and worshiped Him. And
he cried out with a loud voice and said, "What have I to
do with You, Jesus, Son of the Most High God? I implore
You by God that You do not torment me." For He said
to him, "Come out of the man, unclean spirit!" Then He
asked him, "What is your name?" And he answered,
saying, "My name is Legion; for we are many." Also he
begged Him earnestly that He would not send them out
of the country. Now a large herd of swine was feeding
there near the mountains. So all the demons begged Him,
saying, "Send us to the swine, that we may enter them."
And at once Jesus gave them permission. Then the
unclean spirits went out and entered the swine (there
were about two thousand); and the herd ran violently
down the steep place into the sea, and drowned in the
sea. So those who fed the swine fled, and they told it in
the city and in the country. And they went out to see what
it was that had happened. Then they came to Jesus, and
saw the one who had been demon-possessed and had the

legion, sitting and clothed and in his right mind. And they were afraid. And those who saw it told them how it happened to him who had been demon-possessed, and about the swine. Then they began to plead with Him to depart from their region. And when He got into the boat, he who had been demon-possessed begged Him that he might be with Him. However, Jesus did not permit him, but said to him, "Go home to your friends, and tell them what great things the Lord has done for you, and how He has had compassion on you." And he departed and began to proclaim in Decapolis all that Jesus had done for him; and all marveled." *Jesus heals a demon-possessed man in the region of the Gerasenes, demonstrating his authority over evil spirits and their influence.*

Mark: 7:32-35: Then they brought to Him one who was deaf and had an impediment in his speech, and they begged Him to put His hand on him. And He took him aside from the multitude, and put His fingers in his ears, and He spat and touched his tongue. Then, looking up to heaven, He sighed, and said to him, "Ephphatha," that is, "Be opened." Immediately his ears were opened, and the impediment of his tongue was loosed, and he spoke plainly." *Jesus heals a deaf man with a speech impediment, showcasing his ability to restore communication and understanding.*

Mark: 8:22-26: "Then He came to Bethsaida; and they brought a blind man to Him, and begged Him to touch him. So He took the blind man by the hand and led him out of the town. And when He had spit on his eyes and put His hands on him, He asked him if he saw anything.

And he looked up and said, "I see men like trees, walking." Then He put His hands on his eyes again and made him look up. And he was restored and saw everyone clearly. Then He sent him away to his house, saying, "Neither go into the town, nor tell anyone in the town." *Jesus heals a blind man gradually, highlighting the process of faith and progressive restoration.*

Luke:

Luke: 4:40-41: "When the sun was setting, all those who had any that were sick with various diseases brought them to Him; and He laid His hands on every one of them and healed them. And demons also came out of many, crying out and saying, "You are the Christ, the Son of God!" And He, rebuking them, did not allow them to speak, for they knew that He was the Christ." *Jesus heals many sick people at sunset, showcasing his tireless compassion and ability to heal in large numbers.*

Luke: 6:18-19: "as well as those who were tormented with unclean spirits. And they were healed. And the whole multitude sought to touch Him, for power went out from Him and healed them all." *Jesus heals all who come to him, demonstrating his universal availability and desire to offer healing.*

Luke: 8:26-39: "Then they sailed to the country of the Gadarenes, which is opposite Galilee. And when He stepped out on the land, there met Him a certain man from the city who had demons for a long time. And he wore no clothes, nor did he live in a house but in the tombs. When he saw Jesus, he cried out, fell down before Him, and with a loud voice said, "What have I to do with You, Jesus, Son of the Most High God? I beg You, do not torment me!" For He had commanded the unclean spirit to come out of the man. For it had often seized him, and he was kept under guard, bound with chains and shackles; and he broke the bonds and was driven by the demon into the wilderness. Jesus asked him, saying, "What is your name?" And he said, "Legion," because many demons had entered him. And they begged Him that He would not command them to go out into the abyss. Now a herd of many swine was feeding there on the mountain. So they begged Him that He would permit them to enter them. And He permitted them. Then the demons went out of the man and entered the swine, and the herd ran violently down the steep place into the lake and drowned. When those who fed them saw what had happened, they fled and told it in the city and in the country. Then they went out to see what had happened, and came to Jesus, and found the man from whom the demons had departed, sitting at the feet of Jesus, clothed and in his right mind. And they were afraid. They also who had seen it told them by what means he who had been demon-possessed was healed. Then the whole multitude of the surrounding region of the Gadarenes asked Him to depart from them, for they were seized with great fear. And He got into the boat and returned. Now the man from whom the demons had departed begged

Him that he might be with Him. But Jesus sent him away, saying," Return to your own house, and tell what great things God has done for you." And he went his way and proclaimed throughout the whole city what great things Jesus had done for him." *Jesus heals a demon-possessed man in the region of the Gadarenes, illustrating his power over evil forces and their impact on individuals.*

Luke: 13:10-17: "Now He was teaching in one of the synagogues on the Sabbath. And behold, there was a woman who had a spirit of infirmity eighteen years, and was bent over and could in no way raise herself up. But when Jesus saw her, He called her to Him and said to her, "Woman, you are loosed from your infirmity." And He laid His hands on her, and immediately she was made straight, and glorified God. But the ruler of the synagogue answered with indignation, because Jesus had healed on the Sabbath; and he said to the crowd, "There are six days on which men ought to work; therefore come and be healed on them, and not on the Sabbath day." The Lord then answered him and said, "Hypocrite! Does not each one of you on the Sabbath loose his ox or donkey from the stall, and lead it away to water it? So ought not this woman, being a daughter of Abraham, whom Satan has bound think of it for eighteen years, be loosed from this bond on the Sabbath? "And when He said these things, all His adversaries were put to shame; and all the multitude rejoiced for all the glorious things that were done by Him." *Jesus heals a woman crippled by a spirit on the Sabbath, defying religious limitations and prioritizing compassion.*

Luke: 18:35-43: "Then it happened, as He was coming near Jericho, that a certain blind man sat by the road begging. And hearing a multitude passing by, he asked what it meant. So they told him that Jesus of Nazareth was passing by. And he cried out, saying, "Jesus, Son of David, have mercy on me!" Then those who went before warned him that he should be quiet; but he cried out all the more, "Son of David, have mercy on me!" So Jesus stood still and commanded him to be brought to Him. And when he had come near, He asked him, saying, "What do you want Me to do for you?" He said, "Lord, that I may receive my sight." Then Jesus said to him, "Receive your sight; your faith has made you well." And immediately he received his sight, and followed Him, glorifying God. And all the people, when they saw it, gave praise to God. *Jesus heals a blind beggar who calls out to him, demonstrating his response to faith and the need to persevere in seeking healing.*

John:

John: 6:5-14: "Then Jesus lifted up His eyes, and seeing a great multitude coming toward Him, He said to Philip, "Where shall we buy bread, that these may eat?" But this He said to test him, for He Himself knew what He would do. Philip answered Him, "Two hundred denarii worth of bread is not sufficient for them, that every one of them may have a little." One of His disciples, Andrew, Simon Peter's brother, said to Him, "There is a lad here who has five barley loaves and two small fish, but what are they among so many?" Then Jesus said, "Make the people sit down." Now there was much grass in the place. So the men sat down, in number about five thousand. And Jesus took the loaves, and when He had given thanks He distributed them to the disciples, and the disciples to those sitting down; and likewise of the fish, as much as they wanted. So when they were filled, He said to His disciples, "Gather up the fragments that remain, so that nothing is lost." Therefore they gathered them up, and filled twelve baskets with the fragments of the five barley loaves which were left over by those who had eaten. Then those men, when they had seen the sign that Jesus did, said, "This is truly the Prophet who is to come into the world." *Jesus miraculously feeds a large crowd, demonstrating his power over hunger and his provision for those in need.*

John: 9:27-34: "He answered them, "I told you already, and you did not listen. Why do you want to hear it again? Do you also want to become His disciples?" Then they reviled him and said, "You are His disciple, but we are Moses' disciples. We know that God spoke to Moses; as for this fellow, we do not know where He is from." The man answered and said to them, "Why, this is a marvelous thing, that you do not know where He is from; yet He has opened my eyes! Now we know that God does not hear sinners; but if anyone is a worshiper of God and does His will, He hears him. Since the world began it has been unheard of that anyone opened the eyes of one who was born blind. If this Man were not from God, He could do nothing." They answered and said to him, "You were completely born in sins, and are you teaching us?" And they cast him out." *Jesus heals a man born blind and restores his sight, provoking controversy among religious leaders.*

Jesus lived compassion as a compassionate healer who reached out to many individuals suffering from various ailments. They reveal His power over physical limitations, demonic forces, and even death itself. His healing ministry served as an unmistakable sign of God's love and grace for His People, offering hope, healing and restoration to those in need.

JESUS' VICTORIOUS POWER OVER NATURE, HEAVEN, & EARTH:

Mark 4:35-41: "On the same day, when evening had come, He said to them, "Let us cross over to the other side." Now when they had left the multitude, they took Him along in the boat as He was. And other little boats were also with Him. And a great windstorm arose, and the waves beat into the boat, so that it was already filling. But He was in the stern, asleep on a pillow. And they awoke Him and said to Him, "Teacher, do You not care that we are perishing?" Then He arose and rebuked the wind, and said to the sea, "Peace, be still!" And the wind ceased and there was a great calm. But He said to them, "Why are you so fearful? How is it that you have no faith?" And they feared exceedingly, and said to one another, "Who can this be, that even the wind and the sea obey Him!" *Jesus calms the storm at sea, showcasing his power over the forces of nature and his ability to bring peace and security even amidst chaos.*

Matthew 14:25-33: "Now in the fourth watch of the night Jesus went to them, walking on the sea. And when the disciples saw Him walking on the sea, they were troubled, saying, "It is a ghost!" And they cried out for fear. But immediately Jesus spoke to them, saying, "Be of good cheer! It is I; do not be afraid." And Peter answered Him and said, "Lord, if it is You, command me to come to You on the water." So He said, "Come." And when Peter had come down out of the boat, he walked on the water to go to Jesus. But when he saw that the wind was boisterous, he was afraid; and beginning to sink he cried out, saying, "Lord, save me!" And immediately Jesus stretched out His hand and caught him, and said to him, "O you of little faith, why did you doubt?" And when they got into the boat, the wind ceased. Then those who were in the boat came and worshiped Him, saying, "Truly You are the Son of God." _Jesus walks on water, demonstrating his mastery over natural laws and his ability to defy human limitations._

John 6:5-14: "Then Jesus lifted up His eyes, and seeing a great multitude coming toward Him, He said to Philip, "Where shall we buy bread, that these may eat?" But this He said to test him, for He Himself knew what He would do. Philip answered Him, "Two hundred denarii worth of bread is not sufficient for them, that every one of them may have a little." One of His disciples, Andrew, Simon Peter's brother, said to Him, "There is a lad here who has five barley loaves and two small fish, but what are they among so many?" Then Jesus said, "Make the people sit down." Now there was much grass in the place. So the men sat down, in number about five thousand. And Jesus took the loaves, and when He had given thanks He distributed them to the disciples, and the disciples to those sitting down; and likewise of the fish, as much as they wanted. So when they were filled, He said to His disciples, "Gather up the fragments that remain, so that nothing is lost." Therefore they gathered them up, and filled twelve baskets with the fragments of the five barley loaves which were left over by those who had eaten. Then those men, when they had seen the sign that Jesus did, said, "This is truly the Prophet who is to come into the world." *Jesus miraculously feeds five thousand people with five loaves of bread and two fish, revealing his power over hunger and his ability to provide for large numbers with limited resources.*

Mark 11:12-14: "Now the next day, when they had come out from Bethany, He was hungry. And seeing from afar a fig tree having leaves, He went to see if perhaps He would find something on it. When He came to it, He found nothing but leaves, for it was not the season for figs. In response Jesus said to it, "Let no one eat fruit from you ever again." And His disciples heard it." *Jesus curses a fig tree that bears no fruit, highlighting his sovereign authority over creation and his expectations of fruitfulness.*

John 21:5-6: "Then Jesus said to them, "Children, have you any food?" They answered Him, "No. And He said to them, "Cast the net on the right side of the boat, and you will find some." So they cast, and now they were not able to draw it in because of the multitude of fish." _Jesus provides a large catch of fish for his disciples after their unsuccessful attempt, demonstrating his knowledge and control over natural resources._

VICTORIOUS OVER HEAVEN

Matthew 28:18: "And Jesus came and spoke to them, saying, "All authority has been given to Me in heaven and on earth." _Jesus declares, "all authority in heaven and on earth has been given to me," emphasizing his universal dominion and power._

John 3:13: "No one has ascended to heaven but He who came down from heaven, that is, the Son of Man who is in heaven." _Jesus states, "no one has ascended to heaven except the one who descended from heaven, the Son of Man," highlighting his unique connection and authority over the heavenly realm._

Matthew 16:19: "And I will give you the keys of the kingdom of heaven, and whatever you bind on earth will be bound in heaven, and whatever you loose on earth will be loosed in heaven." _Jesus grants Peter the "keys of the kingdom of heaven," indicating his power to grant access and authority within the heavenly realm._

John 14:6: "Jesus said to him, "I am the way, the truth, and the life. No one comes to the Father except through Me." _Jesus declares, "I am the way, and the truth, and the life. No one comes to the Father except through me," emphasizing his exclusive role as the mediator between heaven and earth._

Hebrews 4:14-16: "Seeing then that we have a great High Priest who has passed through the heavens, Jesus the Son of God, let us hold fast our confession. For we do not have a High Priest who cannot sympathize with our weaknesses, but was in all points tempted as we are, yet without sin. Let us therefore come boldly to the throne of grace, that we may obtain mercy and find grace to help in time of need." *Jesus is described as the "great high priest who has passed through the heavens," signifying his access to the heavenly sanctuary and his role as the intercessor for the people of God.*

Earth:

Matthew 8:5-13: "Now when Jesus had entered Capernaum, a centurion came to Him, pleading with Him, saying, "Lord, my servant is lying at home paralyzed, dreadfully tormented." And Jesus said to him, "I will come and heal him." The centurion answered and said, "Lord, I am not worthy that You should come under my roof. But only speak a word, and my servant will be healed. For I also am a man under authority, having soldiers under me. And I say to this one, 'Go,' and he goes; and to another, 'Come,' and he comes; and to my servant, 'Do this,' and he does it." When Jesus heard it, He marveled, and said to those who followed, "Assuredly, I say to you, I have not found such great faith, not even in Israel! And I say to you that many will come from east and west, and sit down with Abraham, Isaac, and Jacob in the kingdom of heaven. But the sons of the kingdom will be cast out into outer darkness. There will be weeping and gnashing of teeth." Then Jesus said to the centurion, "Go your way; and as you have believed, so let it be done for you." And his servant was healed that same hour." *Jesus heals the Centurion's servant at a distance, showcasing his power over physical limitations and his ability to act even without being physically present.*

John 5:1-9: "After this there was a feast of the Jews, and Jesus went up to Jerusalem. Now there is in Jerusalem by the Sheep Gate a pool, which is called in Hebrew, Bethesda, having five porches. In these lay a great multitude of sick people, blind, lame, paralyzed, waiting for the moving of the water. For an angel went down at a certain time into the pool and stirred up the water; then whoever stepped in first, after the stirring of the water, was made well of whatever disease he had. Now a certain man was there who had an infirmity thirty-eight years. When Jesus saw him lying there, and knew that he already had been in that condition a long time, He said to him, "Do you want to be made well?"

The sick man answered Him, "Sir, I have no man to put me into the pool when the water is stirred up; but while I am coming, another steps down before me." Jesus said to him, "Rise, take up your bed and walk." And immediately the man was made well, took up his bed, and walked. And that day was the Sabbath." Jesus heals a man at the pool of Bethesda who has been paralyzed for thirty-eight years, demonstrating his power over illness and his ability to restore mobility and health.

John 11:38-44: " Then Jesus, again groaning in Himself, came to the tomb. It was a cave, and a stone lay against it. Jesus said, "Take away the stone." Martha, the sister of him who was dead, said to Him, "Lord, by this time there is a stench, for he has been dead four days." Jesus said to her, "Did I not say to you that if you would believe you would see the glory of God?" Then they took away the stone from the place where the dead man was lying. And Jesus lifted up His eyes and said, "Father, I thank You that You have heard Me. And I know that You always hear Me, but because of the people who are standing by I said this, that they may believe that You sent Me." Now when He had said these things, He cried with a loud voice, "Lazarus, come forth!" And he who had died came out bound hand and foot with graveclothes, and his face was wrapped with a cloth. Jesus said to them, "Loose him, and let him go." *Jesus raises Lazarus from the dead, showcasing his power over death on earth and offering a glimpse into the future resurrection of all believers.*

Matthew 21:12-13: "Then Jesus went into the temple of God and drove out all those who bought and sold in the temple, and overturned the tables of the money changers and the seats of those who sold doves. And He said to them, "It is written, 'My house shall be called a house of prayer,' but you have made it a 'den of thieves." *Jesus drives the moneychangers and merchants out of the temple, demonstrating his authority over religious institutions and his commitment to cleansing and restoring the house of God before he ascended into heaven.*

Revelation 21:1-5: "Now I saw a new heaven and a new earth, for the first heaven and the first earth had passed away. Also there was no more sea. Then I, John, saw the holy city, New Jerusalem, coming down out of heaven from God, prepared as a bride adorned for her husband. And I heard a loud voice from heaven saying, "Behold, the tabernacle of God is with men, and He will dwell with them, and they shall be His people. God Himself will be with them and be their God. And God will wipe away every tear from their eyes; there shall be no more death, nor sorrow, nor crying. There shall be no more pain, for the former things have passed away."

Then He who sat on the throne said, "Behold, I make all things new." And He said to me, "Write, for these words are true and faithful." *The book of Revelation describes a new heaven and a new earth created by God, with Jesus' reigning as King and bringing ultimate peace and justice to the world.*

Undeniably Jesus' acquired eminent power and authority over the natural world, the heavenly realm, and the earth itself. As the sovereign Lord over all creation, capable of calming storms, multiplying resources, healing the sick, raising the dead, and ultimately bringing about a new and eternal Kingdom. His dominion over nature, heaven, and earth encompasses all aspects of existence, offering believers hope and assurance in his ultimate victory and the fulfillment of God's plan.

SCRIPTURES OF JESUS' VICTORY OVER INJUSTICE, OPPRESSION, AND TEMPTATION:

Victory over Injustice and Oppression:

Matthew 5:3-12: "Blessed are the poor in spirit, For theirs is the kingdom of heaven. Blessed are those who mourn, For they shall be comforted. Blessed are the meek, For they shall inherit the earth. Blessed are those who hunger and thirst for righteousness, For they shall be filled. Blessed are the merciful, For they shall obtain mercy. Blessed are the pure in heart, For they shall see God. Blessed are the peacemakers, For they shall be called sons of God. Blessed are those who are persecuted for righteousness' sake, For theirs is the kingdom of heaven. Blessed are you when they revile and persecute you, and say all kinds of evil against you falsely for My sake. Rejoice and be exceedingly glad, for great is your reward in heaven, for so they persecuted the prophets who were before you." _Jesus through the Beatitudes, proclaims blessings upon the poor, hungry, mourning, persecuted, and righteous, highlighting his concern for the vulnerable and downtrodden._

Matthew 12:10-13: "And behold, there was a man who had a withered hand. And they asked Him, saying, "Is it lawful to heal on the Sabbath?" that they might accuse Him. Then He said to them, "What man is there among you who has one sheep, and if it falls into a pit on the

Sabbath, will not lay hold of it and lift it out? Of how much more value then is a man than a sheep? Therefore it is lawful to do good on the Sabbath." Then He said to the man, "Stretch out your hand." And he stretched it out, and it was restored as whole as the other. *Healing a man with a withered hand on the Sabbath, Jesus challenged religious legalism and prioritizing the well-being of individuals over rigid rules.*

Matthew 21:12-13: "Then Jesus went into the temple of God and drove out all those who bought and sold in the temple, and overturned the tables of the money changers and the seats of those who sold doves. And He said to them, "It is written, 'My house shall be called a house of prayer,' but you have made it a 'den of thieves.'" *Driving the moneychangers and merchants out of the temple, Jesus Challenged corruption and exploitation within religious institutions.*

Mark 3:1-5: "Healing on the Sabbath And He entered the synagogue again, and a man was there who had a withered hand. So they watched Him closely, whether He would heal him on the Sabbath, so that they might accuse Him. And He said to the man who had the withered hand, "Step forward." Then He said to them, "Is it lawful on the Sabbath to do good or to do evil, to save life or to kill?" But they kept silent. And when He had looked around at them with anger, being grieved by the hardness of their hearts, He said to the man, "Stretch out your hand." And he stretched it out, and his hand was restored as whole as the other. *Healing a man with a withered hand on* _the Sabbath, Jesus defied religious restrictions and highlighting the importance of compassion over legalism._

Luke 4:16-21: "So He came to Nazareth, where He had been brought up. And as His custom was, He went into the synagogue on the Sabbath day, and stood up to read. And He was handed the book of the prophet Isaiah. And when He had opened the book, He found the place where it was written: "The Spirit of the Lord is upon Me, Because He has anointed Me To preach the gospel to the poor; He has sent Me to heal the brokenhearted, To proclaim liberty to the captives And recovery of sight to the blind, To set at liberty those who are oppressed; To proclaim the acceptable year of the Lord." Then He closed the book, and gave it back to the attendant and sat down. And the eyes of all who were in the synagogue were fixed on Him. And He began to say to them, "Today this Scripture is fulfilled in your hearing." _Proclaiming good news to the poor, freedom for the captives, and recovery of sight to the blind, Jesus outlined His mission to address societal injustices. He was a God of Justice!_

Luke 6:17-26: "And He came down with them and stood on a level place with a crowd of His disciples and a great multitude of people from all Judea and Jerusalem, and from the seacoast of Tyre and Sidon, who came to hear Him and be healed of their diseases, as well as those who were tormented with unclean spirits. And they healed. And the whole multitude sought to touch Him, for power went out from Him and healed them all.

The Beatitudes

Then He lifted up His eyes toward His disciples, and said:

"Blessed are you poor,
For yours is the kingdom of God.
Blessed are you who hunger now,
For you shall be filled.
Blessed are you who weep now,
For you shall laugh.
Blessed are you when men hate you,
And when they exclude you,
And revile you, and cast out your name as evil,
For the Son of Man's sake.
Rejoice in that day and leap for joy!
For indeed your reward is great in heaven,
For in like manner their fathers did to the prophets.

Jesus Pronounces Woes

"But woe to you who are rich,
For you have received your consolation.
Woe to you who are full,
For you shall hunger.
Woe to you who laugh now,
For you shall mourn and weep.

Woe to you when all men speak well of you, For so did their fathers to the false prophets. *The Sermon on the Mount, emphasized love for enemies, generosity to the poor, and forgiveness of those who trespass against us, challenging traditional norms, emphasizing the cruciality a more compassionate and just society.*

Luke 7:11-15: "Now it happened, the day after, that He went into a city called Nain; and many of His disciples went with Him, and a large crowd. And when He came near the gate of the city, behold, a dead man was being carried out, the only son of his mother; and she was a widow. And a large crowd from the city was with her. When the Lord saw her, He had compassion on her and said to her, "Do not weep." Then He came and touched the open coffin, and those who carried him stood still. And He said, "Young man, I say to you, arise." So he who was dead sat up and began to speak. And He presented him to his mother. *"Raising the son of the widow of Nain from the dead, offering comfort and hope to the marginalized ostracized, socially disadvantaged Jesus demonstrated his power over injustice, oppression and death.*

Luke 10:25-37: "And behold, a certain lawyer stood up and tested Him, saying, "Teacher, what shall I do to inherit eternal life?" He said to him, "What is written in the law? What is your reading of it?" So he answered and said, " 'You shall love the Lord your God with all your heart, with all your soul, with all your strength, and with all your mind,' and 'your neighbor as yourself.' " And He said to him, "You have answered rightly; do this and you will live." But he, wanting to justify himself, said to Jesus, "And who is my neighbor?" Then Jesus answered and said: "A certain man went down from Jerusalem to Jericho, and fell among thieves, who stripped him of his clothing, wounded him, and departed, leaving him half dead. Now by chance a certain priest came down that road. And when he saw him, he passed by on the other side. Likewise a Levite, when he arrived at the place, came and looked, and passed by on the other side. But a certain Samaritan, as he journeyed, came where he was. And when he saw him, he had compassion. So he went to him and bandaged his wounds, pouring on oil and wine; and he set him on his own animal, brought him to an inn, and took care of him. On the next day, when he departed, he took out two denarii, gave them to the innkeeper, and said to him, 'Take care of him; and whatever more you spend, when I come again, I will repay you.' So which of these three do you think was neighbor to him who fell among the thieves?" And he said, "He who showed mercy on him" *The parable of the Good Samaritan, exemplifies Jesus challenging prejudice and advocating for compassion and care for those in need, regardless of their background.*

John 8:3-11: "Then the scribes and Pharisees brought to Him a woman caught in adultery. And when they had set her in the midst, they said to Him, "Teacher, this woman was caught in adultery, in the very act. Now Moses, in the law, commanded us that such should be stoned. But what do You say?" This they said, testing Him, that they might have something of which to accuse Him. But Jesus stooped down and wrote on the ground with His finger, as though He did not hear. So when they continued asking Him, He raised Himself up and said to them, "He who is without sin among you, let him throw a stone at her first." And again He stooped down and wrote on the ground. Then those who heard it, being convicted by their conscience, went out one by one, beginning with the oldest even to the last. And Jesus was left alone, and the woman standing in the midst. When Jesus had raised Himself up and saw no one but the woman, He said to her, "Woman, where are those accusers of yours? Has no one condemned you?" She said, "No one, Lord." And Jesus said to her, "Neither do I condemn you; go and sin no more." *Challenging the crowd's desire to stone an adulterous woman, Jesus outright and publicly advocated for forgiveness and compassion over judgment and condemnation, reminding the spectators all have sinned and fallen short of the glory.*

VICTORY OVER TEMPTATION:

Matthew 4:1-11: "Then Jesus was led up by the Spirit into the wilderness to be tempted by the devil. And when He had fasted forty days and forty nights, afterward He was hungry. Now when the tempter came to Him, he said, "If You are the Son of God, command that these stones become bread." But He answered and said, "It is written, 'Man shall not live by bread alone, but by every word that proceeds from the mouth of God.' " Then the devil took Him up into the holy city, set Him on the pinnacle of the temple, and said to Him, "If You are the Son of God, throw Yourself down. For it is written:

'He shall give His angels charge over you,' and, 'In their hands they shall bear you up, Lest you dash your foot against a stone.' " Jesus said to him, "It is written again, 'You shall not tempt the Lord your God.' "Again, the devil took Him up on an exceedingly high mountain, and showed Him all the kingdoms of the world and their glory. And he said to Him, "All these things I will give You if You will fall down and worship me." Then Jesus said to him, "Away with you, Satan! For it is written, 'You shall worship the Lord your God, and Him only you shall serve." Then the devil left Him, and behold, angels came and ministered to Him." *Jesus' temptation in the wilderness, where he successfully resists the devil's attempts to lead him astray.*

Mark 1:12-13: "Immediately the Spirit drove Him into the wilderness. And He was there in the wilderness forty days, tempted by Satan, and was with the wild beasts; and the angels ministered to Him.*" Jesus being tempted by the devil in the wilderness for forty days did not yield to temptation rather reminded the devil who his Lord was.*

Luke 4:1-13: "And the devil said to Him, "If You are the Son of God, command this stone to become bread." But Jesus answered him, saying, "It is written, 'Man shall not live by bread alone, but by every word of God." Then the devil, taking Him up on a high mountain, showed Him all the kingdoms of the world in a moment of time. And the devil said to Him, "All this authority I will give You, and their glory; for this has been delivered to me, and I give it to whomever I wish. Therefore, if You will worship before me, all will be Yours." And Jesus answered and said to him, "Get behind Me, Satan! For it is written, 'You shall worship the Lord your God, and Him only you shall serve." Then he brought Him to

Jerusalem, set Him on the pinnacle of the temple, and said to Him, "If You are the Son of God, throw Yourself down from here. For it is written: 'He shall give His angels charge over you, To keep you,' and,' In their hands they shall bear you up, Lest you dash your foot against a stone.' "And Jesus answered and said to him, "It has been said, 'You shall not tempt the Lord your God.' "Now when the devil had ended every temptation, he departed from Him until an opportune time. *Jesus' temptation in the wilderness, where he resists the devil's offers of bread, power over kingdoms, and the world's glory.*

Hebrews 2:18: "For in that He Himself has suffered, being tempted, He is able to aid those who are tempted." *For in that he himself has suffered, being tempted, he is able to help them that are tempted."*

Hebrews 4:15: "For we do not have a High Priest who cannot sympathize with our weaknesses, but was in all points tempted as we are, yet without sin." *For we do not have a high priest who cannot sympathize with our weaknesses, but one who in every respect has been tempted as we are, yet without sin."*

James 1:12-14: " Blessed is the man who endures temptation; for when he has been approved, he will receive the crown of life which the Lord has promised to those who love Him. Let no one say when he is tempted, "I am tempted by God"; for God cannot be tempted by evil, nor does He Himself tempt anyone. But each one is tempted when he is drawn away by his own desires and enticed. _for God cannot be tempted with evil, neither tempted he any man: But every man is tempted, when he is drawn away of his own lust, and enticed."_

Henceforth:

- ➤ Jesus' overall life and ministry demonstrate His consistent opposition to injustice and oppression.
- ➤ His kingdom teachings consistently challenged the status quo and advocated for the disregarded and oppressed.
- ➤ His resistance to temptation and commitment to God's will serve as an example for all who strive to overcome sin and live a righteous life.

Jesus' victories over injustice, oppression, and temptation remains consistent, offering a powerful testimony to His character, mission, and the values he embodies.

SCRIPTURES OF JESUS CHALLENGING INJUSTICE AND OPPRESSION:

Matthew

Matthew: 5:3-12: "Blessed are the poor in spirit, For theirs is the kingdom of heaven. Blessed are those who mourn, For they shall be comforted.

Blessed are the meek, For they shall inherit the earth. Blessed are those who hunger and thirst for righteousness, For they shall be filled. Blessed are the merciful, For they shall obtain mercy. Blessed are the pure in heart, For they shall see God. Blessed are the peacemakers, For they shall be called sons of God. Blessed are those who are persecuted for righteousness' sake, For theirs is the kingdom of heaven. Blessed are you when they revile and persecute you, and say all kinds of evil against you falsely for My sake. Rejoice and be exceedingly glad, for great is your reward in heaven, for so they persecuted the prophets who were before you. *Jesus delivers the Beatitudes, proclaiming blessings upon the poor, hungry, mourning, persecuted, and righteous, highlighting his concern for the vulnerable and downtrodden.*

Matthew: 12:10-13: "And behold, there was a man who had a withered hand. And they asked Him, saying, "Is it lawful to heal on the Sabbath?" that they might accuse Him. Then He said to them, "What man is there among you who has one sheep, and if it falls into a pit on the Sabbath, will not lay hold of it and lift it out? Of how much more value then is a man than a sheep? Therefore it is lawful to do good on the Sabbath." Then He said to the man, "Stretch out your hand." And he stretched it out, and it was restored as whole as the other" *Jesus heals a man with a withered hand on the Sabbath, challenging religious legalism and prioritizing the well-being of individuals over rigid rules.*

Matthew: **15:21-28**: "Then Jesus went out from there and departed to the region of Tyre and Sidon. And behold, a woman of Canaan came from that region and cried out to Him, saying, "Have mercy on me, O Lord,

Son of David! My daughter is severely demon-possessed." But He answered her not a word. And His disciples came and urged Him, saying, "Send her away, for she cries out after us." But He answered and said, "I was not sent except to the lost sheep of the house of Israel." Then she came and worshiped Him, saying, "Lord, help me!" But He answered and said, "It is not good to take the children's bread and throw it to the little dogs." And she said, "Yes, Lord, yet even the little dogs eat the crumbs which fall from their masters' table." Then Jesus answered and said to her, "O woman, great is your faith! Let it be to you as you desire." And her daughter was healed from that very hour." *Jesus heals the daughter of a Canaanite woman, demonstrating his willingness to reach out to people beyond the boundaries of his own culture and religion.*

Matthew: 9:35-38: "Then Jesus went about all the cities and villages, teaching in their synagogues, preaching the gospel of the kingdom, and healing every sickness and every disease among the people. But when He saw the multitudes, He was moved with compassion for them, because they were weary and scattered, like sheep having no shepherd. Then He said to His disciples, "The harvest truly is plentiful, but the laborers are few. Therefore pray the Lord of the harvest to send out laborers into His harvest." *Jesus has compassion on the crowds who are like sheep without a shepherd, highlighting their lack of leadership and guidance, and urging his disciples to pray for laborers to work in the harvest.*

Matthew: 19:16-26: "Now behold, one came and said to Him, "Good Teacher, what good thing shall I do that I may have eternal life?" So He said to him," Why do you call Me good? No one is good but One, that is, God. But if you want to enter into life, keep the commandments." He said to Him, "Which ones?" Jesus said, 'You shall not murder,' 'You shall not commit adultery,' 'You shall not steal,' 'You shall not bear false witness,' 'Honor your father and your mother,' and, 'You shall love your neighbor as yourself.' "The young man said to Him, "All these things I have kept from my youth. What do I still lack?" Jesus said to him, "If you want to be perfect, go, sell what you have and give to the poor, and you will have treasure in heaven; and come, follow Me." But when the young man heard that saying, he went away sorrowful, for he had great possessions.

With God All Things Are Possible

Then Jesus said to His disciples, "Assuredly, I say to you that it is hard for a rich man to enter the kingdom of heaven. And again I say to you, it is easier for a camel to go through the eye of a needle than for a rich man to enter the kingdom of God." When His disciples heard it, they were greatly astonished, saying, "Who then can be saved?" But Jesus looked at them and said to them, "With men this is impossible, but with God all things are possible." *Jesus teaches about the importance of wealth and possessions, challenging the values of a society obsessed with material gain and encouraging his disciples to seek first the kingdom of God.*

Matthew: 25:31-46: Then Jesus was led up by the Spirit into the wilderness to be tempted by the devil. And when He had fasted forty days and forty nights, afterward He was hungry. Now when the tempter came to Him, he said, "If You are the Son of God, command that these stones become bread." But He answered and said, "It is written, 'Man shall not live by bread alone, but by every word that proceeds from the mouth of God.' "Then the devil took Him up into the holy city, set Him on the pinnacle of the temple, 6 and said to Him, "If You are the Son of God, throw Yourself down. For it is written:

'He shall give His angels charge over you,' and, 'In their hands they shall bear you up, Lest you dash your foot against a stone. Jesus said to him, "It is written again, 'You shall not tempt the Lord your God.' Again, the devil took Him up on an exceedingly high mountain, and showed Him all the kingdoms of the world and their glory. And he said to Him, "All these things I will give You if You will fall down and worship me." Then Jesus said to him, "Away with you, Satan! For it is written, 'You shall worship the Lord your God, and Him only you shall serve." Then the devil left Him, and behold, angels came and ministered to Him. *Jesus tells the parable of the sheep and the goats, emphasizing the importance of caring for the hungry, thirsty, stranger, naked, sick, and imprisoned, demonstrating that true faith manifests in actions of compassion and justice.*

Mark:

Mark: 7:6-8: "He answered and said to them, "Well did Isaiah prophesy of you hypocrites, as it is written: This people honors Me with their lips, But their heart is far from Me. And in vain they worship Me, Teaching as doctrines the commandments of men.' For laying aside the commandment of God, you hold the tradition of men the washing of pitchers and cups, and many other such things you do." *Jesus critiques the religious leaders for honoring God with their lips but not their hearts, highlighting the hypocrisy of adhering to external rituals while neglecting genuine love and justice.*

Mark: 10:17-22: "Now as He was going out on the road, one came running, knelt before Him, and asked Him, "Good Teacher, what shall I do that I may inherit eternal life?" So Jesus said to him, "Why do you call Me good? No one is good but One, that is, God. You know the commandments: 'Do not commit adultery,' 'Do not murder,' 'Do not steal,' 'Do not bear false witness,' 'Do not defraud,' 'Honor your father and your mother.' "

And he answered and said to Him, "Teacher, all these things I have kept from my youth." Then Jesus, looking at him, loved him, and said to him, "One thing you lack: Go your way, sell whatever you have and give to the poor, and you will have treasure in heaven; and come, take up the cross, and follow Me." But he was sad at this word, and went away sorrowful, for he had great possessions." *Jesus challenges the rich young man to give up his possessions and follow him, exposing the limitations of material wealth and advocating for a life dedicated to serving God and others.*

Mark: 12:13-17: "Then they sent to Him some of the Pharisees and the Herodians, to catch Him in His words. When they had come, they said to Him, "Teacher, we know that You are true, and care about no one; for You do not regard the person of men, but teach the way of God in truth. Is it lawful to pay taxes to Caesar, or not? Shall we pay, or shall we not pay?" But He, knowing their hypocrisy, said to them, "Why do you test Me? Bring Me a denarius that I may see it." So they brought it. And He said to them, "Whose image and inscription is this?" They said to Him, "Caesar's." And Jesus answered and said to them, "Render to Caesar the things that are Caesar's, and to God the things that are God's." And they marveled at Him." *Jesus debates the religious leaders about the lawfulness of paying taxes to Caesar, highlighting the tension between earthly authorities and God's kingdom, and advocating for a balanced approach to respecting both.*

Luke:

Luke: 6:37-38: "Judge not, and you shall not be judged. Condemn not, and you shall not be condemned. Forgive, and you will be forgiven. Give, and it will be given to you: good measure, pressed down, shaken together, and running over will be put into your bosom. For with the same measure that you use, it will be measured back to you." *Jesus teaches about judging others and forgiveness, challenging* *the tendency to condemn and highlighting the importance of generosity and compassion.*

Luke: 7:36-50: "Then one of the Pharisees asked Him to eat with him. And He went to the Pharisee's house, and sat down to eat. And behold, a woman in the city who was a sinner, when she knew that Jesus sat at the table in the Pharisee's house, brought an alabaster flask of fragrant oil, and stood at His feet behind Him weeping; and she began to wash His feet with her tears, and wiped them with the hair of her head; and she kissed His feet and anointed them with the fragrant oil. Now when the Pharisee who had invited Him saw this, he spoke to himself, saying, "This Man, if He were a prophet, would know who and what manner of woman this is who is touching Him, for she is a sinner." And Jesus answered and said to him, "Simon, I have something to say to you." So he said, "Teacher, say it." "There was a certain creditor who had two debtors. One owed five hundred denarii, and the other fifty. And when they had nothing with which to repay, he freely forgave them both. Tell Me, therefore, which of them will love him more?" Simon answered and said, "I suppose the one whom he forgave more." And He said to him, "You have rightly judged." Then He turned to the woman and said to Simon, "Do you see this woman? I entered your house; you gave Me no water for My feet, but she has washed My feet with her tears and wiped them with the hair of her head. You gave Me no kiss, but this woman has not ceased to kiss My feet since the time I came in. You did not anoint My head with oil, but this woman has anointed My feet with fragrant oil. Therefore I say to you, her sins, which are many, are forgiven, for she loved much. But to whom little is forgiven, the same loves little." Then He said to her, "Your sins are forgiven." And those who sat at the table with Him began to say to themselves, "Who is this who even forgives sins?" Then He said to the woman, "Your faith has saved you. Go in peace." *Jesus allows a sinful woman to wash his feet and anoint him, challenging societal judgments and demonstrating his acceptance and forgiveness.*

Luke: 16:19-31: "There was a certain rich man who was clothed in purple and fine linen and fared sumptuously every day. But there was a certain beggar named Lazarus, full of sores, who was laid at his gate, desiring to be fed with the crumbs which fell from the rich man's table. Moreover the dogs came and licked his sores. So it was that the beggar died, and was carried by the angels to Abraham's bosom. The rich man also died and was buried. And being in torments in Hades, he lifted up his eyes and saw Abraham afar off, and Lazarus in his bosom.

"Then he cried and said, 'Father Abraham, have mercy on me, and send Lazarus that he may dip the tip of his finger in water and cool my tongue; for I am tormented in this flame.' But Abraham said, 'Son, remember that in your lifetime you received your good things, and likewise Lazarus evil things; but now he is comforted and you are tormented. And besides all this, between us and you there is a great gulf fixed, so that those who want to pass from here to you cannot, nor can those from there pass to us.'

"Then he said, 'I beg you therefore, father, that you would send him to my father's house, for I have five brothers, that he may testify to them, lest they also come to this place of torment.' Abraham said to him, 'They have Moses and the prophets; let them hear them.' And he said, 'No, father Abraham; but if one goes to them from the dead, they will repent.' But he said to him, 'If they do not hear Moses and the prophets, neither will they be persuaded though one rise from the dead.' " *Jesus tells the parable of the rich man and Lazarus, highlighting the consequences of ignoring the suffering of others and the importance of living a life of compassion and generosity.*

Luke: 18:9-14: "Also He spoke this parable to some who trusted in themselves that they were righteous, and despised others: "Two men went up to the temple to pray, one a Pharisee and the other a tax collector. The Pharisee stood and prayed thus with himself, 'God, I thank You that I am not like other men extortioners, unjust, adulterers, or even as this tax collector. I fast twice a week; I give tithes of all that I possess.' And the tax collector, standing afar off, would not so much as raise his eyes to heaven, but beat his breast, saying, 'God, be merciful to me a sinner!' I tell you, this man went down to his house justified rather than the other; for everyone who exalts himself will be humbled, and he who humbles himself will be exalted." *Jesus tells the parable of the Pharisee and the tax collector, challenging religious pride and self-righteousness, and emphasizing the importance of humility and repentance before God.*

John:

John: 8:2-11: "Now early in the morning He came again into the temple, and all the people came to Him; and He sat down and taught them. Then the scribes and Pharisees brought to Him a woman caught in adultery. And when they had set her in the midst, they said to Him, "Teacher, this woman was caught in adultery, in the very act. Now Moses, in the law, commanded us that such should be stoned. But what do You say?" This they said, testing Him, that they might have something of which to accuse Him. But Jesus stooped down and wrote on the ground with His finger, as though He did not hear. So when they continued asking Him, He raised Himself up and said to them, "He who is without sin among you, let him throw a stone at her first." And again He stooped down and wrote on the ground. Then those who heard it, being convicted by their conscience, went out one by one, beginning with the oldest even to the last. And Jesus was left alone, and the woman standing in the midst. When Jesus had raised Himself up and saw no one but the woman, He said to her, "Woman, where are those accusers of yours? Has no one condemned you?" She said, "No one, Lord." And Jesus said to her, "Neither do I condemn you; go and sin no more." *Jesus challenges the* *crowd's desire to stone an adulterous woman, advocating for forgiveness and compassion over judgment and condemnation.*

John: 10:1-18: "Most assuredly, I say to you, he who does not enter the sheepfold by the door, but climbs up some other way, the same is a thief and a robber. But he who enters by the door is the shepherd of the sheep. To him the doorkeeper opens, and the sheep hear his voice; and he calls his own sheep by name and leads them out. And when he brings out his own sheep, he goes before them; and the sheep follow him, for they know his voice. Yet they will by no means follow a stranger, but will flee from him, for they do not know the voice of strangers." Jesus used this illustration, but they did not understand the things which He spoke to them.

Jesus the Good Shepherd

Then Jesus said to them again, "Most assuredly, I say to you, I am the door of the sheep. All who ever came before Me are thieves and robbers, but the sheep did not hear them. I am the door. If anyone enters by Me, he will be saved, and will go in and out and find pasture. The thief does not come except to steal, and to kill, and to destroy. I have come that they may have life, and that they may have it more abundantly. "I am the good shepherd. The good shepherd gives His life for the sheep. But a hireling, he who is not the shepherd, one who does not own the sheep, sees the wolf coming and leaves the sheep and flees; and the wolf catches the sheep and scatters them. The hireling flees because he is a hireling and does not care about the sheep. I am the good shepherd; and I know My sheep, and am known by My own. As the Father knows Me, even so I know the Father; and I lay down My life for the sheep. And other sheep I have which are not of this fold; them also I must bring, and they will hear My voice; and there will be one flock and one shepherd. "Therefore My Father loves Me, because I lay down My life that I may take it again. No one takes it from Me, but I lay it down of Myself. I have power to lay it down, and I have power to take it again. This command I have received from My Father." _Jesus uses the metaphor of the shepherd and the sheep to illustrate his uniquely intimate relationship He has with his followers and his commitment to protecting and guiding them, challenging the authority of false teachers and oppressive leaders._

John: 13:34-35: "A new commandment I give to you, that you love one another; as I have loved you, that you also love one another. By this all will know that you are My disciples, if you have love for one another." _Jesus gives a new commandment to his disciples to love one another, emphasizing the importance of love as the core principle of his teachings and the foundation for a just and peaceful society._

John 21:12-13 "Most assuredly, I say to you, he who does not enter the sheepfold by the door, but climbs up some other way, the same is a thief and a robber. But he who enters by the door is the shepherd of the sheep. To him the doorkeeper opens, and the sheep hear his voice; and he calls his own sheep by name and leads them out. And when he brings out his own sheep, he goes before them; and the sheep follow him, for they know his voice. Yet they will by no means follow a stranger, but will flee from him, for they do not know the voice of strangers." Jesus used this illustration, but they did not understand the things which He spoke to them.

Jesus the Shephard of His People

Then Jesus said to them again, "Most assuredly, I say to you, I am the door of the sheep. All who ever came before Me are thieves and robbers, but the sheep did not hear them. I am the door. If anyone enters by Me, he will be saved, and will go in and out and find pasture. The thief does not come except to steal, and to kill, and to destroy. I have come that they may have life, and that they may have it more abundantly." I am the good shepherd. The good shepherd gives His life for the sheep. But a hireling, he who is not the shepherd, one who does not own the sheep, sees the wolf coming and leaves the sheep and flees; and the wolf catches the sheep and scatters them. The hireling flees because he is a hireling and does not care about the sheep. I am the good shepherd; and I know My sheep, and am known by My own. As the Father knows Me, even so I know the Father; and I lay down My life for the sheep. And other sheep I have which are not of this fold; them also I must bring, and they will hear My voice; and there will be one flock and one shepherd." Therefore My Father loves Me, because

I lay down My life that I may take it again. No one takes it from Me, but I lay it down of Myself. I have power to lay it down, and I have power to take it again. This command I have received from My Father." *Jesus drives the moneychangers and merchants out of the temple, challenging corruption and exploitation within religious institutions.*

Matthew 23 1-39 Then Jesus spoke to the multitudes and to His disciples, saying: "The scribes and the Pharisees sit in Moses' seat. Therefore whatever they tell you to observe, that observe and do, but do not do according to their works; for they say, and do not do. For they bind heavy burdens, hard to bear, and lay them on men's shoulders; but they themselves will not move them with one of their fingers. But all their works they do to be seen by men. They make their phylacteries broad and enlarge the borders of their garments. They love the best places at feasts, the best seats in the synagogues, greetings in the marketplaces, and to be called by men, 'Rabbi, Rabbi.' But you, do not be called 'Rabbi'; for One is your Teacher, the Christ, and you are all brethren. Do not call anyone on earth your father; for One is your Father, He who is in heaven. And do not be called teachers; for One is your Teacher, the Christ. But he who is greatest among you shall be your servant. And whoever exalts himself will be humbled, and he who humbles himself will be exalted." But woe to you, scribes and Pharisees, hypocrites! For you shut up the kingdom of heaven against men; for you neither go in yourselves, nor do you allow those who are entering to go in. Woe to you, scribes and Pharisees, hypocrites! For you devour widows' houses, and for a pretense make long prayers. Therefore you will receive greater condemnation. "Woe to you, scribes and Pharisees, hypocrites! For you travel land and sea to win one proselyte, and when he is won, you make him twice as much a son of hell as yourselves. "Woe to you, blind guides, who say, 'Whoever swears by the temple, it is nothing; but whoever swears by the gold of the temple, he is obliged to perform it.' Fools and blind! For which is greater, the gold or the temple that sanctifies the gold? And, 'Whoever swears by the altar, it is nothing; but whoever swears by the gift that is on it, he is obliged to perform it.' Fools and blind! For which is greater, the gift or the altar that sanctifies the gift? Therefore he who swears by the altar, swears by it and by all things on it. He who swears by the temple, swears by it and by Him who dwells in it. And he who swears by heaven, swears by the throne of God and by Him who sits on it. "Woe to you, scribes and Pharisees, hypocrites! For you pay tithe of mint and anise and cummin, and have neglected the weightier matters of the law: justice and mercy and faith. These you ought to have done, without leaving the others undone. Blind guides, who strain out a gnat and swallow a camel! "Woe to you, scribes and Pharisees, hypocrites! For you cleanse the outside of the cup and dish, but inside they are full of extortion and self-indulgence. Blind Pharisee, first cleanse the inside of the cup and dish, that the outside of them may be clean also. "Woe to you, scribes and Pharisees, hypocrites! For you are like whitewashed tombs which indeed appear beautiful outwardly, but inside are full of dead men's bones and all uncleanness. Even so you also outwardly appear righteous to men, but inside you are full of hypocrisy and lawlessness. "Woe to you, scribes and Pharisees, hypocrites! Because you build the tombs of the prophets and adorn the monuments of the righteous, and say, 'If we had lived in the days of our fathers, we would not have been partakers with them in the blood of the prophets.' "Therefore you are witnesses against yourselves that you are sons of those who murdered the prophets. Fill up, then, the measure of your fathers' guilt. Serpents, brood of vipers! How can you escape the condemnation of hell? Therefore, indeed, I send you prophets, wise men, and scribes: some of them you will kill and crucify, and some of them you will scourge in your synagogues and persecute from city to city, that on you may come all the righteous blood shed on the earth, from the blood of righteous Abel to the blood of Zechariah, son of Berechiah, whom you murdered between the temple and the altar. Assuredly, I say to you, all these things will come upon this generation.

Jesus Laments over Jerusalem

"O Jerusalem, Jerusalem, the one who kills the prophets and stones those who are sent to her! How often I wanted to gather your children together, as a hen gathers her chicks under her wings, but you were not willing! See! Your house is left to you desolate; for I say to you, you shall see Me no more till you say, 'Blessed is He who comes in the name of the Lord!' *Jesus denounces the hypocrisy and legalism of the religious leaders, exposing their oppression and exploitation of the common people.*

Mark:

Mark: 2:5-12: "When Jesus saw their faith, He said to the paralytic, "Son, your sins are forgiven you." And some of the scribes were sitting there and reasoning in their hearts, "Why does this Man speak blasphemies like this? Who can forgive sins but God alone?" But immediately, when Jesus perceived in His spirit that they reasoned thus within themselves, He said to them, "Why do you reason about these things in your hearts? Which is easier, to say to the paralytic, 'Your sins are forgiven you,' or to say, 'Arise, take up your bed and walk'? But that you may know that the Son of Man has power on earth to forgive sins" He said to the paralytic, "I say to you, arise, take up your bed, and go to your house." Immediately he arose, took up the bed, and went out in the presence of them all, so that all were amazed and glorified God, saying, "We never saw anything like this!" *Jesus heals a paralytic man lowered through the roof, challenging societal limitations and prioritizing the healing of the marginalized.*

Mark: 3:1-5: "Healing on the Sabbath "And He entered the synagogue again, and a man was there who had a withered hand. So they watched Him closely, whether He would heal him on the Sabbath, so that they might accuse Him. And He said to the man who had the withered hand, "Step forward." Then He said to them, "Is it lawful on the Sabbath to do good or to do evil, to save life or to kill?" But they kept silent. And when He had looked around at them with anger, being grieved by the hardness of their hearts, He said to the man, "Stretch out your hand." And he stretched it out, and his hand was restored as whole as the other" *Jesus heals a man with a withered hand on the Sabbath, defying religious restrictions and highlighting the importance of compassion over legalism.*

Mark: 10:46-52: Jesus Heals Blind Bartimaeus "Now they came to Jericho. As He went out of Jericho with His disciples and a great multitude, blind Bartimaeus, the son of Timaeus, sat by the road begging. And when he heard that it was Jesus of Nazareth, he began to cry out and say, "Jesus, Son of David, have mercy on me!" Then many warned him to be quiet; but he cried out all the more, "Son of David, have mercy on me!" So Jesus stood still and commanded him to be called. Then they called the blind man, saying to him, "Be of good cheer. Rise, He is calling you." And throwing aside his garment, he rose and came to Jesus. So Jesus answered and said to him, "What do you want Me to do for you?" The blind man said to Him, "Rabboni, that I may receive my sight." Then Jesus said to him, "Go your way; your faith has made you well." And immediately he received his sight and followed Jesus on the road. Jesus heals Bartimaeus, a blind beggar, responding to his faith and challenging societal disregard for the disabled.

Luke:

Luke: 4:16-21: Jesus Himself Rejected at Nazareth

"So He came to Nazareth, where He had been brought up. And as His custom was, He went into the synagogue on the Sabbath day, and stood up to read. And He was handed the book of the prophet Isaiah. And when He had opened the book, He found the place where it was written: "The Spirit of the Lord is upon Me, Because He has anointed Me To preach the gospel to the poor; He has sent Me to heal the brokenhearted, To proclaim liberty to the captives And recovery of sight to the blind,

To set at liberty those who are oppressed; To proclaim the acceptable year of the Lord." Then He closed the book, and gave it back to the attendant and sat down. And the eyes of all who were in the synagogue were fixed on Him. And He began to say to them, "Today this Scripture is fulfilled in your hearing." *Jesus reads from Isaiah in the synagogue, proclaiming good news to the poor, freedom for the captives, and recovery of sight to the blind, outlining his mission to address societal injustices.*

Luke: 6:17-26: Jesus Heals a Great Multitude "And He came down with them and stood on a level place with a crowd of His disciples and a great multitude of people from all Judea and Jerusalem, and from the seacoast of Tyre and Sidon, who came to hear Him and be healed of their diseases, as well as those who were tormented with unclean spirits. And they were healed. And the whole multitude sought to touch Him, for power went out from Him and healed them all. The Beatitudes Then He lifted up His eyes toward His disciples, and said: "Blessed are you poor, For yours is the kingdom of God. Blessed are you who hunger now, For you shall be filled. Blessed are you who weep now, For you shall laugh. Blessed are you when men hate you, And when they exclude you, And revile you, and cast out your name as evil, For the Son of Man's sake. Rejoice in that day and leap for joy! For indeed your reward is great in heaven, For in like manner their fathers did to the prophets.

Jesus Pronounces Woes

"But woe to you who are rich, For you have received your consolation. Woe to you who are full, For you shall hunger. Woe to you who laugh now, For you shall mourn and weep. Woe to you when all men speak well of you,

For so did their fathers to the false prophets. *Jesus delivers the Sermon on the Plain, emphasizing love for enemies, generosity to the poor, and forgiveness of those who trespass against us, challenging societal norms and promoting a more compassionate and just society.*

Luke: 7:11-15: "Jesus Raises the Son of the Widow of Nain Now it happened, the day after, that He went into a city called Nain; and many of His disciples went with Him, and a large crowd. And when He came near the gate of the city, behold, a dead man was being carried out, the only son of his mother; and she was a widow. And a large crowd from the city was with her. When the Lord saw her, He had compassion on her and said to her, "Do not weep." Then He came and touched the open coffin, and those who carried him stood still. And He said, "Young man, I say to you, arise." So he who was dead sat up and began to speak. And He presented him to his mother" *Jesus raises the son of the widow of Nain from the dead, offering comfort and hope to the marginalized and demonstrating his power over death.*

Luke: 10:25-37: The Parable of the Good Samaritan And behold, a certain lawyer stood up and tested Him, saying, "Teacher, what shall I do to inherit eternal life?" He said to him, "What is written in the law? What is your reading of it?" So he answered and said, " 'You shall love the Lord your God with all your heart, with all your soul, with all your strength, and with all your mind,' and 'your neighbor as yourself.' "And He said to him, "You have answered rightly; do this and you will live." But he, wanting to justify himself, said to Jesus, "And who is my neighbor?" Then Jesus answered and said: "A certain man went down from Jerusalem to Jericho, and fell among thieves, who stripped him of his clothing, wounded him, and departed, leaving him half dead. Now by chance a certain priest came down that road. And when he saw him, he passed by on the other side. Likewise a Levite, when he arrived at the place, came and looked, and passed by on the other side. But a certain Samaritan, as he journeyed, came where he was. And when he saw him, he had compassion. So he went to him and bandaged his wounds, pouring on oil and wine; and he set him on his own animal, brought him to an inn, and took care of him. On the next day, when he departed, he took out two denarii, gave them to the innkeeper, and said to him, 'Take care of him; and whatever more you spend, when I come again, I will repay you.' So which of these three do you think was neighbor to him who fell among the thieves?" And he said, "He who showed mercy on him." Then Jesus said to him, "Go and do likewise." _Jesus tells the parable of the Good Samaritan, challenging prejudice and advocating for compassion and care for those in need, regardless of their background._

Luke: 14:12-14: "Then He also said to him who invited Him, "When you give a dinner or a supper, do not ask your friends, your brothers, your relatives, nor rich neighbors, lest they also invite you back, and you be repaid. But when you give a feast, invite the poor, the maimed, the lame, the blind. And you will be blessed, because they cannot repay you; for you shall be repaid at the resurrection of the just." _Jesus instructs his disciples to invite the poor, the crippled, the lame, and the blind to a feast, challenging social hierarchies and prioritizing the inclusion and dignity of the marginalized._

John

John: 4:7-26: "The woman said to Him, "Sir, You have nothing to draw with, and the well is deep. Where then do You get that living water? Are You greater than our father Jacob, who gave us the well, and drank from it himself, as well as his sons and his livestock?" Jesus answered and said to her, "Whoever drinks of this water will thirst again, but whoever drinks of the water that I shall give him will never thirst. But the water that I shall give him will become in him a fountain of water springing up into everlasting life." The woman said to Him, "Sir, give me this water, that I may not thirst, nor come here to draw." Jesus said to her, "Go, call your husband, and come here." The woman answered and said, "I have no husband." Jesus said to her, "You have well said, 'I have no husband,' for you have had five husbands, and the one whom you now have is not your husband; in that you spoke truly." The woman said to Him, "Sir, I perceive that You are a prophet. Our fathers worshiped on this mountain, and you Jews say that in Jerusalem is the place where one ought to worship." Jesus said to her, "Woman, believe Me, the hour is coming when you will neither on this mountain, nor in Jerusalem, worship the Father. You worship what you do not know; we know what we worship, for salvation is of the Jews. But the hour is coming, and now is, when the true worshipers will worship the Father in spirit and truth; for the Father is seeking such to worship Him. God is Spirit, and those who worship Him must worship in spirit and truth." The woman said to Him, "I know that Messiah is coming" (who is called Christ). "When He comes, He will tell us all things." Jesus said to her, "I who speak to you am He."

Jesus converses with a Samaritan woman at a well, breaking down _cultural barriers and engaging with those traditionally excluded from religious discourse._

John: 8:3-11: "Then the scribes and Pharisees brought to Him a woman caught in adultery. And when they had set her in the midst, they said to Him, "Teacher, this woman was caught in adultery, in the very act. Now Moses, in the law, commanded us that such should be stoned. But what do You say?" This they said, testing Him, that they might have something of which to accuse Him. But Jesus stooped down and wrote on the ground with His finger, as though He did not hear. So when they continued asking Him, He raised Himself up and said to them, "He who is without sin among you, let him throw a stone at her first." And again He stooped down and wrote on the ground. Then those who heard it, being convicted by their conscience, went out one by one, beginning with the oldest even to the last. And Jesus was left alone, and the woman standing in the midst. When Jesus had raised Himself up and saw no one but the woman, He said to her, "Woman, where are those accusers of yours? Has no one condemned you?"

She said, "No one, Lord." And Jesus said to her, "Neither do I condemn you; go and sin no more." _Jesus challenges the crowd's desire to stone an adulterous woman, advocating for forgiveness and compassion over judgment and condemnation._

John: 13:1-17: Jesus Washes the Disciples' Feet. Now before the Feast of the Passover, when Jesus knew that His hour had come that He should depart from this world to the Father, having loved His own who were in the world, He loved them to the end. And supper being ended, the devil having already put it into the heart of Judas Iscariot, Simon's son, to betray Him, Jesus, knowing that the Father had given all things into His hands, and that He had come from God and was going to God, rose from supper and laid aside His garments, took a towel and girded Himself. After that, He poured water into a basin and began to wash the disciples' feet, and to wipe them with the towel with which He was girded. Then He came to Simon Peter. And Peter said to Him, "Lord, are You washing my feet?" Jesus answered and said to him, "What I am doing you do not understand now, but you will know after this." Peter said to Him, "You shall never wash my feet!" Jesus answered him, "If I do not wash you, you have no part with Me." Simon Peter said to Him, "Lord, not my feet only, but also my hands and my head!" Jesus said to him, "He who is bathed needs only to wash his feet, but is completely clean; and you are clean, but not all of you." For He knew who would betray Him; therefore He said, "You are not all clean. "So when He had washed their feet, taken His garments, and sat down again, He said to them, "Do you know what I have done to you? You call Me Teacher and Lord, and you say well, for so I am. If I then, your Lord and Teacher, have washed your feet, you also ought to wash one another's feet. For I have given you an example, that you should do as I have done to you. Most assuredly, I say to you, a servant is not greater than his master; nor is he who is sent greater than he who sent him. If you know these things, blessed are you if you do them. *Jesus washes the feet of his disciples, demonstrating humility and service, challenging societal expectations of power and dominance.*

These sacred texts of the gospels offer a powerful glimpses of Jesus Christ "active engagement" into challenging the injustices and oppressions of His time. His actions and teachings divulge a deep concern for the disregarded, marginalized and cast out , epitomizing a commitment to justice, and a passionate desire to see God's kingdom established on earth, where love, compassion, forgiveness prevail. His declarations continue to inspire and guide believers in their pursuit of a more spiritually just world. For the Just live by faith. Jesus' commitment to social justice and His bold active resistance against various forms of oppression and injustice was made known outrightly. He challenged the societal norms of his time, advocated for the marginalized, and offered a vision of a world renovated by compassion, love, and equality. His teachings and actions continue to inspire individuals and communities to work towards building a more just and equitable world, reflecting the values of his kingdom.

VICTORY OVER DEATH:

Matthew 28:5-7: "But the angel answered and said to the women, "Do not be afraid, for I know that you seek Jesus who was crucified. He is not here; for He is risen, as He said. Come, see the place where the Lord lay. And go quickly and tell His disciples that He is risen from the dead, and indeed He is going before you into Galilee; there you will see Him. Behold, I have told you." _This passage describes the empty tomb and announces Jesus' resurrection, marking the beginning of his victory over death._

John 11:25-26: "Jesus declares, "I am the resurrection and the life. Whoever believes in me, though he die, yet shall he live, and everyone who lives and believes in me shall never die. Do you believe this?" _In this verse Jesus authoritatively declared his power over death and offers the promise of eternal life to those who follow him._

1 Corinthians 15:54-57: "When the perishable puts on the imperishable, and the mortal puts on immortality, then shall come to pass the saying that is written: 'Death is swallowed up in victory.' 'O Death, where is your sting? O Sheol, where is your victory?' The sting of death is sin, and the power of sin is the law. But thanks be to God, who gives us the victory through our Lord Jesus Christ." Jesus boldly denounces the assignment of death. _Jesus' declares victory over death and its sting, which is sin. Through His sacrifice, He offers believers the gift of eternal life._

Revelation 1:18: "I died, and behold I am alive forevermore, and I have the keys of Death and Hades." _This report by the resurrected Jesus affirms his authority over death and even Hell._

Revelation 21:4: "He will wipe away every tear from their eyes, and death shall be no more, neither shall there be mourning, nor crying, nor pain anymore, for the former things have passed away." _This passage describes the future state of heaven, where death and suffering are abolished, and believers experience eternal joy and peace._

Isaiah 53, illustrates the most profound powerful prophecy that demonstrates Jesus Christ's ultimate victory over death, let's delve into the details ....

Substitutionary Atonement

Isaiah 53:8 "For the transgression of my people he was punished." This verse highlights that Jesus, as the suffering servant, bore the punishment for our sins. His sacrificial death on the cross serves as a substitute for our guilt. _Through His death, we are set free from condemnation and the penalty of sin. When Jesus declared, "It is finished!" on the cross, He fulfilled the just requirements of the law against us, once and for all_

Victory Over Death

Jesus' death was a decisive victory. Just as Samson's last victory over the Philistines involved pulling down the house and sacrificing himself, Jesus conquered death itself. His cry, "It is finished," signified the completion of God's redemptive plan. By **_dying_** and **_rising again_**, Jesus destroyed the power of death.

Securing Our Justification

Jesus secured our justification before God. His perfect life, fulfilling God's laws, is credited to us when we put our faith in Him and are faithful to His redemptive plan. He paid the penalty for our sins, satisfying God's justice. His resurrection demonstrated God's acceptance of His sacrifice. By grace through faith in Christ alone. All our sins past, present, and future are forgiven through His sacrificial atonement to sins. Justification is based on an objective legal agreement which is acceptable to God, not our feelings. However, if an individual does not accept Jesus Christ as Lord and Savior, and will not allow Christ's blood to pay the detrimental debt of sin, the only recourse is for his life to be taken as "restitutional-payment" for his sin. If thus said individual is determined to live in opposition to God, unconcerned about obeying God's commands, that person risk being given the gift of eternal life for eternal everlasting punishment. False teachers, who will, over time, detrimentally pervert and damage the faith on which we stand teach that once you are saved it is impossible to lose Gods Grace. "Not TRUE", Titus 3 warns every believer to "Maintain Good Works; {Prayer, compassion, repentance & doing Gods Will] "*But when the kindness and the love of God our Savior toward man appeared, not by works of righteousness which we have done, but according to His mercy He saved us, through the washing of regeneration and renewing of the Holy Spirit, whom He poured out on us abundantly through Jesus Christ our Savior, that having been justified by His grace we should become heirs according to the hope of eternal life.* This is a faithful saying, and these things I want you to affirm constantly, that those who have believed in God should be careful to maintain good works.

Triumph Over Evil

Jesus' resurrection proclaims God's triumph over the forces of evil. Accepting His atonement assures our final victory over sin and death. His Lordship is acknowledged by all, as every knee will bow before Him.

Isaiah 53 *declares Jesus Christ's victory over death through His sacrificial work, securing our redemption, justification, and eternal life. His triumphant cry echoes through the ages: "It is finished!"*

VICTORY OVER HELL (SHEOL):

Acts 2:27-31: Peter, quoting David, declares that "You will not abandon my soul to Hades[Hell], nor let your Holy One see corruption." *This verse emphasizes that Jesus' soul was not left in the realm of the dead, foreshadowing his resurrection.*

Romans 10:7: Paul asks, "Or who will descend into the deep?" *Referring to Hades, implying that Christ did descend into this realm and conquered it.*

Ephesians 4:9: "(Now this, "He ascended" what does it mean but that He also first descended into the lower parts of the earth?" *This verse states that Christ "descended into the lower parts of the earth." This could be interpreted as referring to his descent into Hades before his resurrection.*

Matthew 12:40: "For as Jonah was three days and three nights in the belly of the great fish, so will the Son of Man be three days and three nights in the heart of the earth. "*Jesus declares that just as Jonah was in the belly of the fish, so the Son of Man (referring to Himself) would be in the heart of the earth (referring to Hell) for three days and three nights. This statement points directly to Jesus' impending death, burial, and subsequent resurrection".*

VICTORY OVER THE GRAVE (HADES):

Acts 2:24: Peter declares that God raised Jesus from the dead, "breaking the pangs of death, because it was not possible for him to be held by it." *This verse emphasizes God's power over death and his release of Jesus from the grave.*

1 Corinthians 15:55: Paul declares, "O grave, where is your victory? O death, where is your sting?" *This verse again celebrates Jesus' victory over death and its dominion over the grave.*

Matthew 12:40: "For as Jonah was three days and three nights in the belly of the great fish, so will the Son of Man be three days and three nights in the heart of the earth" *He descended into the realm of the dead, proclaiming His authority and defeating the enemy. His resurrection shattered the gates of hell, securing eternal life for all who believe in Him.*

161

Victory over the Abyss (Greek Word: "abyssos")

Revelation 20:1-3: "Then I saw an angel coming down from heaven, having the key to the bottomless pit and a great chain in his hand. He laid hold of the dragon, that serpent of old, who is the Devil and Satan, and bound him for a thousand years; and he cast him into the bottomless pit, and shut him up, and set a seal on him, so that he should deceive the nations no more till the thousand years were finished. But after these things he must be released for a little while." *This passage describes the binding of Satan for a thousand years, symbolizing the ultimate triumph of God and his kingdom over the forces of evil, including the abyss.*

Luke 8:31: "And they begged Him that He would not command them to go out into the abyss." *Demons beg Jesus not to command them to go to the "abyss," suggesting a place of confinement and judgment for evil spirits.*

Jesus Christ victory over death, hell, the grave, and the abyss were carried out like no other. His triumph over these domains signifies the ultimate power of God and His love for humanity. He conquered death and opened the way for eternal life for those who believe in him.

JESUS BEING VICTORIOUS OVER THIRST & FAMINE

Responding to Hunger

Matthew 14:13-21: "When Jesus heard it, He departed from there by boat to a deserted place by Himself. But when the multitudes heard it, they followed Him on foot from the cities. And when Jesus went out He saw a great multitude; and He was moved with compassion for them, and healed their sick. When it was evening, His disciples came to Him, saying, "This is a deserted place, and the hour is already late. Send the multitudes away, that they may go into the villages and buy themselves food." But Jesus said to them, "They do not need to go away. You give them something to eat."

And they said to Him, "We have here only five loaves and two fish." He said, "Bring them here to Me." Then He commanded the multitudes to sit down on the grass. And He took the five loaves and the two fish, and looking up to heaven, He blessed and broke and gave the loaves to the disciples; and the disciples gave to the multitudes. So they all ate and were filled, and they took up twelve baskets full of the fragments that remained. Now those who had eaten were about five thousand men, besides women and children." *Jesus miraculously feeds five thousand people with five loaves of bread and two fish, demonstrating his power to multiply resources and provide for large crowds with limited supplies. Jesus' compassion and power in addressing the needs of the hungry and spiritually thirsty.*

Matthew 25:35-36: "for I was hungry and you gave Me food; I was thirsty and you gave Me drink; I was a stranger and you took Me in; I was naked and you clothed Me; I was sick and you visited Me; I was in prison and you came to Me." *In the parable of the sheep and the goats, Jesus emphasizes the importance of feeding the hungry and caring for those in need.*

Luke 14:12-14: "Then He also said to him who invited Him, "When you give a dinner or a supper, do not ask your friends, your brothers, your relatives, nor rich neighbors, lest they also invite you back, and you be repaid. But when you give a feast, invite the poor, the maimed, the lame, the blind. And you will be blessed, because they cannot repay you; for you shall be repaid at the resurrection of the just." *Jesus instructs His host to invite the poor, the crippled, the lame, and the blind to a feast, prioritizing the inclusion and care of those who were often marginalized and neglected.*

John 6:5-13: "Then Jesus lifted up His eyes, and seeing a great multitude coming toward Him, He said to Philip, "Where shall we buy bread, that these may eat?" But this He said to test him, for He Himself knew what He would do. Philip answered Him, "Two hundred denarii worth of bread is not sufficient for them, that every one of them may have a little." One of His disciples, Andrew, Simon Peter's brother, said to Him, "There is a lad here who has five barley loaves and two small fish, but what are they among so many?" Then Jesus said, "Make the people sit down." Now there was much grass in the place. So the men sat down, in number about five thousand. And Jesus took the loaves, and when He had given thanks He distributed them to the disciples, and the disciples to those sitting down; and likewise of the fish, as much as they wanted. So when they were filled, He said to His disciples, "Gather up the fragments that remain, so that nothing is lost." Therefore they gathered them up, and filled twelve baskets with the fragments of the five barley loaves which were left over by those who had eaten." *Jesus feeds five thousand people with five loaves and two fish, showcasing his ability to overcome hunger and care for the needs of others.*

Acts 6:1-7: "Now in those days, when the number of the disciples was multiplying, there arose a complaint against the Hebrews by the Hellenists, because their widows were neglected in the daily distribution. Then the twelve summoned the multitude of the disciples and said, "It is not desirable that we should leave the word of God and serve tables. Therefore, brethren, seek out from among you seven men of good reputation, full of the Holy Spirit and wisdom, whom we may appoint over this business; but we will give ourselves continually to prayer and to the ministry of the word." And the saying pleased the whole multitude. And they chose Stephen, a man full of faith and the Holy Spirit, and Philip, Prochorus, Nicanor, Timon, Parmenas, and Nicolas, a proselyte from Antioch, whom they set before the apostles; and when they had prayed, they laid hands on them. Then the word of God spread, and the number of the disciples multiplied greatly in Jerusalem, and a great many of the priests were obedient to the faith. *The early church establishes a system to ensure the fair distribution of food among widows and other vulnerable members, reflecting Jesus' teachings on caring for the less fortunate.*

James 2:14-17: " What does it profit, my brethren, if someone says he has faith but does not have works? Can faith save him? If a brother or sister is naked and destitute of daily food, and one of you says to them, "Depart in peace, be warmed and filled," but you do not give them the things which are needed for the body, what does it profit? Thus also faith by itself, if it does not have works, is dead." *James, Jesus Disciple emphasizes the importance of accompanying faith with action, encouraging believers to demonstrate their love for God through acts of compassion and service, such as providing food for the hungry.*

OFFERING WATER:

Isaiah 41:17-18: "The poor and needy seek water, but there is none, Their tongues fail for thirst. I, the Lord, will hear them; I, the God of Israel, will not forsake them.

I will open rivers in desolate heights, And fountains in the midst of the valleys; I will make the wilderness a pool of water, And the dry land springs of water." *The prophet Isaiah speaks of God's promise to open springs in the desert and provide water for the thirsty, foreshadowing the future provision of Jesus' living water.*

John 7:39: "On the last day, that great day of the feast, Jesus stood and cried out, saying, "If anyone thirsts, let him come to Me and drink. He who believes in Me, as the Scripture has said, out of his heart will flow rivers of living water." But this He spoke concerning the Spirit, whom those believing in Him would receive; for the Holy Spirit was not yet given, because Jesus was not yet glorified." *This verse clarifies the previous statement about rivers of living water, stating that "He spoke of the Spirit that those who believed in him were to receive." This highlights the connection between Jesus' offer of living water and the gift of the Holy Spirit.*

Revelation 22:17: 17 And the Spirit and the bride say, "Come!" And let him who hears say, "Come!" And let him who thirsts come. Whoever desires, let him take the water of life freely." *This verse reiterates the invitation for anyone who is thirsty to come and drink of the water of life freely, emphasizing the universal accessibility of God's grace and forgiveness(freely Jesus Gives).*

Jesus Christ commitment to addressing both physical and spiritual hunger and thirst. He not only miraculously provided for the immediate needs of people, but also offered a deeper source of nourishment and fulfillment through his teachings and the gift of the Holy Spirit. His example inspires individuals and communities to continue to work for a world where everyone has access to the necessities of life and the hope and peace found in Christ.

John 4:7-14: "Then the woman of Samaria said to Him, "How is it that You, being a Jew, ask a drink from me, a Samaritan woman?" For Jews have no dealings with

Samaritans. Jesus answered and said to her, "If you knew the gift of God, and who it is who says to you, 'Give Me a drink,' you would have asked Him, and He would have given you living water." The woman said to Him, "Sir, You have nothing to draw with, and the well is deep. Where then do You get that living water? Are You greater than our father Jacob, who gave us the well, and drank from it himself, as well as his sons and his livestock?" Jesus answered and said to her, "Whoever drinks of this water will thirst again, but whoever drinks of the water that I shall give him will never thirst. But the water that I shall give him will become in him a fountain of water springing up into everlasting life." *Jesus encounters a Samaritan woman at a well and offers her living water, symbolizing his ability to provide spiritual refreshment and quench the deepest thirst for meaning and purpose.*

John 7:37-38: "On the last day, that great day of the feast, Jesus stood and cried out, saying, "If anyone thirsts, let him come to Me and drink. He who believes in Me, as the Scripture has said, out of his heart will flow rivers of living water." *During the Feast of Tabernacles, Jesus declares, "Let anyone who is thirsty come to me and drink. Whoever believes in me, as the Scripture has said, rivers of living water will flow from within them." This statement emphasizes his ability to quench spiritual thirst and offer eternal life.*

Revelation 21:6: "On the last day, that great day of the feast, Jesus stood and cried out, saying, "If anyone thirsts, let him come to Me and drink. He who believes in Me, as the Scripture has said, out of his heart will flow rivers of living water" *In the vision of the New Jerusalem, God declares, "I will freely give to the one who is thirsty from the spring of the water of life." This verse symbolizes the abundant provision of God's grace and blessings for all who seek him.*

These powerful scriptures illustrate Jesus' power to provide for the physical and spiritual needs of others. His compassionate acts of feeding the hungry and offering living water demonstrates His commitment to alleviating suffering and offering hope and sustenance to those in need.

JESUS' VICTORY OVER PERSECUTION:

New Testament:

Matthew 2:13-18: The Flight into Egypt "Now when they had departed, behold, an angel of the Lord appeared to Joseph in a dream, saying, "Arise, take the young Child and His mother, flee to Egypt, and stay there until I bring you word; for Herod will seek the young Child to destroy Him." When he arose, he took the young Child and His mother by night and departed for Egypt, and was there until the death of Herod, that it might be fulfilled which was spoken by the Lord through the prophet, saying, "Out of Egypt I called My Son."

Massacre of the Innocents

Then Herod, when he saw that he was deceived by the wise men, was exceedingly angry; and he sent forth and put to death all the male children who were in Bethlehem and in all its districts, from two years old and under, according to the time which he had determined from the wise men. Then was fulfilled what was spoken by Jeremiah the prophet, saying:

"A voice was heard in Ramah,
Lamentation, weeping, and great mourning,
Rachel weeping for her children,
Refusing to be comforted,
Because they are no more."

King Herod sought to kill the infant Jesus, forcing the Holy Family to flee to Egypt, highlighting the persecution faced by Jesus from an early age.

Matthew 10:16-22: "Persecutions Are Coming "Behold, I send you out as sheep in the midst of wolves. Therefore be wise as serpents and harmless as doves. But beware of men, for they will deliver you up to councils and scourge you in their synagogues. You will be brought before governors and kings for My sake, as a testimony to them and to the Gentiles. But when they deliver you up, do not worry about how or what you should speak. For it will be given to you in that hour what you should speak; for it is not you who speak, but the Spirit of your Father who speaks in you.

"Now brother will deliver up brother to death, and a father his child; and children will rise up against parents and cause them to be put to death. And you will be hated by all for My name's sake. But he who endures to the end will be saved." *Jesus warns his disciples that they will be "like sheep among wolves," facing persecution and opposition for their beliefs. However, he encourages them to be fearless and trust in God's protection.*

Matthew 26:57-68: Jesus Faces the Sanhedrin "And those who had laid hold of Jesus led Him away to Caiaphas the high priest, where the scribes and the elders were assembled. But Peter followed Him at a distance to the high priest's courtyard. And he went in and sat with the servants to see the end. Now the chief priests, the elders, and all the council sought false testimony against Jesus to put Him to death, but found none. Even though many false witnesses came forward, they found none. But at last two false witnesses came forward and said, "This fellow said, 'I am able to destroy the temple of God and to build it in three days.'" And the high priest arose and said to Him, "Do You answer nothing? What is it these men testify against You?" But Jesus kept silent. And the high priest answered and said to Him, "I put You under oath by the living God: Tell us if You are the Christ, the Son of God!" Jesus said to him, "It is as you said. Nevertheless, I say to you, hereafter you will see the Son of Man sitting at the right hand of the Power, and coming on the clouds of heaven." Then the high priest tore his clothes, saying, "He has spoken blasphemy! What further need do we have of witnesses? Look, now you have heard His blasphemy! What do you think?" They answered and said, "He is deserving of death." Then they spat in His face and beat Him; and others struck Him with [d]the palms of their hands, saying, "Prophesy to us, Christ! Who is the one who struck You?" *Jesus is arrested, falsely accused, and physically abused by the authorities, demonstrating his willingness to endure suffering for the salvation of many.*

Mark 13:9-13: "But watch out for yourselves, for they will deliver you up to councils, and you will be beaten in the synagogues. You will be brought before rulers and kings for My sake, for a testimony to them. And the gospel must first be preached to all the nations. But when they arrest you and deliver you up, do not worry beforehand, or premeditate what you will speak. But whatever is given you in that hour, speak that; for it is not you who speak, but the Holy Spirit. Now brother will betray brother to death, and a father his child; and children will rise up against parents and cause them to be put to death. And you will be hated by all for My name's sake. But he who endures to the end shall be saved. *Jesus warns of the future persecution of Christians, stating that they will be "betrayed even by parents and brothers and relatives and friends, and some of you they will put to death." This emphasizes the potential severity of persecution and the need for endurance.*

Mark 14:65: "Then some began to spit on Him, and to blindfold Him, and to beat Him, and to say to Him, "Prophesy!" And the officers struck Him with the palms of their hands." *After Jesus' arrest, some began to spit on him, blindfold him, and mock him, showcasing the intense persecution he faced.*

Luke 9:23-26: "Then He said to them all, "If anyone desires to come after Me, let him deny himself, and take up his cross daily, and follow Me. For whoever desires to save his life will lose it, but whoever loses his life for My sake will save it. For what profit is it to a man if he gains the whole world, and is himself destroyed or lost? For whoever is ashamed of Me and My words, of him the Son of Man will be ashamed when He comes in His own glory, and in His Father's, and of the holy angels." *Jesus calls his disciples to take up their crosses and follow him, emphasizing the willingness to suffer and endure hardship for the sake of the gospel.*

Luke 23:26-49: "Now as they led Him away, they laid hold of a certain man, Simon a Cyrenian, who was coming from the country, and on him they laid the cross that he might bear it after Jesus. And a great multitude of the people followed Him, and women who also mourned and lamented Him. But Jesus, turning to them, said, "Daughters of Jerusalem, do not weep for Me, but weep for yourselves and for your children. For indeed the days are coming in which they will say, 'Blessed are the barren, wombs that never bore, and breasts which never nursed!' Then they will begin 'to say to the mountains, "Fall on us!" and to the hills, "Cover us!" ' For if they do these things in the green wood, what will be done in the dry?"

There were also two others, criminals, led with Him to be put to death. And when they had come to the place called Calvary, there they crucified Him, and the criminals, one on the right hand and the other on the left. Then Jesus said, "Father, forgive them, for they do not know what they do." And they divided His garments and cast lots. And the people stood looking on. But even the rulers with them sneered, saying, "He saved others; let Him save Himself if He is the Christ, the chosen of God." The soldiers also mocked Him, coming and offering Him sour wine, and saying, "If You are the King of the Jews, save Yourself." And an inscription also was written over Him in letters of Greek, Latin, and Hebrew:

THIS IS THE KING OF THE JEWS.

"Then one of the criminals who were hanged blasphemed Him, saying, If You are the Christ, save Yourself and us." But the other, answering, rebuked him, saying, "Do you not even fear God, seeing you are under the same condemnation? And we indeed justly, for we receive the due reward of our deeds; but this Man has done nothing wrong." Then he said to Jesus, "Lord, remember me when You come into Your kingdom." And Jesus said to him, "Assuredly, I say to you, today you will be with Me in Paradise."

JESUS DIES ON THE CROSS

Now it was about the sixth hour, and there was darkness over all the earth until the ninth hour. Then the sun was darkened, and the veil of the temple was torn in two. And when Jesus had cried out with a loud voice, He said, "Father, 'into Your hands I commit My spirit.' " Having said this, He breathed His last. So when the centurion saw what had happened, he glorified God, saying, "Certainly this was a righteous Man!" And the whole crowd who came together to that sight, seeing what had been done, beat their breasts and returned. But all His acquaintances, and the women who followed Him from Galilee, stood at a distance, watching these things." *Jesus is crucified alongside criminals, enduring physical pain and humiliation, yet demonstrating his forgiveness and compassion even towards his tormentors.*

John 15:18-20: "If the world hates you, you know that it hated Me before it hated you. If you were of the world, the world would love its own. Yet because you are not of the world, but I chose you out of the world, therefore the world hates you. Remember the word that I said to you, 'A servant is not greater than his master.' If they persecuted Me, they will also persecute you. If they kept My word, they will keep yours also." *Jesus warns his disciples about the persecution they will face, stating, "If the world hates you, know that it has hated me before it hated you." This emphasizes the connection between his own experience and the struggles of his followers.*

John 16:33: " These things I have spoken to you, that in Me you may have peace. In the world you will have tribulation; but be of good cheer, I have overcome the world." _Jesus comforts his disciples by stating, "I have overcome the world." This statement implies his victory not only over death but also over the forces of evil and opposition to his message._

Hebrews 12:1-2: "Therefore we also, since we are surrounded by so great a cloud of witnesses, let us lay aside every weight, and the sin which so easily ensnares us, and let us run with endurance the race that is set before us, looking unto Jesus, the author and finisher of our faith, who for the joy that was set before Him endured the cross, despising the shame, and has sat down at the right hand of the throne of God" _The author encourages believers to persevere in the face of trials and persecution, reminding them of the "great cloud of witnesses" who have gone before them and the reward that awaits them in heaven._

Acts 7:54-60: "Stephen the Martyr "When they heard these things they were cut to the heart, and they gnashed at him with their teeth. But he, being full of the Holy Spirit, gazed into heaven and saw the glory of God, and Jesus standing at the right hand of God, and said, "Look! I see the heavens opened and the Son of Man standing at the right hand of God!" Then they cried out with a loud voice, stopped their ears, and ran at him with one accord; and they cast him out of the city and stoned him. And the witnesses laid down their clothes at the feet of a young man named Saul. And they stoned Stephen as he was calling on God and saying, "Lord Jesus, receive my spirit." Then he knelt down and cried out with a loud voice, "Lord, do not charge them with this sin." And when he had said this, he fell asleep." *Stephen, the first Christian martyr, is stoned to death for his faith, demonstrating the willingness of early Christians to endure persecution rather than deny their beliefs.*

Romans 8:35-39: "Who shall separate us from the love of Christ? Shall tribulation, or distress, or persecution, or famine, or nakedness, or peril, or sword? As it is written: "For Your sake we are killed all day long; We are accounted as sheep for the slaughter."

Yet in all these things we are more than conquerors through Him who loved us. For I am persuaded that neither death nor life, nor angels nor principalities nor powers, nor things present nor things to come, nor height nor depth, nor any other created thing, shall be able to separate us from the love of God which is in Christ Jesus our Lord." *Paul declares that nothing can separate believers from the love of God, including persecution, implying a sense of victory even amidst suffering.*

Revelation 2:10: "Do not fear any of those things which you are about to suffer. Indeed, the devil is about to throw some of you into prison, that you may be tested, and you will have tribulation ten days. Be faithful until death, and I will give you the crown of life." *Jesus encourages the church in Smyrna, facing persecution, to "be faithful unto death,* *and I will give you the crown of life." This promise highlights the reward awaiting those who endure persecution for their faith.*

Old Testament:

Isaiah 53:3-7: "He is despised and rejected by men, A Man of sorrows and acquainted with grief. And we hid, as it were, our faces from Him; He was despised, and we did not esteem Him. Surely He has borne our griefs And carried our sorrows; Yet we esteemed Him stricken, Smitten by God, and afflicted. But He was wounded for our transgressions, He was bruised for our iniquities;

The chastisement for our peace was upon Him, And by His stripes we are healed. All we like sheep have gone astray; We have turned, every one, to his own way; And the Lord has laid on Him the iniquity of us all. He was oppressed and He was afflicted, Yet He opened not His mouth; He was led as a lamb to the slaughter, And as a sheep before its shearers is silent, So He opened not His mouth." *This passage describes the suffering servant who is despised and rejected, yet bears the sins of many, foreshadowing Jesus' sacrifice and his ultimate victory over sin and death.*

Daniel 3:16-18: "Shadrach, Meshach, and Abed-Nego answered and said to the king, "O Nebuchadnezzar, we have no need to answer you in this matter. If that is the case, our God whom we serve is able to deliver us from the burning fiery furnace, and He will deliver us from your hand, O king. But if not, let it be known to you, O king, that we do not serve your gods, nor will we worship the gold image which you have set up." *Shadrach, Meshach, and Abednego are thrown into a fiery furnace for refusing to worship the king's idol, showcasing their unwavering faith even in the face of potential death.*

***Hebrews 12:1-2*:**" Therefore we also, since we are surrounded by so great a cloud of witnesses, let us lay aside every weight, and the sin which so easily ensnares us, and let us run with endurance the race that is set before us, looking unto Jesus, the author and finisher of our faith, who for the joy that was set before Him endured the cross, despising the shame, and has sat down at the right hand of the throne of God. *The author encourages believers to persevere in the face of trials and persecution, reminding them of the "great cloud of witnesses" who have gone before them and the reward that awaits them in heaven.*

Jesus' showcased courage and resilience in the face of persecution. He endured suffering and injustice without retaliation, demonstrating his unwavering commitment to His mission and His love for His sheep. Jesus a victorious Lord & Savior who victoriously overcame persecution and hardship. His astonishing leadership serves as a "Bread of Life" and encouragement for believers facing similar challenges, reminding them of the promises of God and the ultimate triumph of good over evil. His victory over persecution ultimately paved the way for the spread of the gospel and the offer of salvation to all.

JESUS BEING VICTORIOUS OVER HYPOCRISY

New Testament

Matthew 7:1-5: "Judge not, that you be not judged. For with what judgment you judge, you will be judged; and with the measure you use, it will be measured back to you. And why do you look at the speck in your brother's eye, but do not consider the plank in your own eye? Or how can you say to your brother, 'Let me remove the speck from your eye'; and look, a plank is in your own eye? Hypocrite! First remove the plank from your own eye, and then you will see clearly to remove the speck from your brother's eye." *Jesus warns against judging others while ignoring one's own shortcomings, emphasizing the importance of self-reflection and humility.*

Matthew 15:7-9: "Hypocrites! Well did Isaiah prophesy about you, saying: 'These people draw near to Me with their mouth, And honor Me with their lips,

But their heart is far from Me. And in vain they worship Me, Teaching as doctrines the commandments of men." *Jesus quotes Isaiah, criticizing the religious leaders for honoring God with their lips but not their hearts, highlighting the hypocrisy of adhering to external rituals without genuine love and devotion.*

Matthew 23:1-39: "Then Jesus spoke to the multitudes and to His disciples, saying: "The scribes and the Pharisees sit in Moses' seat. Therefore whatever they tell you to observe, that observe and do, but do not do according to their works; for they say, and do not do. For they bind heavy burdens, hard to bear, and lay them on men's shoulders; but they themselves will not move them with one of their fingers. But all their works they do to be seen by men. They make their phylacteries broad and enlarge the borders of their garments. They love the best places at feasts, the best seats in the synagogues, greetings in the marketplaces, and to be called by men, 'Rabbi, Rabbi.' But you, do not be called 'Rabbi'; for One is your Teacher, the Christ, and you are all brethren. Do not call anyone on earth your father; for One is your Father, He who is in heaven. And do not be called teachers; for One is your Teacher, the Christ. But he who is greatest among you shall be your servant. And whoever exalts himself will be humbled, and he who humbles himself will be exalted.

"But woe to you, scribes and Pharisees, hypocrites! For you shut up the kingdom of heaven against men; for you neither go in yourselves, nor do you allow those who are entering to go in. Woe to you, scribes and Pharisees, hypocrites! For you devour widows' houses, and for a pretense make long prayers. Therefore you will receive greater condemnation.

"Woe to you, scribes and Pharisees, hypocrites! For you travel land and sea to win one proselyte, and when he is won, you make him twice as much a son of hell as yourselves.

"Woe to you, blind guides, who say, 'Whoever swears by the temple, it is nothing; but whoever swears by the gold of the temple, he is obliged to perform it.' Fools and blind! For which is greater, the gold or the temple that sanctifies the gold? And, 'Whoever swears by the altar, it is nothing; but whoever swears by the gift that is on it, he is obliged to perform it.' Fools and blind! For which is greater, the gift or the altar that sanctifies the gift? Therefore he who swears by the altar, swears by it and by all things on it. He who swears by the temple, swears by it and by Him who dwells in it. And he who swears by heaven, swears by the throne of God and by Him who sits on it.

"Woe to you, scribes and Pharisees, hypocrites! For you pay tithe of mint and anise and cummin, and have neglected the weightier matters of the law: justice and mercy and faith. These you ought to have done, without leaving the others undone. Blind guides, who strain out a gnat and swallow a camel!

"Woe to you, scribes and Pharisees, hypocrites! For you cleanse the outside of the cup and dish, but inside they are full of extortion and self-indulgence. Blind Pharisee, first cleanse the inside of the cup and dish, that the outside of them may be clean also.

"Woe to you, scribes and Pharisees, hypocrites! For you are like whitewashed tombs which indeed appear beautiful outwardly, but inside are full of dead men's bones and all uncleanness. Even so you also outwardly appear righteous to men, but inside you are full of hypocrisy and lawlessness.

"Woe to you, scribes and Pharisees, hypocrites! Because you build the tombs of the prophets and [m]adorn the monuments of the righteous, and say, 'If we had lived in the days of our fathers, we would not have been partakers with them in the blood of the prophets.'

"Therefore you are witnesses against yourselves that you are sons of those who murdered the prophets. Fill up, then, the measure of your fathers' guilt. Serpents, brood of vipers! How can you escape the condemnation of hell? Therefore, indeed, I send you prophets, wise men, and scribes: some of them you will kill and crucify, and some of them you will scourge in your synagogues and persecute from city to city, that on you may come all the righteous blood shed on the earth, from the blood of righteous Abel to the blood of Zechariah, son of Berechiah, whom you murdered between the temple and the altar. Assuredly, I say to you, all these things will come upon this generation." *This entire chapter is a scathing rebuke of the scribes and Pharisees, exposing their hypocrisy, legalism, and pride and unprofitable traditions. Jesus criticizes them for focusing on outward appearances and neglecting justice, mercy, and faithfulness.*

Luke 18:9-14: "Also He spoke this parable to some who trusted in themselves that they were righteous, and despised others: "Two men went up to the temple to pray, one a Pharisee and the other a tax collector. The

Pharisee stood and prayed thus with himself, 'God, I thank You that I am not like other men extortioners, unjust, adulterers, or even as this tax collector. I fast twice a week; I give tithes of all that I possess.' And the tax collector, standing afar off, would not so much as raise his eyes to heaven, but beat his breast, saying, 'God, be merciful to me a sinner!' I tell you, this man went down to his house justified rather than the other; for everyone who exalts himself will be humbled, and he who humbles himself will be exalted" *Jesus tells the parable of the Pharisee and the tax collector, contrasting the self-righteousness and pride of the Pharisee with the humility and repentance of the tax collector, demonstrating that true righteousness comes from a genuine heart, not outward displays.*

Mark 7:1-23: "Then the Pharisees and some of the scribes came together to Him, having come from Jerusalem. Now when they saw some of His disciples eat bread with defiled, that is, with unwashed hands, they found fault. For the Pharisees and all the Jews do not eat unless they wash their hands in a special way, holding the tradition of the elders. When they come from the marketplace, they do not eat unless they wash. And there are many other things which they have received and hold, like the washing of cups, pitchers, copper vessels, and couches. Then the Pharisees and scribes asked Him, "Why do Your disciples not walk according to the tradition of the elders, but eat bread with unwashed hands?" He answered and said to them, "Well did Isaiah prophesy of you hypocrites, as it is written: "These people honors Me with their lips, But their heart is far from Me. And in vain they worship Me, Teaching as doctrines the commandments of men.' For laying aside the commandment of God, you hold the tradition of men the washing of pitchers and cups, and many other such things you do." He said to them, "All too well you reject the commandment of God, that you may keep your tradition. For Moses said, 'Honor your father and your mother'; and, 'He who curses father or mother, let him be put to death.' But you say, 'If a man says to his father or mother, "Whatever profit you might have received from me is Corban" (that is, a gift to God), then you no longer let him do anything for his father or his mother, making the word of God of no effect through your tradition which you have handed down. And many such things you do." When He had called all the multitude to Himself, He said to them, "Hear Me, everyone, and understand: There is nothing that enters a man from outside which can defile him; but the things which come out of him, those are the things that defile a man. If anyone has ears to hear, let him hear!" When He had entered a house away from the crowd, His disciples asked Him concerning the parable. So He said to them, "Are you thus without understanding also? Do you not perceive that whatever enters a man from outside cannot defile him, because it does not enter his heart but his stomach, and is eliminated, thus purifying all foods?" And He said, "What comes out of a man, that defiles a man. For from within, out of the heart of men, proceed evil thoughts, adulteries, fornications, murders, thefts, covetousness, wickedness, deceit, lewdness, an evil eye, blasphemy, pride, foolishness. All these evil things come from within and defile a man." *Jesus criticizes the Pharisees for their emphasis on ritual purity while neglecting weightier matters of the law, such as justice, mercy, and faithfulness. He highlights the hypocrisy of focusing on external regulations while neglecting the inner condition of the heart.*

John 8:7: "So when they continued asking Him, He raised Himself up and said to them, "He who is without sin among you, let him throw a stone at her first." *Jesus confronts the woman caught in adultery, challenging the hypocrisy of those who want to stone her while ignoring their own sinfulness.*

Romans 2:1-11: "Therefore you are inexcusable, O man, whoever you are who judge, for in whatever you judge another you condemn yourself; for you who judge practice the same things. But we know that the judgment of God is according to truth against those who practice such things. And do you think this, O man, you who judge those practicing such things, and doing the same, that you will escape the judgment of God? Or do you despise the riches of His goodness, forbearance, and longsuffering, not knowing that the goodness of God leads you to repentance? But in accordance with your hardness and your impenitent heart you are treasuring up for yourself wrath in the day of wrath and revelation of the righteous judgment of God, who "will render to each one according to his deeds": eternal life to those who by patient continuance in doing good seek for glory, honor, and immortality; but to those who are self-seeking and do not obey the truth, but obey unrighteousness indignation and wrath, tribulation and anguish, on every soul of man who does evil, of the Jew first and also of the Greek; but glory, honor, and peace to everyone who works what is good, to the Jew first and also to the Greek. For there is no partiality with God." *Paul reminds believers that they are just as guilty of sin as those they judge, emphasizing the need for humility and self-awareness before criticizing others.*

Galatians 2:11-14: "Now when Peter had come to Antioch, I withstood him to his face, because he was to be blamed; for before certain men came from James, he would eat with the Gentiles; but when they came, he withdrew and separated himself, fearing those who were of the circumcision. And the rest of the Jews also played the hypocrite with him, so that even Barnabas was carried away with their hypocrisy. But when I saw that they were not straightforward about the truth of the gospel, I said to Peter before them all, "If you, being a Jew, live in the manner of Gentiles and not as the Jews, why do you compel Gentiles to live as Jews?" *Paul publicly confronts Peter for his hypocrisy in withdrawing from eating with Gentile Christians, highlighting the importance of consistency and living according to one's convictions.*

Jesus unwavering commitment to truth and authenticity in faith pertaining to Gods Word and expectations was matched to no-one. He challenged the hypocrisy of religious leaders and exposed the emptiness of outward displays without genuine love and compassion. His teachings emphasize the need for a heart transformed by grace, manifested in acts of justice, mercy, and love.

Old Testament:

Isaiah 58:6-7: "Is this not the fast that I have chosen: To loose the bonds of wickedness, To undo the heavy burdens, To let the oppressed go free, And that you break every yoke? Is it not to share your bread with the hungry, And that you bring to your house the poor who are cast out; When you see the naked, that you cover him, And not hide yourself from your own flesh?" *This passage criticizes those who observe religious fasts while neglecting to care for the poor and oppressed, emphasizing the importance of social justice & sincere compassion alongside religious practices.*

Amos 5:21-24: "I hate, I despise your feast days, And I do not savor your sacred assemblies. Though you offer Me burnt offerings and your grain offerings, I will not accept them, Nor will I regard your fattened peace offerings. Take away from Me the noise of your songs, For I will not hear the melody of your stringed instruments. But let justice run down like water,

And righteousness like a mighty stream. *Amos condemns the religious practices of the people while they ignore injustice and oppression, highlighting the need for faith to be accompanied by righteous actions.*

God's consistent message against hypocrisy and the call for true devotion expressed through love, justice, compassion and care for the marginalized.

JESUS IS VICTORIOUS IN CASTING OUT DEMONS:

The New Testament

Matthew

Matthew: 8:16-17: "When evening had come, they brought to Him many who were demon-possessed. And He cast out the spirits with a word, and healed all who were sick, that it might be fulfilled which was spoken by Isaiah the prophet, saying: "He Himself took our infirmities And bore our sicknesses." *Jesus heals various demon-possessed people, including a man with a mute demon, demonstrating his power to heal physical and spiritual ailments.*

Matthew: 8:28-34: "When evening had come, they brought to Him many who were demon-possessed. And He cast out the spirits with a word, and healed all who were sick, that it might be fulfilled which was spoken by Isaiah the prophet, saying: "He Himself took our infirmities And bore our sicknesses" *Jesus encounters two demon-possessed men living in tombs, demonstrating his ability to confront and conquer even the most powerful evil forces.*

Matthew: 9:32-33: "As they went out, behold, they brought to Him a man, mute and demon-possessed. And when the demon was cast out, the mute spoke. And the multitudes marveled, saying, "It was never seen like this in Israel!" *Jesus heals a demon-possessed mute man, restoring his speech and highlighting his authority over speech impediments and demonic influence.*

Matthew: 12:22-28: "A House Divided Cannot Stand: Then one was brought to Him who was demon-possessed, blind and mute; and He healed him, so that the blind and mute man both spoke and saw. And all the multitudes were amazed and said, "Could this be the Son of David?" Now when the Pharisees heard it they said, "This fellow does not cast out demons except by Beelzebub, the ruler of the demons." But Jesus knew their thoughts, and said to them: "Every kingdom divided against itself is brought to desolation, and every city or house divided against itself will not stand. If Satan casts out Satan, he is divided against himself. How then will his kingdom stand? And if I cast out demons by Beelzebub, by whom do your sons cast them out? Therefore they shall be your judges. But if I cast out demons by the Spirit of God, surely the kingdom of God has come upon you." *Jesus heals a demon-possessed blind and mute man, sparking debate about his source of power and ultimately exposing the blasphemy of attributing his miracles to Beelzebul.*

Matthew: 17:14-18: "And when they had come to the multitude, a man came to Him, kneeling down to Him and saying, "Lord, have mercy on my son, for he is an epileptic and suffers severely; for he often falls into the fire and often into the water. So I brought him to Your disciples, but they could not cure him." Then Jesus answered and said, "O faithless and perverse generation, how long shall I be with you? How long shall I bear with you? Bring him here to Me." And Jesus rebuked the demon, and it came out of him; and the child was cured from that very hour. *Jesus casts out a deaf and mute spirit from a boy, displaying his compassion and ability to heal even the most challenging cases.*

Mark:

Mark: 1:23-26: " Then they went into Capernaum, and immediately on the Sabbath He entered the synagogue and taught. And they were astonished at His teaching, for He taught them as one having authority, and not as the scribes. Now there was a man in their synagogue with an unclean spirit. And he cried out, saying, "Let us alone! What have we to do with You, Jesus of Nazareth? Did You come to destroy us? I know who You are — the Holy One of God!" But Jesus rebuked him, saying, Be quiet, and come out of him!" *Jesus commands a demon in a synagogue to be quiet and come out of the man, demonstrating his authority over evil spirits and their disruptive influence.*

Mark: 5:1-20: "Then they came to the other side of the sea, to the country of the Gadarenes. And when He had come out of the boat, immediately there met Him out of the tombs a man with an unclean spirit, who had his dwelling among the tombs; and no one could bind him, not even with chains, because he had often been bound with shackles and chains. And the chains had been pulled apart by him, and the shackles broken in pieces; neither could anyone tame him. And always, night and day, he was in the mountains and in the tombs, crying out and cutting himself with stones. When he saw Jesus from afar, he ran and worshiped Him. And he cried out with a loud voice and said, "What have I to do with You, Jesus, Son of the Most High God? I implore You by God that You do not torment me." For He said to him, "Come out of the man, unclean spirit!" Then He asked him, "What is your name?" And he answered, saying, "My name is Legion; for we are many." Also he begged Him earnestly that He would not send them out of the country. Now a large herd of swine was feeding there near the mountains. So all the demons begged Him, saying, "Send us to the swine, that we may enter them." And at once Jesus gave them permission. Then the unclean spirits went out and entered the swine (there were about two thousand); and the herd ran violently down the steep place into the sea, and drowned in the sea. So those who fed the swine fled, and they told it in the city and in the country. And they went out to see what it was that had happened. Then they came to Jesus, and saw the one who had been demon-possessed and had the legion, sitting and clothed and in his right mind. And they were afraid. And those who saw it told them how it happened to him who had been demon-possessed, and about the swine. Then they began to plead with Him to depart from their region. And when He got into the boat, he who had been demon-possessed begged Him that he might be with Him. However, Jesus did not permit him, but said to him, "Go home to your friends, and tell them what great things the Lord has done for you, and how He has had compassion on you." And he departed and began to proclaim in Decapolis all that Jesus had done for him; and all marveled." *Jesus encounters and liberates a demon-possessed man in the region of the Gerasenes, showcasing his power over even the most violent and destructive manifestations of evil.*

Mark: 7:25-30: " For a woman whose young daughter had an unclean spirit heard about Him, and she came and fell at His feet. The woman was a Greek, a Syro-Phoenician by birth, and she kept asking Him to cast the demon out of her daughter. But Jesus said to her, "Let the children be filled first, for it is not good to take the children's bread and throw it to the little dogs." And she answered and said to Him, "Yes, Lord, yet even the little dogs under the table eat from the children's crumbs." Then He said to her, "For this saying go your way; the demon has gone out of your daughter." And when she had come to her house, she found the demon gone out, and her daughter lying on the bed." *Jesus heals a Syrophoenician woman's daughter from a demon, demonstrating his willingness to reach out to people beyond Jewish boundaries and offer healing and liberation.*

Mark: 9:14-29: "And when He came to the disciples, He saw a great multitude around them, and scribes disputing with them. Immediately, when they saw Him, all the people were greatly amazed, and running to Him, greeted

Him. And He asked the scribes, "What are you discussing with them?" Then one of the crowd answered and said, "Teacher, I brought You my son, who has a mute spirit. And wherever it seizes him, it throws him down; he foams at the mouth, gnashes his teeth, and becomes rigid. So I spoke to Your disciples, that they should cast it out, but they could not." He answered him and said, "O faithless generation, how long shall I be with you? How long shall I bear with you? Bring him to Me." Then they brought him to Him. And when he saw Him, immediately the spirit convulsed him, and he fell on the ground and wallowed, foaming at the mouth. So He asked his father, "How long has this been happening to him?" And he said, "From childhood. And often he has thrown him both into the fire and into the water to destroy him. But if You can do anything, have compassion on us and help us." Jesus said to him, "If you can believe, all things are possible to him who believes." Immediately the father of the child cried out and said with tears, "Lord, I believe; help my unbelief! When Jesus saw that the people came running together, He rebuked the unclean spirit, saying to it, "Deaf and dumb spirit, I command you, come out of him and enter him no more!" Then the spirit cried out, convulsed him greatly, and came out of him. And he became as one dead, so that many said, "He is dead." But Jesus took him by the hand and lifted him up, and he arose. And when He had come into the house, His disciples asked Him privately, "Why could we not cast it out?" So He said to them, "This kind can come out by nothing but prayer and fasting." *Jesus heals a boy experiencing* _seizures and demon possession, highlighting his ability to overcome both physical and spiritual afflictions._

Luke:

Luke: 4:33-35: "Now in the synagogue there was a man who had a spirit of an unclean demon. And he cried out with a loud voice, saying, "Let us alone! What have we to do with You, Jesus of Nazareth? Did You come to destroy us? I know who You are the Holy One of God!" But Jesus rebuked him, saying, "Be quiet, and come out of him!" And when the demon had thrown him in their midst, it came out of him and did not hurt him._" Jesus commands an unclean spirit in a synagogue to be silent and come out of the man, showcasing his authority over evil spirits in public settings._

Luke: 8:26-39: "Then they sailed to the country of the Gadarenes, which is opposite Galilee. And when He stepped out on the land, there met Him a certain man from the city who had demons for a long time. And he wore no clothes, nor did he live in a house but in the tombs. When he saw Jesus, he cried out, fell down before Him, and with a loud voice said, "What have I to do with You, Jesus, Son of the Most High God? I beg You, do not torment me!" For He had commanded the unclean spirit to come out of the man. For it had often seized him, and he was kept under guard, bound with chains and shackles; and he broke the bonds and was driven by the demon into the wilderness. Jesus asked him, saying,

"What is your name?" And he said, "Legion," because many demons had entered him. And they begged Him that He would not command them to go out into the abyss. Now a herd of many swine was feeding there on the mountain. So they begged Him that He would permit them to enter them. And He permitted them. Then the demons went out of the man and entered the swine, and the herd ran violently down the steep place into the lake and drowned. When those who fed them saw what had happened, they fled and told it in the city and in the country. Then they went out to see what had happened, and came to Jesus, and found the man from whom the demons had departed, sitting at the feet of Jesus, clothed and in his right mind. And they were afraid. They also who had seen it told them by what means he who had been demon-possessed was healed. Then the whole multitude of the surrounding region of the Gadarenes asked Him to depart from them, for they were seized with great fear. And He got into the boat and returned. Now the man from whom the demons had departed begged Him that he might be with Him. But Jesus sent him away, saying, "Return to your own house, and tell what great things God has done for you." And he went his way and proclaimed throughout the whole city what great things Jesus had done for him." *Jesus encounters and liberates a demon-possessed man in the region of the Gadarenes, demonstrating his power over even the most entrenched and destructive demonic forces.*

Luke: 11:14-26*:*" And He was casting out a demon, and it was mute. So it was, when the demon had gone out, that the mute spoke; and the multitudes marveled. But some of them said, "He casts out demons by Beelzebub, the ruler of the demons." Others, testing Him, sought from Him a sign from heaven. But He, knowing their thoughts, said to them: "Every kingdom divided against itself is brought to desolation, and a house divided against a house falls. If Satan also is divided against himself, how will his kingdom stand? Because you say I cast out demons by Beelzebub. And if I cast out demons by Beelzebub, by whom do your sons cast them out? Therefore they will be your judges. But if I cast out demons with the finger of God, surely the kingdom of God has come upon you. When a strong man, fully armed, guards his own palace, his goods are in peace. But when a stronger than he comes upon him and overcomes him, he takes from him all his armor in which he trusted, and divides his spoils. He who is not with Me is against Me, and he who does not gather with Me scatters." *Jesus casts out a demon from a mute man, sparking controversy and exposing the hypocrisy of those who accuse him of using the power of the devil.*

Luke: 13:10-17: "Now He was teaching in one of the synagogues on the Sabbath. And behold, there was a woman who had a spirit of infirmity eighteen years, and was bent over and could in no way raise herself up. But when Jesus saw her, He called her to Him and said to her, "Woman, you are loosed from your infirmity." And He laid His hands on her, and immediately she was made straight, and glorified God. But the ruler of the synagogue answered with indignation, because Jesus had healed on the Sabbath; and he said to the crowd, "There are six days on which men ought to work; therefore come and be healed on them, and not on the Sabbath day." The Lord then answered him and said, "Hypocrite! Does not each one of you on the Sabbath loose his ox or donkey from the stall, and lead it away to water it? So ought not this woman, being a daughter of Abraham, whom Satan has bound think of it for eighteen years, be loosed from this bond on the Sabbath?" And when He said these things, all His adversaries were put to shame; and all the multitude rejoiced for all the glorious things that were done by Him." *Jesus liberates a woman crippled by a spirit for eighteen years, demonstrating his compassion for the marginalized and his ability to restore health and wholeness.*

John:

John: 10:21: "Others said, "These are not the words of one who has a demon. Can a demon open the eyes of the blind?" *Jesus casts out a demon from a man born blind, showcasing his power over spiritual blindness and his ability to restore sight and understanding.*

Jesus' authority over demonic forces was historically unmatched. He consistently confronted and conquered evil spirits, demonstrating his power to heal physical and spiritual ailments, restore speech and sight, and liberate individuals from the grip of darkness. His victories over demons serve as a reminder of his ultimate triumph over evil and the promise of freedom and healing available to all who seek him.

CHALLENGING RELIGIOUS VILENESS

Matthew 21:12-13: "Then Jesus went into the temple of God and drove out all those who bought and sold in the temple, and overturned the tables of the money changers and the seats of those who sold doves. And He said to them, "It is written, 'My house shall be called a house of prayer,' but you have made it a 'den of thieves." *Jesus drives out the moneychangers and merchants from the temple, challenging corruption and exploitation within religious institutions.*

Luke 14:12-14: "Then He also said to him who invited Him, "When you give a dinner or a supper, do not ask your friends, your brothers, your relatives, nor rich neighbors, lest they also invite you back, and you be repaid. But when you give a feast, invite the poor, the maimed, the lame, the blind. And you will be blessed, because they cannot repay you; for you shall be repaid at the resurrection of the just." *Jesus instructs his host to invite the poor, the crippled, the lame, and the blind to a feast, prioritizing the inclusion and care of those who were often marginalized and neglected.*

Luke 19:1-10: "Then Jesus entered and passed through Jericho. Now behold, there was a man named Zacchaeus who was a chief tax collector, and he was rich. And he sought to see who Jesus was, but could not because of the crowd, for he was of short stature. So he ran ahead and climbed up into a sycamore tree to see Him, for He was going to pass that way. And when Jesus came to the place, He looked up and saw him, and said to him, "Zacchaeus, make haste and come down, for today I must stay at your house." So he made haste and came down, and received Him joyfully. But when they saw it, they all complained, saying, "He has gone to be a guest with a man who is a sinner." Then Zacchaeus stood and said to the Lord, "Look, Lord, I give half of my goods to the poor; and if I have taken anything from anyone by false accusation, I restore fourfold." And Jesus said to him, "Today salvation has come to this house, because he also is a son of Abraham; for the Son of Man has come to seek and to save that which was lost." *Jesus visits Zacchaeus, a tax collector known for his dishonesty, demonstrating his willingness to reach out to those considered outcasts and offer them redemption and forgiveness.*

John 8:3-11: "Then the scribes and Pharisees brought to Him a woman caught in adultery. And when they had set her in the midst, they said to Him, "Teacher, this woman was caught in adultery, in the very act. Now Moses, in the law, commanded us that such should be stoned. But what do You say?" This they said, testing Him, that they might have something of which to accuse Him. But Jesus stooped down and wrote on the ground with His finger, as though He did not hear. So when they continued asking Him, He raised Himself up and said to them, "He who is without sin among you, let him throw a stone at her first." And again He stooped down and wrote on the ground. Then those who heard it, being convicted by their conscience, went out one by one, beginning with the oldest even to the last. And Jesus was left alone, and the woman standing in the midst. When Jesus had raised Himself up and saw no one but the woman, He said to her, "Woman, where are those accusers of yours? Has no one condemned you?" She said, "No one, Lord." And Jesus said to her, "Neither do I condemn you; go and sin no more" *Jesus challenges the crowd's desire to stone an adulterous woman, advocating for forgiveness and compassion over judgment and condemnation.*

JESUS OFFERING COMFORT AND HOPE

Matthew 11:28-30: "Come to Me, all you who labor and are heavy laden, and I will give you rest. Take My yoke upon you and learn from Me, for I am gentle and lowly in heart, and you will find rest for your souls. For My yoke is easy and My burden is light." *Jesus offers rest and peace to those who are weary and burdened, highlighting his compassion and desire to offer solace and hope amidst suffering.*

John 14:1-3: "Let not your heart be troubled; you believe in God, believe also in Me. In My Father's house are many mansions; if it were not so, I would have told you. I go to prepare a place for you. And if I go and prepare a place for you, I will come again and receive you to Myself; that where I am, there you may be also." *Jesus assures his* *disciples that he will prepare a place for them in his Father's house, offering comfort and hope in the face of death and separation.*

Revelation 21:4: "And God will wipe away every tear from their eyes; there shall be no more death, nor sorrow, nor crying. There shall be no more pain, for the former things have passed away." *This passage describes the future state of heaven, where death and suffering are abolished, and believers experience eternal joy and peace.*

The core of Jesus' ministry embodies His commitment and devotion in overcoming various forms of evil and suffering. He healed the sick, challenged social injustices, offered comfort to the downtrodden, and ultimately offered a brand-new hope for a brand-new future. His actions and teachings of His kingdom ministry continue to inspire believers, worshipers and church communities to work towards a world that exemplifies love, compassion, forgiveness, repentance and justice, reflecting the core values of His Heavenly kingdom.

John 16:33 *"These things I have spoken to you, that in Me you may have peace. In the world you will have tribulation; but be of good cheer, I have overcome the world."*

Matthew 5:10 *"Blessed are those who are persecuted for righteousness' sake, for theirs is the kingdom of heaven,"*

John 13 1-17 Jesus washed the feet of His disciples as a demonstration of "humility and servanthood". By performing this act, Jesus showed that genuine, fervent leadership involves selflessness and a willingness to serve others. He emphasized the importance of servanthood and demonstrated that true greatness comes from serving others, not from being served. This revolutionary act of selflessness challenged His followers to be like Him and to serve others with humility. The act of washing feet is a powerful symbol as to how we should live our lives, serving and loving others selflessly. Jesus' direct instructions left no room for confusion: "*I have set you an example that you should do as I have done to you*" (***John 13:15***). He called His disciples to a radical restructuring of life's priorities, where greatness is measured not by power, titles or positions, but by the depth of our service. Compassion and love, (not self-assertion), become the trademark of our works. "Jesus' action was unprecedented and unheard of as such a task was often assigned to that of a servant or slave. Through this seemingly simple act, the most-high Lord & Savior humbly, with all meekness took on the position of one of the most-low. Washing the disciples' feet metaphorically embodied this historically "radical symbolic act", representing the "divine spiritual cleansing" that would come later, as a result of Jesus Christ devotion in Ransoming sinners from death with his love that ultimately led to death on the cross. Jesus' foot-washing was a call to action for believers to serve one another with humility and selflessness. "The foot washing first signified salvation offered through Jesus' death. As Jesus explained to Peter, Unless I wash you, you have no part with me *John13:8*. Washing the disciples' feet was a predecessor to the sacrificial love He would soon model on the cross. And Jesus goes on to say that He intends for the disciples to display this same humility and self-sacrifice to others. When He had finished washing their feet, he put on his clothes and returned to his place. "Do you understand what I have done for you?" he asked them. *"You call me 'Teacher' and 'Lord,' and rightly so, for that is what I am. Now that I, your Lord and Teacher, have washed your feet, you also should wash one another's feet. I have set you an example that you should do as I have done for you. Very truly I tell you, no servant is greater than his master, nor is a messenger greater than the one who sent him. Now that you know these things, you will be blessed if you do them"* (*John 13:12-17*). Later on, during their reflection, Jesus tells the disciples that displaying this humble, self-sacrificing love is how people will recognize His followers. "A new command I give you: Love one another. As I have loved you, so you must love one another. By this everyone will know that you are my disciples, if you love one another" (*John 13:34–35*).

As we seek to follow Christ's example, we need to extend our humility toward those who will never return our acts of service, will take advantage of us, and never thank us. Jesus' foot-washing was a call to action for believers to serve one another with humility and selflessness

NO OTHER WAS AS VICTORIOUS AS JESUS CHRIST! OUR PROMISED, RISEN-MESSIAH

Jesus' resurrection marked a pivotal moment in human History, as it defied the natural order and provided undeniable proof of His divinity and the power of God over death. It offered hope for eternal life and transformed the lives of His disciples. The empty tomb served as tangible evidence that Jesus had indeed risen from the dead. It dispelled any doubts about His victory over death and provided a lasting symbol of His resurrection for future generations. Jesus' appearances to His disciples after His resurrection served multiple purposes. They provided reassurance and comfort to His grieving followers, confirmed their faith in His resurrection, and commissioned them to continue His work on earth. Jesus faced temptations in the wilderness that represented the most common human desires, material possessions, power, and recognition. He resisted these temptations through prayer, scripture, and reliance on God's power, demonstrating that it is possible to live a sinless life, even amidst temptation. Jesus Boldy confronted hypocrisy and judgment outright and publicly, of religious leaders by rebuking and correcting their fruitless inconsistencies, showing compassion and forgiveness to the woman caught in adultery. This act challenged societal norms and demonstrated that God's grace extends to everyone, regardless of their past. In the Garden of Gethsemane, Jesus wrestled with His impending death, recognizing the pain and suffering it would bring. He ultimately surrendered to God's will, demonstrating His obedience and commitment to fulfilling His mission of redemption. Casting out demons, Jesus' ability to cast out demons demonstrated His authority over the spiritual realm and His infinite power to liberate people from demonic oppression and slavery. This act revealed the reality of spiritual warfare and the power of Jesus to overcome it. Healing the sick and disabled, Jesus' miracles of healing were not only acts of compassion but also signs of God's kingdom breaking into the world. They brought hope and restoration to those suffering from physical limitations and revealed Jesus' power over illness and disease. Jesus' calming of the storm at sea was a powerful demonstration of His authority over nature and His ability to bring peace and calm even amidst chaos. This event strengthened the faith of His disciples and revealed His control over the elements. Crucifixion! although often viewed as a defeat, Jesus' death on the cross was actually an act of ultimate love, sacrifice and devotion. He willingly bore the punishment for all human sin, thereby defeating sin's power and offering forgiveness and reconciliation to humanity. Harrowing of Hell, Jesus descended into hell after His death and triumphed over the devil and the forces of darkness. This act ensured the final victory over evil and secured the salvation of those who believe in Him. Jesus' ascension to heaven marked the beginning of His reign as the rightful King of Kings and Lord of Lords. This event signified the transfer of authority from earthly to heavenly realms and the inauguration of a new era under His leadership. The Second Coming, Jesus' promised return marks the culmination of His victory and the final establishment of God's kingdom on earth. This event signifies the end of evil, the judgment of the wicked, and the eternal reign of Jesus with His followers. Sending the Holy Spirit; the Holy Spirit empowered Jesus' disciples to continue His work of spreading the gospel, performing miracles, and building the church. This event marked the beginning of the Christian Church and ensured that Jesus' mission would continue after His departure. The Great Commission, Jesus' Great Commission to His disciples to "make disciples of all nations" signifies His intention to expand His kingdom and offer salvation to all people. This mission continues today, and Christians are called to participate in it by sharing the gospel and spreading the message of Christ's love. There you have it. The evidence is clear and the proof is in the pudding. Satan may have bruised His heel but a victorious Jesus crushed satan under his feet. He awaits at the right hand of God in his heavenly estate until he makes every enemy His footstool. Only a fool, in his heart says there is no God.

Bible References for the Victories of Jesus Christ:

Overcoming temptation and sin:

> Temptation in the wilderness: Matthew 4:1-11, Luke 4:1-13
> The woman caught in adultery: John 8:1-11

Gethsemane: Matthew 26:36-46, Mark 14:32-42, Luke 22:39-46

Overcoming death and the grave:

Resurrection: Matthew 28:1-10, Mark 16:1-8, Luke 24:1-12, John 20:1-18
Empty tomb: Matthew 28:1-7, Mark 16:1-8, Luke 24:1-3, John 20:1-10
Appearances to his disciples: Matthew 28:16-20, Mark 16:9-20, Luke 24:36-49, John 20:19-29, Acts 1:3-8

Overcoming evil and darkness:

Casting out demons: Matthew 8:28-34, Mark 1:23-28, Luke 4:33-35
Healing the sick and disabled: Matthew 9:2-8, Mark 2:1-12, Luke 5:17-26
Calming the storm: Matthew 8:23-27, Mark 4:35-41, Luke 8:22-25

Establishing his kingdom and defeating the enemy:

Ascension: Acts 1:9-11
Sending the Holy Spirit: Acts 2:1-4
Great Commission: Matthew 28:18-20, Mark 16:15-18, Luke 24:46-49

Ultimate victory over sin, death, and the devil:

> Crucifixion: Matthew 27:32-56, Mark 15:20-41, Luke 23:26-46, John 19:17-37
>
> Harrowing of Hell: 1 Peter 3:18-20, Ephesians 4:8-10
>
> Second Coming: Matthew 24:27-31, Mark 13:24-27, Luke 21:25-28, Revelation 19:11-21

Additional References:

> Romans 5:6-8 (Victory over sin)
>
> 1 Corinthians 15:54-57 (Victory over death)
>
> Hebrews 2:14-15 (Victory over the devil)
>
> Revelation 1:18 (Victory over death and hell)
>
> Revelation 20:10 (Ultimate victory over the devil)

Establishing his kingdom and defeating the enemy:

> Ascension: Acts 1:9-11.
>
> Sending the Holy Spirit: Acts 2:1-4.
>
> Great Commission: Matthew 28:18-20, Mark 16:15-18, Luke 24:46-49, Acts 1:8.

Ultimate victory over sin, death, and the devil:

> Crucifixion: Matthew 27:32-56, Mark 15:21-41, Luke 23:26-46, John 19:17-30.
>
> Harrowing of Hell: Jesus' descent into hell can be found in 1 Peter 3:18-19 and 4:6.
>
> Second Coming: Matthew 24:27-31, Mark 13:24-27, Luke 21:25-28, Revelation 19:11-21.

1 Cross
3 Nails
4 Given

210

Jesus Accomplished Victories	
Isahia 53 Jesus Paid it all, *Jesus was Victorious*	
Over sin	*Over death*
Over satan	*Over sickness and disease*
Over nature, heaven & earth	*Over injustice and oppression*
Over temptation	*Over death, hell the grave and abyss*
Over thirst & famine	*Over persecution*
Over hypocrisy	*Over demons*
Over false Prophesy	*Over the tomb*

Isbia 53: "And He was wounded for our transgressions, He was bruised for our iniquities; The chastisement for our peace was upon Him, And by His stripes we are healed. All we like sheep have gone astray; We have turned, every one, to his own way; And the Lord has laid on Him the iniquity of us all..."

"Then the seventh angel blew his trumpet, and there were loud voices in heaven, saying, "The kingdom of the world has become the kingdom of our Lord and of his Christ, and he shall reign forever and ever."
Revelation 11:15

Daniel 2:44 "And in the days of those kings the God of heaven will set up a kingdom that shall never be destroyed, nor shall the kingdom be left to another people. It shall break in pieces all these kingdoms and bring them to an end, and it shall stand forever."

Matthew 11:12 "From the days of John the Baptist until now the kingdom of heaven has suffered violence, and the violent take it by force."

THE ULTIMATE COST
OF DISIPLESHIP

A disciple of Jesus Christ requires a deep commitment and willingness to endure hardship as a good soldier, abuse, persecution, and suffering for the sake of His name. The challenges faced by disciples were both internal and external. Internally, disciples must be willing to give up their own desires and follow Jesus' teachings, which can be difficult and require a great deal of self-discipline. Externally, disciples may face persecution, separation, ostracization, ridicule, and even death for their faith.

The Apostle Paul is an example of someone who faced many challenges and hardships as he lived out his faith and dedication to Jesus Christ. He was imprisoned, beaten, and stoned for preaching the gospel. Despite these challenges, he remained steadfast in his faith and continued to spread the message of Jesus Christ. The ultimate cost of discipleship is a deep commitment to

Jesus Christ that requires a willingness to endure hardship, abuse, persecution, and suffering for the sake of Christ name. Disciples must be willing to put Jesus above all else, even their own lives, and follow His teachings. The challenges faced by disciples are both internal and external, but with faith and dedication, they can overcome these challenges and live a life that is pleasing to God. The Cost of Discipleship as explained in the Bible relates to how following Jesus as His believers came at a high price for His disciples. They faced various challenges and hardships, both internal and external, as they lived out their faith. Here's a list of some of the costs they endured.

PERSECUTION AND DANGER: Early Christians faced relentless persecution from both Jewish and Roman authorities. They were accused of blasphemy, treason, and disturbing the peace. This often led to violence, imprisonment, and even death.

> ➤ **_Matthew 10:21-23_**: "Brother will betray brother to death, and a father his child; children will rebel against their parents and bring them to death. <u>You will be hated by everyone because of my name. But the one who endures to the end will be saved.</u>"

> ➤ **_John 15:20:_** "Remember the word I spoke to you, 'No servant is greater than his master.' <u>If they persecuted me, they will persecute you also.</u>"

Rejection and religious ostracism: Following Jesus often meant going against the grain of society. Disciples were ostracized by their families, communities, and synagogues. They were mocked, ridiculed, and excluded.

> ➢ *Luke 6:22:* "Blessed are you when people hate you, when they exclude you and insult you, and spit on your name as something evil, because of the Son of Man."

> ➢ *John 17:14:* "I have given them your word and the world has hated them, for they are not of the world any more than I am of the world."

LOSS OF POSSESSIONS AND LIVELIHOOD: In

some cases, discipleship meant giving up everything they owned. Jesus called for radical commitment, urging his followers to sell their possessions and give to the poor. This left many vulnerable and dependent on the generosity of others.

> ➢ *Luke 14:33:* "Therefore, anyone of you who does not give up everything he has cannot be my disciple."

> ➢ *Matthew 19:21*: "Jesus said to him, 'If you want to be perfect, go, sell your possessions *and give to the poor, and you will have* treasure in heaven. And come, follow me."

INTERNAL STRUGGLES AND TEMPTATION:
The path of discipleship is not always easy. Doubts, fears, insecurities and temptations can arise, testing one's faith and resolve. The disciples themselves struggled with these issues throughout their journey with Jesus.

> ➢ ***Matthew 26:39***: "Going a little farther, he fell with his face to the ground and prayed, 'My Father, if it is possible, let this cup pass from me. Yet not as I will, but as you will.'"
> ➢ ***Mark 14:38:*** "Watch and pray so that you will not fall into temptation. The spirit is willing, but the flesh is weak."

SEPARATION FROM LOVED ONES: Following Jesus could sometimes lead to division within families and communities. Some family members might not accept the new faith, leading to estrangement and conflict.

> ➢ ***Matthew 10:34-35:*** "'Do not think that I have come to bring peace to the earth; I have not come to bring peace, but a sword. For I have come to set a man against his father, a daughter against her mother, a daughter-in-law against her mother-in-law and a man's enemies will be the members of his own household.'"

> ➢ ***Luke 14:26:*** "Whoever comes to me and does not love father and mother, wife and children, brothers and sisters, yes, and even his own life, cannot be my disciple."

REJECTION AND DIVISION: Family and Friends: Following Jesus' teachings could lead to estrangement from family and friends who didn't share the same beliefs.

> ➤ ***Matthew 10:34-35:*** "'Do not think that I have come to bring peace to the earth; I have not come to bring peace, but a sword. For I have come to set a man against his father, a daughter against her mother, a daughter-in-law against her mother-in-law and a man's enemies will be the members of his own household.'"

COMFORT AND SECURITY: Following Jesus often meant leaving behind a comfortable life and embracing uncertainty and hardship.

> ➤ ***Mark10:21:*** Looking at him, Jesus loved him and said, "One thing you lack. Go, sell all you have and give to the poor, and you will have treasure in heaven. Then come, follow me."

> ➤ ***Acts 4:32-35:*** "All the believers were one in heart and mind. No one claimed that any of his possessions was his own, but they shared everything they had. With great power the apostles gave witness to the resurrection of Jesus, and great grace was upon them all."

SELF-DENIAL: Discipleship requires constant self-examination and a willingness to deny oneself for the sake of God's will.

Living a Life Not One's Own: Ultimately, the cost of discipleship is the surrender of one's own desires and ambitions to fully embrace God's purpose.

> ➤ *Mark 8:34-35:* "Then he called the crowd to him along with his disciples and said, 'Whoever wants to be my disciple must deny themselves and take up their cross and follow me. For whoever wants to save their life will lose it, but whoever loses their life for me and for the gospel will save it.'"

> ➤ *Luke 14:27:* "Whoever does not carry his own cross and come after me cannot be my disciple."

FULL SURRENDER TO GODS WILL: Living a Life Not One's Own a complete surrender to God's will, even if it means suffering or hardship. It's a call to prioritize God's kingdom above all else, even one's own life.

DENYING YOURSELF AND TAKING UP YOUR CROSS:

> ➤ **Luke 9:23:** "Then he said to them all, "Whoever wants to be my disciple must deny themselves and take up their cross daily and follow me."

➢ *Matthew 16:24*: "Then Jesus said to his disciples, "Whoever wants to be my disciple must deny themselves and take up their cross and follow me."

➢ *Galatians 2:20:* "I have been crucified with Christ and I no longer live, but Christ lives in me. The life I live now in the flesh I live by faith in the Son of God, who loved me and gave himself for me.

SEEKING GOD'S KINGDOM FIRST:

➢ *Matthew 6:33:* "But seek first his kingdom and his righteousness, and all these things will be given to you as well."

➢ *Luke 12:31:* "But seek his kingdom, and these things will be added to you."

➢ *Philippians 3:7-8:* "But whatever was to my gain I now consider loss for the sake of Christ. What is more, I consider everything a loss compared to the surpassing greatness of knowing Christ Jesus my Lord, for whose sake I have lost all things. I consider them rubbish, that I may gain Christ."

TRUST AND OBEDIENCE:

- ➢ *John 14:23:* "Whoever loves me will keep my word, and my Father will love him, and we will come to him and make our home with him."

- ➢ *Hebrews 11:6:* "And without faith it is impossible to please him, for whoever would draw near to God must believe that he exists and that he rewards those who seek him."

DEATH, PERSECUTION: Capital Punishment: imposition of the death penalty

- ➢ *Simon Peter:* Was crucified upside down in Rome around 64 AD. He reportedly felt unworthy to be crucified in the same manner as Jesus.

- ➢ *Paul:* According to tradition, Paul was beheaded in Rome around 67 AD under the reign of Nero.

- ➢ *Thomas*: Thomas was martyred in India, either stabbed with a spear or shot with arrows.

- ➢ *James:* The brother of Jesus, the leader of the early Jerusalem church, was reportedly stoned to death by a mob in 62 AD.

John 15:20: "Remember the word I spoke to you: 'No servant is greater than his master.' If they persecuted me, they will persecute you also."

- ➤ ***Matthew 10:22-23:*** "You will be hated by everyone because of my name. But whoever stands firm to the end will be saved."

- ➤ ***Acts 8:1:*** "On that day a great persecution broke out against the church in Jerusalem, and all except the apostles were scattered throughout Judea and Samaria."

The Word of God teaches that following Jesus Christ requires an unrelenting spiritual commitment and an unwavering willingness to *sacrifice everything*. Jesus requires putting Him above everything else, including family and personal desires. The cost of discipleship is high, and it includes persecution, rejection, and even death. The apostle Paul, suffered great publicly for his faith. He was beaten, imprisoned, and eventually executed for preaching the gospel. Other disciples also faced persecution and death for their faith, including Stephen, who was stoned to death for preaching about Jesus. Despite the high cost of discipleship, the Bible teaches that the rewards of following Jesus are immeasurable. Jesus said, "Whoever wants to be my disciple must deny themselves and take up their cross and follow me. For whoever wants to save their life will lose it, but whoever loses their life for me will find it". This statement emphasizes that following Jesus requires self-denial and sacrifice, but it also promises eternal life for those who are faithful. The ultimate cost of discipleship is high, but the rewards are invaluable. The Bible teaches that following Jesus requires a solid commitment and a willingness to sacrifice everything, but it also promises eternal life for those who are faithful.

Following Jesus Christ requires an unrelenting spiritual commitment and an unwavering willingness to sacrifice everything because it is a journey that requires complete surrender to God's will and a willingness to put Him above all else. The Holy Scriptures teaches that being a disciple of Jesus Christ requires a deep commitment and willingness to endure hardship as a good soldier, abuse, persecution, and suffering for the sake of His name. Disciples must be willing to put Jesus above all else, even their own lives. In **Matthew 16:24-25**, Jesus said, "If anyone would come after me, let him deny himself and take up his cross and follow me. For whoever would save his life will lose it, but whoever loses his life for my sake will find it". This verse emphasizes the importance of self-denial and sacrifice in following Jesus Christ. The Apostle Paul faced many challenges and hardships as he lived out his faith and dedication to Jesus Christ. He was imprisoned, beaten, and stoned for preaching the gospel. Despite these challenges, he remained steadfast in his faith and continued to spread the message of Jesus Christ. Jesus warns potential disciples that following him comes with a cost. He says, "No one who puts a hand to the plow and looks back is fit for the kingdom of God" (Luke 9:62). This means being willing to sacrifice anything that hinders our relationship with God, be it relationships, possessions, or even our own lives. This sacrifice requires unwavering faith and trust in God's ultimate plan.

Scriptural Examples:

Matthew 10:37-39: "Whoever loves their father or mother more than me is not worthy of me; and whoever loves their son or daughter more than me is not worthy of me; and whoever does not take up their cross and follow me is not worthy of me. Whoever finds their life will lose it, and whoever loses their life for my sake will find it."

Mark 8:34-35: "Whoever wants to be my disciple must deny themselves and take up their cross and follow me. For whoever wants to save their life will lose it, but whoever loses their life for me and for the gospel will save it."

Philippians 3:7-8: "But whatever was to my profit I now consider loss for the sake of Christ. What is more, I consider everything a loss compared to the surpassing greatness of knowing Christ Jesus my Lord, for whose sake I have lost all things. I consider them rubbish, that I may gain Christ."

2 Corinthians 5:17: "Therefore, if anyone is in Christ, he is a new creation; old things have passed away; behold, all things have become new."

The Bible paints a clear picture of following Jesus Christ as a "faith walk" demanding an unwavering spiritual commitment and a willingness to sacrifice everything. This call to radical devotion stems from several key themes:

RENOUNCING THE WORLD

Matthew 10:37: "Whoever loves their father or mother more than me is not worthy of me; whoever loves their son or daughter more than me is not worthy of me; and whoever does not take up their cross and follow me is not worthy of me." This verse highlights that aligning oneself with Jesus requires prioritizing Him above all earthly attachments, even family.

Luke 14:33: "Therefore no one who does not renounce everything they have can be my disciple." This verse emphasizes the complete dedication expected, demanding a willingness to let go of possessions, desires, and ambitions that conflict with following Jesus.

Embracing the Cross

Mark 8:34: "Whoever wants to be my disciple must deny themselves and take up their cross and follow me." The cross was a symbol of suffering and death in Jesus' time. This verse signifies the hardships and challenges often faced by those who truly follow Christ.

John 12:25: "Whoever loves their life will lose it, but whoever hates their life in this world will keep it for eternal life." This verse emphasizes the paradox of Christian living losing ourselves to truly find life in Christ, even if it means facing trials and tribulations.

Obedience and Humility

Philippians 2:5-8: "Have the same mindset as Christ Jesus: Who, being in very nature God, did not consider equality with God something to be grasped, but made himself nothing, taking the very nature of a servant, being made in human likeness. And being found in appearance as a man, he humbled himself and became obedient to death, even death on a cross!" This passage exemplifies Jesus' radical humility and obedience, setting the standard for disciples to follow.

Matthew 23:11-12: "The greatest among you will be your servant. For whoever exalts themselves will be humbled, and whoever humbles themselves will be exalted." This verse emphasizes that true greatness in the Kingdom of God is measured by servanthood and humility, not earthly accomplishments or status.

Radical Transformation of Mind & Heart

Jesus calls for a complete transformation of our hearts and minds. He says, "Whoever wants to be my disciple must deny themselves and take up their cross and follow me" *(Matthew 16:24).* This means putting aside our own desires, ambitions, and even comfort zones to align ourselves with God's will. This transformation can be challenging and requires a constant effort to overcome our natural tendencies.

COMMITMENT TO GOD, CHRIST AND THE KINGDOM

Following Jesus is not just about individual salvation; it's about participating in the building of God's kingdom on earth and winning souls to Christ. This kingdom is characterized by justice, repentance, compassion and love, and it requires active participation from believers. God needs you to level up like never before *for the Harvest is plenty and the Laborers are few.* This commitment often involves standing up for what is right, even when it's difficult or an unpopular opinion, demanding bold courage and unwavering conviction. Following Jesus Christ is not a "casual chore". It requires a lifelong commitment marked by unwavering faith, selfless devotion, and a willingness to face challenges for the sake of the Gospel. The scriptures provide a strong foundation for this challenging path, reminding us that the rewards of eternal life and true fulfillment only come through radical commitment and sacrifice.

It's important to realize that the call to sacrifice "everything" is not always literal. The key is to surrender our hearts, minds, desires, and priorities to God, placing

Him above all else. This may involve letting go of certain possessions, relationships, or ambitions, but ultimately it leads to a deeper spiritual transformation and a life lived in accordance with God's will.

The Lamb of God, Promised Messiah

Genesis 9:9

THE GREAT
COMMANDMENT

But when the Pharisees heard that he had silenced the Sadducees, they came together. And one of them, a lawyer, asked him a question, to test him. "Teacher, which is the great commandment in the Law?" And he said to him, "You shall love the Lord your God with all your heart, and with all your soul, and with all your mind. This is the great and first commandment. And a second is like it, You shall love your neighbor as yourself. On these two commandments depend all the Law and the Prophets." (*Matt 22: 34-40*).

Jesus' reply surprises them. He doesn't point to one of the ten commandments in "Mosaic Law", but rather mentions two that are not specifically part of it. First, he cites a text from the Old Testament that is part of the prayer the Jews called the *Shemá*, found in the book of Deuteronomy: "Hear, O Israel: The Lord our God is one Lord; and you shall love the Lord your God with all your heart, and with all your soul, and with all your might" *(Deut 6:4-5).* The second, "you shall love your neighbor as yourself" *(Lev 19:18),* is one of the many precepts included in what is called the "Code of Holiness" in the book of Leviticus.

Matthew 22:34-40, in these concise verses, Jesus articulates two core principles that intricately integrates the core essence of the "Greatest Commandment and the First Commandment which essentially operate as conjoined twin's inseparable yet very different in its core essence: love for God and love for neighbor.

> ➤ *"Love the Lord your God with all your heart, and with all your soul, and with all your mind". (**Matthew 22: 37**)* This first commandment demands complete and unwavering devotion to God, prioritizing Him above all other earthly concerns. It encompasses intellectual, emotional, and volitional engagement with the divine, urging a total surrender to God's will and purpose. *Jesus eloquently cites a text from the Old Testament that is part of the prayer the Jews called the Shemá, found in the book of Deuteronomy: "Hear, O Israel: The Lord our God is one Lord; and you shall love the Lord your God with all your heart, and with all your soul, and with all your might" (Deut 6:4-5).*

> ➤ *Love your neighbor as yourself. (**Matthew 22: 39**)* This second commandment expands the realm of love, indicative of agape, selfless love,

demanding compassionate and ethical action towards fellow citizens and believers. The "neighbor" encompasses all individuals, regardless of social standing, ethnicity, denomination or religious affiliation. Jesus' intentional use of the word "as yourself" underscores the radical nature of this love, urging Christians to treat others with the same care and consideration they extend to themselves. *The second, "you shall love your neighbor as yourself" (Lev 19:18), is one of the many precepts included in what is called the "Code of Holiness" in the book of Leviticus.*

LOVING GOD WITH ALL HEART & SOUL

This stretches beyond the scope of emotions or conception. It encompasses an absolute surrender of ones' heart, mind, and soul to God. We prioritize Him above all else, aligning our thoughts, desires, and actions with His will. It's not about compartmentalizing God into a specific aspect of our lives; rather it's about infusing His presence into every aspect of our lives, soul and purpose.

LOVE AS (SELF-EMPTYING)

This concept, rooted in **Philippians 2:5-8**, describes how Jesus emptied Himself, taking on the form of a servant. Similarly, our love for God and neighbor calls for a similar " self-humbling." We willingly let go of self-centeredness, pride, and carnal vain ambitions to make room for God's love, His priorities and His will.

Love as Sacrifice:

Following Jesus will require putting the needs of others before our own. This may involve sacrificing time, resources, comfort, feeling and emotions, even personal desires. The ultimate example is Jesus' sacrifice on the cross, giving His life for the love of sinners like us.

SERVANTHOOD EMBODIED AS LOVE:

The statement connects love, to taking on the role of a servant, putting ourselves last and others first. This isn't just about acts of charity; it's about a fundamental shift in our mindset, that we may through faith adapt the same mind of Christ Jesus through the neutrality of our actions. We ought to adore service as a high privilege, an opportunity to express our love through sincere actions that meet the needs of others.

Examples of Love in Action:

Caring for a sick neighbor, donating time to a worthy cause, or offering forgiveness to someone who has wronged us these are all expressions of love that go beyond empty platitudes. They involve tangible actions and sacrifices that reflect the depth of our commitment.

BEYOND EMOTION:

While emotions play a role in our love, the statement emphasizes that true love transcends fleeting feelings. It's a conscious choice, a daily commitment to live a life rooted in God's love and directed towards serving others.

CONTINUOUS JOURNEY:

This "*Love in Action*" isn't a one-time achievement but a lifelong journey. We continually strive to deepen our love for God and neighbor, embracing the challenges and sacrifices that come with such a radical commitment.

The statement is strongly emphasized in various Biblical passages. **Matthew 22:37-39** highlights the greatest commandments loving God with all your heart. **John 13:1-15** showcases Jesus' act of washing the disciples' feet, a powerful symbol of servanthood. **Philippians 2:5-8** exemplifies Jesus' self-emptying and calls us to follow His example.

Illustrating Gods "agape love" as an active force, not just a doormat passive feeling. It demands a constant self-emptying, a willingness to sacrifice one's own feelings and desires, aiming for a life dedicated to Loving and serving God and as well as our neighbors. By actively expressing our love through profitable actions, we truly embody the core essence of what it means to follow Jesus. Loving God with all our heart, all our soul and all our minds and live a life filled with Christ-centered love.

It is crucial to recognize that these commandments presented as separate entities, essentially, they are as two sides of the same coin. Loving God cannot be fully realized without loving one's neighbor, and vice versa. True love for God overflows into concrete acts of care, compassion, charity and service towards others. This resonates with Jesus' earlier teachings on the Good Samaritan *(Luke 10:25-37),* where He demonstrates that love for God manifests in tangible acts of mercy and compassion towards those in need.

Opusdei.org commentary on "The Gospel, The Greatest Commandment" concluded that "Benedict the 16th specified "*in God and with God, I love even the person whom I do not like or even know.*" ... *This can only take place on the basis of an intimate encounter with God, an encounter which has become a communion of will, even affecting ones' own feelings. Then I learn to look on this other person, not simply with my eyes and my feelings, but from the perspective of Jesus Christ. His friend is my friend. Going beyond exterior appearances, I perceive in others an interior desire for a sign of love, of concern ... Seeing with the eyes of Christ, I can give to others much more than their outward necessities; I can give them the look of love which they crave." "If we want to help others, we must love them. I insist with a love clothed in understanding, dedication, affection and voluntary humility. Then we will understand why our Lord summed up the whole law in that double commandment, which is really just one: love of God, and love of one's neighbor, with all our heart.*"

The Greatest Commandment is a fundamental love, rooted in scripture and exemplified by Jesus Christ life himself. It's a powerful selfless act of continual evolving service demanding radical self-emptying, unwavering sacrifice, and a life transformed by unconditional love and charity.

Matthew 22 34-40 "But when the Pharisees heard that He {Jesus} had silenced the Sadducees, they gathered together. Then one of them, a lawyer, asked Him a question, testing Him, and saying, "Teacher, which is the great commandment in the law?" Jesus said to him, "You shall love the Lord your God with all your heart, with all your soul, and with all your mind.' This is the first and great commandment. And the second is like it: 'You shall love your neighbor as yourself.' On these two commandments hang all the Law and the Prophets." Inevitably we the believers are bankrupt without love. ***1 Corinthians 13:13,*** elegantly states *"And now these three remain: faith, hope and love. But the greatest of these is love." Without love, followers of Jesus Christ believe their faith is incomplete or "bankrupt" because love is the foundation of all commandments and teachings in Christianity. It is through love that believers reflect the nature of God, as God Himself is described as love in **1 John 4:8**, "Whoever does not love does not know God, because God is love."* Therefore, without love, Christians would not be able to fully live out their faith or reflect the character of God, rendering their spiritual life "bankrupt." Love is seen as the driving force behind acts of kindness, forgiveness, and sacrifice, which are all key components of the sacred doctrines of Jesus Christ and God His Father. Without love, these actions would be devoid of their true meaning and sole purpose. Thus, love is not just a part of our faith and belief in Jesus who spared us retribution of sin, it is the core essence of it.

Bankrupt Without Love 1 Corinthians 13 "*Though I speak with the tongues of men and of angels, but have not love, I have become sounding brass or a clanging cymbal. And though I have the gift of prophecy, and understand all mysteries and all knowledge, and though I have all faith, so that I could remove mountains, but have not love, I am nothing. And though I bestow all my goods to feed the poor, and though I give my body to be burned, but have not love, it profits me nothing. Love suffers long and is kind; love does not envy; love does not parade itself, is not puffed up; does not behave rudely, does not seek its own, is not provoked, thinks no evil; does not rejoice in iniquity, but rejoices in the truth; bears all things, believes all things, hopes all things, endures all things. Love never fails. But whether there are prophecies, they will fail; whether there are tongues, they will cease; whether there is knowledge, it will vanish away. For we know in part and we prophesy in part. But when that which is perfect has come, then that which is in part will be done away. When I was a child, I spoke as a child, I understood as a child, I thought as a child; but when I became a man, I put away childish things. For now we see in a mirror, dimly, but then face to face. Now I know in part, but then I shall know just as I also am known. And now abide faith, hope, love, these three; but the greatest of these is love.*

THE SUPREME TEACHER

Jesus Christ, not only "Lord and Savior" but incomparable master of "kingdom wisdom", stands as history's most extraordinary teacher yet. Jesus, the unrivaled master, didn't just speak wisdom, He ignited an inner revolution of the hearts and minds of those looking for salvation and received His sovereign knowledge. His words, like holy ghost fire, pierced the hearts of those who followed Him seeking God. Yes indeed! It's true His lessons were like "fire shut off in my bones". His profound biblical wisdom still resonates through the ages, leaving an undeniable mark on the hearts and minds of believers alike. Jesus's teachings were not mere empty words; they were living parables that resonated with the souls of his disciples and believers. His spiritual accounts, like the Good Samaritan and the Prodigal Son, spoke vividly of Biblical truths relating to compassion, repentance, sin, forgiveness, and love. During His ministerial sermons on earth, Jesus asserted: "What I teach is not mine, but belongs to him that sent me." (John 7:16) Another time he said: "I do nothing on my own authority, but speak just as the Father taught me." (John 8:28) Here, we see that Jesus gave all of the attention to His heavenly Father. Although He was the long-awaited Messiah, the Son of God; he was moved to glorify the Father, not himself. (Matthew 6:9; John 17:26) It was this noteworthy humble attitude that made Jesus the excellent yet exceptional teacher that He was. The profound impact of Jesus's teachings extends beyond intellectual understanding they are in fact, a lifeline to our spiritual survival that navigates His believers to Gods imperishable plan of salvation. Christ is often considered the greatest teacher in history for several reasons.

- ➤ *Diverse Teaching Methods:* Jesus employed a wide array of teaching styles and strategies, always choosing the most effective method for any particular person, group, or situation.

- ➤ *Nationwide Attention*: Jesus fearlessly captured attention and interest of followers across the world. He utilized shocking profound spiritual parables to grab the attention of His believers that propelled them to intricate thought.

- ➤ *Teaching with Authority*: Jesus stood apart from other men because no other man resided in heaven before being born on earth. In His heavenly estate, Jesus had been a good Son, one who obediently listened to His Father. Jesus was therefore able to teach people what he had learned and observed from God.

> ➤ **Instructing Salvation:** Jesus is the definitive instructor on the attainment of salvation. Predecessors tried to impart knowledge about salvation, but their teachings although some were guided by the Spirit of God, most was structured in anticipation of His {Promised Messiah] teachings.

> ➤ **Supremacy in Person:** The supremacy of Jesus Christ is also highlighted in His relation to God, creation, and the church.

> ➤ **Relation to the Church:** As the head of the church, Jesus' teachings form the foundation of Christian doctrine and practice. His supremacy as a teacher is recognized and followed by the church.

Jesus' teachings continue to inspire and guide millions throughout history, shaping religious traditions, ethical principles, and cultural values.

DIVINE AUTHORITY

Jesus spoke with God's own authority, not just interpreting existing scriptures. He declared, "*I speak not on my own authority, but the Father who sent me has commanded me what to say and what to speak*" (**John 12:49**). This direct connection to God placed his teachings on a higher level than those of other human teachers.

UNMATCHED WISDOM

The Bible portrays Jesus as possessing perfect wisdom and understanding, exceeding that of any human scholar. He could answer complex questions with simple yet profound parables, leaving audiences amazed. For example, when asked about the greatest commandment, he summarized the entire Law and Prophets into two: "Love the Lord your God with all your heart, and with all your soul, and with all your mind, and love your neighbor as yourself" *(Matthew 22:37-39)*.

REVOLUTIONARY POWER

Jesus' teachings weren't mere theory; they had the power to change lives. His words could heal the sick, raise the dead, and even forgive sins. This practical demonstration of his message's truth further solidified his position as a supreme teacher.

ENDURING IMPACT

Unlike other teachers whose teachings faded over time, Jesus' message has resonated for centuries, inspiring countless individuals and shaping entire cultures. The spread of Christianity and its continued influence throughout history stand as a testament to the enduring impact of his teachings.

PROPHETIC FULFILLMENT

Jesus fulfilled numerous prophecies from the Old Testament, further solidifying his divine authority and the weight of his teachings. This aspect resonated deeply with his Jewish audience, accustomed to looking for fulfillment of prophetic promises.

Matthew 4:23 "Jesus was going throughout all Galilee, teaching in their synagogues and proclaiming the gospel of the kingdom, and healing every kind of disease and every kind of sickness among the people".

Matthew 7:29 "for He was teaching them as one having authority, and not as their scribes".

Matthew 23:9-12 "Do not call anyone on earth your father; for One is your Father, He who is in heaven. And do not be called teachers; for One is your Teacher, the Christ. But he who is greatest among you shall be your servant. And whoever exalts himself will be [a]humbled, and he who humbles himself will be exalted".

JESUS' KNOWLEDGE CAME FROM SEVERAL SOURCES

Divine Wisdom: As the Son of God, Jesus had divine wisdom and understanding imparted by God His father even before His ministerial call was activated. His knowledge was grounded in Himself and in His own determinations. He was eternally omniscient.

Holy Spirit: Christians gain the knowledge of Christ through the Holy Spirit who enlightens them to Christ.

Self-Education: There's a story in the Gospel of Luke about a 12-year-old Jesus debating scholars in the Temple, which raises the question of where He got His education. The Talmud (Tora books of Moses) suggested that every town should have a Bet ha-Sefer, or "House of the Book," where boys could be taught in the Law. Jesus studied "Mosaic Law" faithfully until His ministerial time came.

ADDITIONALLY

Yes, studying the Holy Scrolls of the Prophets was indeed a significant part of Jesus' education. The Bible provides several references to Jesus' familiarity with the Scriptures:

> ➤ *Childhood Learning:* As a child, Jesus was taught from the scrolls of the prophets at His mother's knee. This early exposure to the Scriptures likely laid the foundation for His deep understanding of them.

> *Self-Study:* Jesus continued to study the Scriptures throughout His youth and adulthood. He often spent quiet hours in prayer and the study of God's word.

> **Public Reading:** There are instances in the Bible where Jesus publicly read and interpreted the Scriptures. For example, in *Luke 4:17,* Jesus was handed the scroll of the prophet Isaiah, and He read from it in the synagogue

> *Teaching and Debating:* Jesus demonstrated His intimate knowledge of the Scriptures through His teachings and debates with religious leaders. His insights often astonished those who heard Him.

These references suggest that Jesus had direct access to the scrolls of Scripture and spent considerable time studying them. This deep and personal engagement with the Scriptures was a key part of His ministry and teachings.

Matthew 4:23, it is mentioned that Jesus was going throughout all Galilee, teaching in their synagogues and proclaiming the gospel of the kingdom, and healing every kind of disease and every kind of sickness among the people. The Gospel proves Jesus' knowledge is unsurpassed to no other, drawing from unreachable sources that highlight His unique nature as both God in Flesh and ruler over His heavenly Estate:

➢ **Divine Inheritance**: As the Son of God, Jesus possessed inherent knowledge and wisdom directly from God the Father. **John 1:1-5** states, "In the beginning was the Word, and the Word was with God, and the Word was God. He was with God in the beginning. Through him all things were made; without him nothing was made that has been made." This divine origin implies access to infinite knowledge and understanding.

➢ **Scripture and Jewish Tradition:** Throughout his life, Jesus was immersed in Jewish scripture and traditions. He studied the Torah, participated in religious practices, and engaged in discussions with religious leaders. **Luke 2:41-52** describes Jesus at the Temple at age 12, "listening and asking questions." This suggests his active engagement with religious knowledge.

➢ **Personal Experiences and Observations**: Despite his divine nature, Jesus also lived a fully human life and gained knowledge through experiences like any other person. This included interactions with people, exposure to different cultures, and observation of the world around him. Hebrews 5:8 refers to "what he suffered he learned obedience."

➢ **Holy Spirit Guidance:** The Bible also portrays Jesus as receiving guidance and inspiration from the Holy Spirit. **_John 3:34_** states, "For the one whom God has sent speaks the words of God, for he gives the Spirit without limit." This suggests that the Holy Spirit played a role in shaping Jesus' teachings and insights.

In Matthew 5:2, it is mentioned that Jesus opened His mouth and began to teach them, saying....

Jesus Teaches His Opponent Nicodemus, the Pharisee

Jesus taught Nicodemus. This encounter is described in the Gospel of *John 3:12*. Nicodemus was a Pharisee and a prominent member of the Jewish ruling council. *He came to Jesus at night and acknowledged that Jesus was a teacher who had come from God.* In this conversation, Jesus introduced the concept of being "born again" or "born from above," explaining that to see the kingdom of God, one must be born of water and the Spirit. This teaching puzzled Nicodemus, leading to further explanation from Jesus about spiritual rebirth. This dialogue between Jesus and Nicodemus is one of the most well-known teachings of Jesus, and it includes the famous verse *John 3:16*: "*For God so loved the world that he gave his one and only Son, that whoever believes in him shall not perish but have eternal life*"

Matthew 7:29, "it is mentioned that the people were astonished at Jesus' teaching, for He taught them as one having authority, and not as the scribes."

Mya A Chavis

Jesus taught His opponents for several reasons

Exposing Motives: Jesus often used His teachings to expose the motives of His opponents, false teachers, hypocrites and those exploiting the Gospel and Gods Church for monitary or political gain. For example, in Mark, Jesus challenged the Pharisees who were watching to see if He would heal on the Sabbath.

Seeking Peacful, Non Violent resolutions: Jesus was non violent and compassionate even to the unGodly. At times He sought peace, even with His opponents. When Peter cut off the ear of the high priest's servant during Jesus' arrest, Jesus not only condemned this act of violence but also healed the man's ear.

Applying Scripture: Jesus used Scripture to challenge the hardened hearts of His opponents. For example, in Matthew, Jesus quoted **Hosea 6:6** to the Pharisees who questioned why He ate with tax collectors and sinners.

Revealing True Identity: Jesus used His teachings to reveal both His true identity and the true identity of His opponents. In **John 8:31-59**, Jesus made it clear that His opponents were not the children of Abraham as they claimed, but were really children of the devil.

Teaching According to Divine Will: In Matthew, Jesus is portrayed as the lawgiver who teaches according to the divine will. He used His teachings to announce divine judgment on His foes.

In essence, it could be said Jesus taught His opponents to expose their motives, seek peace on non violent terms, apply Scripture, reveal true identities, and teach according to the divine will of God. His teachings were a reflection of His mission to spread the message of love, peace, and salvation to all, including His opponents. ***Mark 6:34***, it is mentioned that when Jesus went ashore, He saw a large crowd, and He felt compassion for them because they were like sheep without a shepherd; and He began to teach them many things.

False teachers challenged the "fullness" and sufficiency of the gospel. Indeed, throughout history, there have been instances where false teachers have challenged the "fullness" and sufficiency of the gospel. These individuals often deviate from the core teachings of Christianity, introducing doctrines that are not aligned with the Bible. In the Word of God, Jesus warns about false prophets in ***Matthew 7:15-20***. He describes them as wolves in sheep's clothing and emphasizes that their true nature will be revealed by their fruits. This means that their teachings and actions will ultimately reveal their true intentions. False teachers can come from various backgrounds. They may appear within prominent religious establishments, and their teachings can lead people away from the narrow path of truth. The Apostle Paul also warns about false teachers in his letters. For example, in his letter to Timothy, he emphasizes the importance of refuting falsehoods that are not based on the objective truth from God.

It's crucial for believers to have discernment to recognize these false teachings and not be led astray. This discernment often comes from a deep understanding of the Bible and the teachings of Jesus Christ. Remember, the gospel message in its fullness and sufficiency is centered on the life, death, and resurrection of Jesus Christ for the salvation of mankind. Any teaching that adds to, takes away from, or distorts this central message could be considered a false teaching. *It's always important to go back to the source, the Bible, for guidance and truth.*

Downplaying the significance of Jesus Christ.

Emphasis on human works or additional practices. False teachers might diminish the importance of faith in Jesus Christ for salvation, instead emphasizing adherence to specific rituals, following dietary restrictions, or performing certain works. This diminishes the grace offered through Jesus and potentially traps people in a cycle of striving and self-reliance.

Introducing alternative figures or teachings:

Some false teachers might elevate other spiritual figures or un factual philosophies alongside of Jesus, suggesting their teachings hold equal or even greater weight. This creates confusion and dilutes the unique message of salvation through Jesus alone.

DISTORTING KEY DOCTRINES.

Misinterpretation of grace.

False teachers might misinterpret the concept of grace, implying that it allows for a life of sin without consequences. This contradicts the biblical call to live a holy life as a response to God's grace.

Twisting the nature of God or Jesus.

Some false teachings might depict God as wrathful and vengeful, or Jesus as simply a moral teacher rather than the divine Son of God. This alters the core understanding of God's character and the significance of Jesus' sacrifice.

Focusing on worldly rewards or prosperity.

Promising material blessings or success in exchange for Money or Monatary Seed. False teachers might exploit people's desire for prosperity by claiming their teachings guarantee wealth, health, or earthly advantages, for a cost, fee or seed. This manipulates people's faith and distracts from the true focus of seeking God's kingdom first.

Appealing to sensational experiences or emotionalism. Some false teachers might rely on emotionally charged experiences or dramatic claims to attract followers. This can bypass rational reflection and critical thinking, potentially leading people astray.

REJECTING BIBLICAL AUTHORITY OR PROMOTING SELECTIVE INTERPRETATIONS.

"Twisting or Distorting" the inspiration or accuracy of scripture. False teachers might doubt the Bible's authority or selectively interpret verses to support their own agendas. This undermines the foundational source of Christian faith and introduces confusion.

Promoting personal interpretations or agendas over established doctrine: Some false teachings might prioritize individual feelings or interpretations over the collective factual sound understanding of Christian traditions and core doctrines. This can lead to fragmentation and personal distortions of the gospel.

Mixing the Gospel with Other Religions, Witchcraft or Philosophies: Some false teachings attempt to blend the gospel with elements from other religions or philosophies, such as New Age beliefs, occult practices, or Eastern mysticism. This creates a syncretistic mixture that dilutes the unique message of the Christian faith.

It's important to remember that the true "fullness" and sufficiency of Gods Word lies in the complete work of Jesus Christ on the cross and the evolutionary power of the Holy Spirit in the lives of true believers. False teachings, by contrast, often seek to add to, manipulate, or distort this core message, leading people away from the redemptive grace ,life and salvation found in Jesus Christ alone.

As Christians, it's crucial to pray, fast, find quiet time alone with God, remain grounded in scripture, hold fast to core doctrines that Jesus taught, and seek discernment to recognize and resist the distortions of false teachings. By staying true to the gospel in its fullness, we can continue to experience its transformational power in our lives and faithfully share it with others.

In **Luke 4:15**, it is mentioned that Jesus began teaching in their synagogues and was praised by all.

Jesus Christ did not charge for His teachings.

He shared His message freely. This was in line with his mission to spread the teachings of love, compassion, repentance, and salvation to all, regardless of their ability to pay. His teachings were meant to be accessible to everyone, rich or poor, and he often emphasized the importance of spiritual wealth over material wealth in his teachings. This approach allowed his teachings to reach a wide audience and have a profound impact on many lives. It's also worth noting that his teachings were not just verbal; they were demonstrated through his actions, miracles, and personal interactions, which were all offered freely.

The phrase "*Freely you have received, freely give*" comes from the Bible, specifically **Matthew 10:81**. This verse is part of the instructions that Jesus gave to his disciples when he sent them out to preach the message of the kingdom of heaven.

The disciples had received the power to perform miracles, such as healing the sick, raising the dead, cleansing those with leprosy, and casting out demons. These miracles were meant to authenticate their message and demonstrate that they were truly representing Jesus. Importantly, the disciples did not perform these miracles through their own power, but in Jesus' name and by His authority.

When Jesus said, "Freely you have received, freely give," he was instructing His disciples not to sell their gifts of healing, preaching, etc for riches or material gain. They were not to make a money-making business of it. The disciples had received these gifts for free from Jesus, and they were to offer them freely to all who would come and hear and believe. This firm , direct instruction accentuates the grace of God, which is always a free gift. Connecting faith to material prosperity is a "great grave mistake" that God is highly displeased with; attempting to "sell" salvation or spiritual gifts is a despicable sin. The disciples were not to seek much in the way of support. They were to travel and preach, but they were not to "work" or ask to be paid. In essence, Jesus taught His disciples and us the core principles of generositya and compassion, love , charity and service. Just as they had freely received from God, they were to freely give to others. This principle applies not only to material wealth but also to spiritual wealth. It's a reminder that the blessings we receive from God are not meant to be hoarded but shared liberally and freely. This is a key aspect of Christian discipleship and a reflection of God's own generosity towards us. Acts of service and giving driven by the generosity of a pure heart is what pleases God. It serves as a reminder that true fulfillment comes from serving others and sharing the good fortune we receive freely.

Beautiful are the Feet that deliver the Good News!

The phrase "Beautiful are the feet that deliver the good news of the gospel" appears in two places in the Bible:

Romans 10:15: "And how shall they preach, unless they be sent? as it is written, How beautiful are the feet of them that preach the gospel of peace, and bring glad tidings of good things!"

Isaiah 52:7: "How beautiful upon the mountains are the feet of him that bringeth good tidings, that publisheth peace, that bringeth good tidings of happiness, that publisheth salvation, that saith unto Zion, Thy God reigneth!"

In both instances, the metaphor of "beautiful feet" refers to the messengers who bring the good news of the gospel. This beautiful imagery carries several layers of meaning. The beauty of the feet isn't literal; it represents the importance and value of the message they carry. The gospel, the news of God's salvation and love, is seen as the most beautiful and transformative message imaginable. Reaching people with the gospel often requires considerable effort devotion, dedication and sacrifice. Some Ambassadors of Christ may travel long distances, face hardships, and encounter rejection. The "beautiful feet" acknowledge the dedication and perseverance of those who share the message despite challenges. The phrase "Beautiful are the feet that deliver the Good News of the Gospel" is derived from the Bible, specifically *Romans 10:15*. This verse is a quotation from *Isaiah 52:7* in the Old Testament. The "Good News" or "Gospel" refers to the message of salvation through Jesus Christ. The "feet" symbolize the bearers of this message, typically referring to preachers, missionaries, or any believers who share the Gospel. The term "beautiful" in this context does not refer to physical attractiveness, but rather to the preciousness and value of the task being performed. The feet are described as "beautiful" because they are bringing a message of hope, peace, and salvation.

This verse underscores the importance and value of evangelism the act of sharing the Gospel. It highlights the beauty and joy that come from delivering the message of God's love and salvation to others. It's a reminder to Christians of their calling to spread the Gospel and a commendation of those who undertake this task. In essence, this scripture emphasizes the nobility and significance of the mission to spread the Gospel, and it commends those who undertake this mission, regardless of the challenges they may face.

The Bible tells that , Jesus Christ knowledge is unsurpassed to no other, drawing from unreachable sources that highlight His unique nature as both God in Flesh and ruler over His heavenly Estate.

> ➤ **Divine Inheritance:** As the Son of God, Jesus possessed inherent knowledge and wisdom directly from God the Father. ***John 1:1-5*** states, "In the beginning was the Word, and the Word was with God, and the Word was God. He was with God in the beginning. Through him all things were made; without him nothing was made that has been made." *This divine origin implies access to infinite knowledge and understanding.*

> ➤ **Scripture and Jewish Tradition**: Throughout His life, Jesus was immersed in Jewish scripture and traditions. He studied the Torah, participated in religious practices, and engaged in discussions with older religious leaders. ***Luke 2:41-52*** describes Jesus at the Temple at age 12, "listening and asking questions." *This suggests his active engagement with religious knowledge.*

> ➤ **Personal Experiences and Observations:** Despite his supreme supereior nature, Jesus also lived a fully human life and gained knowledge through experiences like any other person. This

included interactions with people, exposure to different cultures, and observation of the world ,people and nature around Him. ***Hebrews 5:8*** refers to "what he suffered he learned obedience."

➤ ***Holy Spirit Guidance:*** According to the Holy Bible Jesus received guidance and inspiration from the Holy Spirit continually especially through prayer and fasting. ***John 3:34*** states, "For the one whom God has sent speaks the words of God, for he gives the Spirit without limit." <u>This suggests that the Holy Spirit played a role in shaping Jesus' teachings and insights.</u>

Jesus Christ's supremacy as the "Supreme Teacher" is highlighted in His authoritative teachings, diverse teaching methods, and His unique relations to God, creation, and the church. Jesus's teachings provide the path to salvation and eternal life. His wisdoms include faith in Christ, repentance, sin, baptism, keeping God's commandments, receiving the Holy Ghost, and enduring to the end.

The core principle doctrines of Jesus Christ form the foundation of Christian faith and practice and way of life. They are the bedrock on which His Gospel is built. His teachings have been preserved and passed down through the apostolic witness all throughout the New Testament. His teachings provide guidance for salvation and form the foundation of Christian faith and practice. His teachings have had a profound impact on the world and continue to guide millions of people today. Jesus Christ, the unsurpassed master of wisdom and Supreme Teacher stands as history's most extraordinary giver of knowledge yet. His profound spiritual impact is still prevalent through the ages, leaving a permanent mark on the hearts, minds, and souls of believers alike. His unparalleled wisdom, radical love, stern rebukes, firm ethical foundations, game-changing influence, and sacrificial redemption continue to motivate and encourage seekers, believers, and scholars across cultures, generations, and relations today.

HIS STANCE AGAINST
FALSE PROPHESY

Throughout the Bible, Jesus Christ consistently and sternly condemned hypocrisy and false teachers. Jesus' condemnation of hypocrisy, the importance of humility, compassion, repentance and the need for genuine righteousness, beyond mere outward appearance. Jesus acknowledges the authority of the Scribes and Pharisees, who sit on Moses' seat. However, He openly criticizes their hypocrisy: emphasizing they preach but do not practice what they teach. Jesus emphasizes humility, instructing that the greatest among them should be a servant. Jesus pronounces several "woes" upon the scribes and Pharisees. Jesus criticizes their meticulous tithing of minor herbs (mint, dill, cumin) while neglecting justice, mercy, and faithfulness. He equates them to blind guides who strain out gnats but swallow camels. Jesus rebukes their focus on external outward appearances metaphorically equating them to partially clean cups; while neglecting inner purity. He calls for cleansing from within, so that the outside may also be clean. Here are some key examples, Mathew 23:

> *Hypocrisy:* Jesus exposes their outward displays of religiousness while neglecting the core principles of the Law (justice, mercy, and faithfulness). He calls them "hypocrites" and "blind guides" for misleading the people.

> *Pride and Self-righteousness:* Jesus condemns their arrogance and self-importance. They elevate themselves above others, claiming authority and reverence, while neglecting their true role as servants of God and the people.

> *Exploitation:* They exploit the people for their own gain(material and spiritual), burdening them with heavy religious rules while they themselves don't follow them. Jesus compares them to "whitewashed tombs" - beautiful on the outside but full of dark decay on the inside.

> *Spiritual Blindness:* They are blind to the true meaning of faith and focus on outward appearances. Jesus compares them to "blind guides" leading others astray.

> *Woes:* Jesus delivers seven pronouncements of "woe" upon them, highlighting their specific sins and the terrible consequences they will face for leading God's people astray.

Denouncing Hypocrisy

Sermon on the Mount: In **Matthew 6:1-8,** Jesus criticizes hypocritical acts like praying and giving charities just to be seen by others. He emphasizes the importance of sincerity and acting from the heart in religious practices.

Scribes and Pharisees: Jesus repeatedly criticized the religious leaders of his time, the Scribes and Pharisees, for their outward displays of religiousness while neglecting the inward transformation of their hearts. He called them "blind guides" and "whitewashed tombs" **(Matthew 23).**

CONFRONTING FALSE TEACHERS:

Parable of the Weeds: In **Matthew 13:24-30,** Jesus compares false teachers to weeds sown among the wheat, seeking to deceive and mislead people. He warns against being misled by their false teachings and emphasizes the importance of discerning true faith from false claims.

Wolves in Sheep's Clothing: Jesus cautioned his disciples against false teachers who disguise themselves as harmless sheep but are in reality "ravenous wolves" **(Matthew 7:15**). He urged them to identify them by their fruits, meaning their actions and teachings.

Direct Stances: Matthew 23

Woe to You: Several times in the Gospel of Matthew, Jesus pronounces harsh pronouncements ("Woe to you!") on the religious leaders who mislead the people and burden them with heavy traditions. These pronouncements directly highlight the severity of their actions and the consequences they face.

"I am the way, the truth, and the life": *John 14:6* clearly establishes Jesus as the sole source of truth and salvation. This statement implicitly refutes any claims made by false teachers who offer alternative paths or teachings.

Matthew 23 is a fiery, "emotional spicey" powerful chapter where Jesus unleashes a serious fiery rebuke against the Pharisees and Scribes, the religious leaders, elders , chief priest and legalistics of His time. Let's delve into it and understand his passionate disgust at their actions:Jesus, addressing a large crowd observers and religious elite anxiously assembled at the Temple Mount. He launches into a series of seven pronouncements of "woe" against the Pharisees and Scribes. *His warnings were more than mere minor reproaches; they were critical denunciations of their hypocrisy, greed, and spiritual blindness.*

Unmasking the Hypocrisy:

Jesus exposed the inner darkness and private agenda behind their outward religiosity. He calls those "hypocrites" who. Preach but don't practice: They impose burdensome rules on others while ignoring them themselves *(Matt 23 : 3-4).*

- ➤ Love appearances: They prioritize artificial public displays of devotion over genuine love for God and neighbor *(Matt 23 : 5-7).*
- ➤ Exploit people: They devour widows' houses and use prayer as a smokescreen for greed *(Matt 23 : 14, 25).*
- ➤ Stumble the innocent: They meticulously follow man-made traditions while neglecting the weightier matters of justice, mercy, and faithfulness *(Matt 23: 23-24).*

The Source of Jesus' Disgust:

What fueled Jesus' anger wasn't mere disagreement; it was a deep love for God and his people. He saw how these false teachers were leading God's flock astray, trapping them in legalistic rituals and superficiality. Their objectionable actions ...

- ➤ *Offended God:* Their hypocrisy dishonored God's name and misrepresented His true nature.
- ➤ *Harmed the people:* Their misleading teachings burdened and exploited the vulnerable, hindering their spiritual growth.
- ➤ *Blocked the way to God:* Their emphasis on outward appearances obscured the true path to salvation through faith in Jesus.

Beyond Anger: Compassion and Warning:

Despite his disgust, Jesus' words also revealed a deep compassion to not allow his sheep to be deceived. He warns the people about being deceived by these false teachers *(Matt :8-12)*. He longs for them to encounter the genuine love and grace of God.

Mathew 23 challenges us to

> ➢ *Examine our own motives:* Are we focused on genuine love for God and others, or do we fall into the trap of outward performance?
> ➢ *Discern true teachers:* We must critically evaluate teachings against the light of scripture and the life and message of Jesus.
> ➢ *Live authentically:* Let our faith be embodied in our actions, not just our words for faith without works are dead.

Matthew 23 is both a wake-up call for all Christians to guard against hypocrisy as well as a stern warning against false teachings. Jesus' passionate words remind us to not take Gods will or His word in vain, compassion, and pure authentic faith over appearances and self-serving agendas.

Jesus' Devotion to His Sheep:

> ➢ His words are filled with anger and disgust, reflecting his deep love for God and his people. The deception and harm these false teachers are causing is disturbing & alarming.

- ➤ He asserts strong imagery and metaphors to accentuate their wickedness and the gravity of their actions.
- ➤ His tone is a stark contrast to his usual gentle and compassionate teachings.
- ➤ Overall, Jesus' stance against hypocrisy and false teachers was clear and uncompromising. He exposed their deceptive practices, condemned their self-righteousness, and called for genuine repentance and inner reformation. His teachings remain a powerful reminder for all Christians to prioritize authenticity, love, and faithfulness over outward appearances and empty rituals.
- ➤ Jesus Christ rebuked false teachers and hypocrites in a number of ways according to the Bible:

Public Censure: Jesus publicly addressed the toxic doctrine of religious leaders for the benefit of their victims and potential victims. He did not water down his speech to give them the benefit of the doubt. Instead, He specified their doctrinal error and unrighteous actions, warned of the consequences of their error, and called his listeners to reject the false teachers and their deadly doctrine.

Stern Language: Authoritatively Jesus calls the scribes and Pharisees "hypocrites" six times. Besides that, he calls them "blind guides," "blind fools," "blind men," "whitewashed tombs," "sons of those who murdered the prophets," "serpents," and "brood of vipers".

Exposing Doctrinal Errors: Jesus confronted their error by telling the crowd, "They tie up heavy burdens, hard to bear, and lay them on people's shoulders, but they themselves are not willing to move them with their finger" *(Matthew 23:4)*.

Seven Woes: Matthew 23, Jesus pronounces seven "woes" upon the Pharisees and teachers of the law. The word "woe" used in this passage goes beyond the typical expression of grief, regret, or anger. The Greek word, "ouai" carries the connotation of warning that precedes judgment or impending doom.

Calling Out Neglect of Justice, Mercy, and Faithfulness to Gods Will: Jesus accused them of giving a tenth of their spices (as a tithe), but of neglecting the more important matters of justice, mercy, and faithfulness.

These instances show that *Jesus was not hesitant to call out hypocrisy and false teachings, and he did so with conviction and authority.* His rebukes served as a warning to others about the dangers of such behavior and teachings.

Confronting False Teachers:

> ➤ Parable of the Weeds: In ***Matthew 13:24-30***, Jesus compares false teachers to weeds sown among the wheat, seeking to deceive and mislead people. He warns against being misled by their

false teachings and emphasizes the importance of discerning true faith from false claims.

➢ **Wolves in Sheep's Clothing:** Jesus cautioned his disciples against false teachers who disguise themselves as harmless sheep but are in reality "ravenous wolves" **(Matthew 7:15)**. He urged them to identify them by their fruits, meaning their actions and teachings.

Denouncing Hypocrisy:

➢ **Sermon on the Mount:** In **Matthew 6:1-8**, Jesus criticizes those who practice religious acts for public display rather than genuine devotion. He condemns hypocrisy in prayer, fasting, and giving contributions, urging his followers to act with sincerity and humility.

➢ **Parable of the Pharisee and the Tax Collector:** In **Luke 18:9-14**, Jesus reveals the dangers of self-righteousness through the parable. The Pharisee boasts about his outward piety, while the tax collector humbly seeks forgiveness. Jesus commends the tax collector's humility and warns against hypocrisy.

➢ **Woes to the Scribes and Pharisees:** In **Matthew 23**, Jesus delivers a series of scathing pronouncements against the religious leaders of His time. He accuses them of hypocrisy, greed, and burdening the people with heavy traditions.

Confronting False Teachers:

> ➤ *Sermon on the Mount*: In *Matthew 7:15-20*, Jesus warns against false prophets who appear like sheep but are inwardly ravenous wolves. He encourages his followers to discern true teachings by their fruits, emphasizing the importance of living out the message of the gospel.

> ➤ *Parable of the Weeds: Matthew 13:24-30,* Jesus uses the parable to illustrate the presence of both good and bad seeds within the kingdom of God. He warns against confusing false teachings with the true message of the gospel.

> ➤ *Confrontation with the Sadducees: Matthew 22:23-33,* Jesus exposes the Sadducees' misinterpretation of scripture regarding the resurrection. He demonstrates the importance of rightly interpreting scripture and avoiding false doctrines.

Matthew 23 serves as a imposing warning against hypocrisy, false teachings, and spiritual blindness. It reminds us of the importance of genuine faith, compassion, repentance, love, God's Will and living a life that aligns with Jesus Teachings. It challenges us to be discerning of religious leaders and their motives pertaining to leading people to salvation, ensuring they align with the true, authentic message of the Gospel.

Vitality of Jesus Christ Warnings

Matthew 23 obliges a serious warning against <u>hypocrisy,</u> <u>false teachings</u>, and <u>spiritual blindness</u>. It reminds us of the importance of genuine faith, humility, and living a life that aligns with our beliefs. It outwardly challenges us to be ***discerning*** of religious leaders and their teachings, ensuring they align with the true message of the Gospel.

Woe to the Scribes and Pharisees (Matthew 23 NKJV)

Then Jesus spoke to the multitudes and to His disciples, saying "The scribes and the Pharisees sit in Moses' seat. Therefore whatever they tell you to observe, that observe and do, but do not do according to their works; for they say, and do not do. For they bind heavy burdens, hard to bear, and lay them on men's shoulders; but they themselves will not move them with one of their fingers. But all their works they do to be seen by men. They make their phylacteries broad and enlarge the borders of their garments. They love the best places at feasts, the best seats in the synagogues, greetings in the marketplaces, and to be called by men, 'Rabbi, Rabbi.' But you, do not be called 'Rabbi'; for One is your Teacher, the Christ, and you are all brethren. Do not call anyone on earth your father; for One is your Father, He who is in heaven. And do not be called teachers; for One is your Teacher, the Christ. But he who is greatest among you shall be your servant. And whoever exalts himself will be humbled, and he who humbles himself will be exalted.

"But woe to you, scribes and Pharisees, hypocrites! For you shut up the kingdom of heaven against men; for you neither go in yourselves, nor do you allow those who are entering to go in. Woe to you, scribes and Pharisees, hypocrites! For you devour widows' houses, and for a pretense make long prayers. Therefore you will receive greater condemnation. "Woe to you, scribes and Pharisees, hypocrites! For you travel land and sea to win one proselyte, and when he is won, you make him twice as much a son of hell as yourselves.

"Woe to you, blind guides, who say, 'Whoever swears by the temple, it is nothing; but whoever swears by the gold of the temple, he is obliged to perform it.' Fools and blind! For which is greater, the gold or the temple that sanctifies the gold? And, 'Whoever swears by the altar, it is nothing; but whoever swears by the gift that is on it, he is obliged to perform it.' Fools and blind! For which is greater, the gift or the altar that sanctifies the gift? Therefore he who swears by the altar, swears by it and by all things on it. He who swears by the temple, swears by it and by Him who dwells in it. And he who swears by heaven, swears by the throne of God and by Him who sits on it.

"Woe to you, scribes and Pharisees, hypocrites! For you pay tithe of mint and anise and cummin, and have neglected the weightier matters of the law: justice and mercy and faith. These you ought to have done, without leaving the others undone. Blind guides, who strain out a gnat and swallow a camel!

"Woe to you, scribes and Pharisees, hypocrites! For you cleanse the outside of the cup and dish, but inside they are full of extortion and self-indulgence. Blind Pharisee, first cleanse the inside of the cup and dish, that the outside of them may be clean also.

"Woe to you, scribes and Pharisees, hypocrites! For you are like whitewashed tombs which indeed appear beautiful outwardly, but inside are full of dead men's bones and all uncleanness. Even so you also outwardly appear righteous to men, but inside you are full of hypocrisy and lawlessness.

"Woe to you, scribes and Pharisees, hypocrites! Because you build the tombs of the prophets and adorn the monuments of the righteous, and say, 'If we had lived in the days of our fathers, we would not have been partakers with them in the blood of the prophets.'

"Therefore you are witnesses against yourselves that you are sons of those who murdered the prophets. Fill up, then, the measure of your fathers' guilt. Serpents, brood of vipers! How can you escape the condemnation of hell? Therefore, indeed, I send you prophets, wise men, and scribes: some of them you will kill and crucify, and some of them you will scourge in your synagogues and persecute from city to city, that on you may come all the righteous blood shed on the earth, from the blood of righteous Abel to the blood of Zechariah, son of Berechiah, whom you murdered between the temple and the altar. Assuredly, I say to you, all these things will come upon this generation.

JESUS STERN REBUKE

Why did Jesus rebuke the scribes and Pharisees so harshly in *Matthew 23:13–36?* gotquestions.org in there commentary on "Jesus Rebuke" elaborates below ... .

"In Matthew 23 Jesus pronounces "woes" on the scribes and Pharisees, the religious elite of the day. The word woe is an exclamation of grief, denunciation, or distress. This was not the first time Jesus had some harsh words for the religious leaders of His day. Why did Jesus rebuke them so harshly here? Looking at each woe gives some insight.Before pronouncing the woes, Jesus told His listeners to respect the scribes and Pharisees due to their position of authority but not to emulate them, "for they do not practice what they preach. They tie up heavy, cumbersome loads and put them on other people's shoulders, but they themselves are not willing to lift a finger to move them. Everything they do is done for people to see" (*Matthew 23:3–5*). The scribes and Pharisees were supposed to know God and help others know Him and follow His ways. Instead, the religious leaders added to God's Law, making it a cumbersome and onerous burden. And they did not follow God with a pure heart. Their religion was not true worship of God; rather, it was rooted in a prideful heart. Jesus' Sermon on the Mount emphasizes the true intent of the Law over the letter of the Law. The scribes and Pharisees emphasized the letter, completely missing its spirit.

The first woe is, "Woe to you, teachers of the law and Pharisees, you hypocrites! You shut the door of the kingdom of heaven in people's faces. You yourselves do not enter, nor will you let those enter who are trying to" *(Matthew 23:13)*. Jesus cares for people. He desires for them to know Him and to enter into His kingdom *(John 3:16–17; 10:10, 17; 2 Peter 3:9)*. After rebuking the scribes and Pharisees, Jesus lamented over rebellious Jerusalem (Matthew 23:37-39). Clearly, His heart is for people to find life in Him. It stands to reason, then, that He would have harsh words for those who prevented people from finding salvation. The teachers of the Law and Pharisees were not truly seeking after God, though they acted as if they were. Their religion was empty, and it was preventing others from following the Messiah.

In the second woe, Jesus condemns the scribes and Pharisees for making strenuous efforts to win converts and then leading those converts to be "twice as much" children of hell as the scribes and Pharisees were *(Matthew 13:15)*. In other words, they were more intent on spreading their religion than on maintaining the truth.

The third woe Jesus pronounces against the scribes and Pharisees calls the religious leaders "blind guides" and "blind fools" (*Matthew 23:16–17*). Specifically, Jesus points out, they nit-picked about which oaths were binding and which were not, ignoring the sacred nature of all oaths and significance of the temple and God's holiness*(Matthew15–22).*

The fourth woe calls out the scribes and Pharisees for their practice of diligently paying the tithe while neglecting to actually care for people. While they were counting their mint leaves to make sure they gave one tenth to the temple, they "neglected the more important matters of the law justice, mercy and faithfulness" *(Matthew 23:23).* Once again, they focused on the letter of the Law and obeyed it with pride, but they missed the weightier things of God. Their religion was external; their hearts were not transformed.

Jesus elaborates on their hypocrisy in the fifth woe. He tells the religious leaders they appear clean on the outside, but they have neglected the inside. They perform religious acts but do not have God-honoring hearts. It does no good, Jesus says, to clean up the outside when the inside is "full of greed and self-indulgence" *(Matthew 23:25).* The Pharisees and scribes are blind and do not recognize that, when the inside is changed, the outside, too, will be transformed.

In the sixth woe, Jesus claims the scribes and Pharisees are "like whitewashed tombs, which look beautiful on the outside but on the inside are full of the bones of the dead and everything unclean" *(Matthew 23:27).* The deadness inside of tombs is likened to the "hypocrisy and wickedness" inside the religious leaders *(Matthew 23:28).* Once again, they appear to obey God, but their hearts are far from Him *(see Matthew 15:7–9 and Isaiah 29:13).*

Jesus concludes His seven-fold rebuke by telling the religious leaders that they are just like their fathers, who persecuted the prophets of old. In building monuments to the prophets, they testify against themselves, openly admitting that it was their ancestors who killed the prophets *(Matthew 23:29–31).* Although they arrogantly claim that they would not have done so, they are the ones who will soon plot the murder of the Son of God Himself *(Matthew:26:4).*

Jesus' words are harsh because there was so much at stake. Those who followed the Pharisees and scribes were being kept from following God. So much of the teaching in Jesus' day was in direct contradiction of God's Word *(see Matthew 15:6).* The religious leaders made a mockery out of following God. They did not truly understand God's ways, and they led others away from God. Jesus' desire was that people would come to know God and be reconciled with Him. In *Matthew 11:28–30* Jesus said, "Come to me, all you who are weary and burdened, and I will give you rest. Take my yoke upon you and learn from me, for I am gentle and humble in heart, and you will find rest for your souls. For my yoke is easy and my burden is light." Unlike the burdens the scribes and Pharisees laid on the people in a human effort to gain reconciliation with God, Jesus gives true rest. The religious leaders spread lies covered in a veneer of godliness *(John 8:44)*; Jesus spoke harshly against them because He came to bring life *(John 10:10)*.

Also, the word woe carries with it a tinge of sorrow. There is an element of imprecation, to be sure, but with it an element of compassionate sadness. The seven woes that Jesus pronounces on the religious leaders are solemn declarations of future misery. The stubbornness of the sinners to whom He speaks is bringing a judgment to be feared. The scribes and Pharisees are calling down God's wrath upon themselves, and they are to be commiserated.

Immediately after Jesus' rebuke of the scribes and Pharisees, we see Jesus' compassion. He asks, "How will you escape being condemned to hell?" *(Matthew 23:33)*. Jesus then expresses His desire to gather the people of Israel to Himself for safety, if only they were willing *(Matthew 23: 37)*. Latsly they close by saying, God longs for His people to come to Him and find forgiveness. Jesus was not harsh to be mean. He was not having a temper tantrum. Rather, love guided His actions. Jesus spoke firmly against the deception of Satan out of a desire for people to know truth and find life in Him".

False prophets often lead people astray, promoting teachings that deviate from God's truth. Their actions can cause confusion, division, and spiritual harm. False prophets typically do not care for the spiritual needs of others. They appear loving to the "carnal eye", but "Spiritually Mature Discerned" Christians can spot their hypocrisy a mile away. False prophets often lead people astray, promoting teachings that deviate from God's truth. Their actions can cause confusion, division, and spiritual harm. False prophets typically do not care for the spiritual needs of others but more so their own agenda deviating from God's plan and God's will. They appear loving to the "carnal eye", but "Spiritually Mature Discerned" Christians can spot their hypocrisy a mile away. Recognizing and avoiding false prophets is essential for maintaining spiritual steadfastness and discerning God's truth amidst deception. Please see ....

Matthew 7:15: "Beware of false prophets, who come to you in sheep's clothing but inwardly are ravenous wolves."

1 John 4:1: "Beloved, do not believe every spirit, but test the spirits to see whether they are from God, for many false prophets have gone out into the world."

Matthew 24:24: "For false christs' and false prophets will arise and perform great signs and wonders, so as to lead astray, if possible, even the elect."

2 Peter 2:1: "But false prophets also arose among the people, just as there will be false teachers among you, who will secretly bring in destructive heresies, even denying the Master who bought them, bringing upon themselves swift destruction."

Matthew 24:11: "And many false prophets will arise and lead many astray."

Colossians 2-8 "Beware lest anyone cheat you through philosophy and empty deceit, according to the tradition of men, according to the basic principles of the world, and not according to Christ".

Ezekial 34:1-4 "The word of the Lord came to me: "Son of man, prophesy against the shepherds of Israel; prophesy, and say to them, even to the shepherds, Thus says the Lord God: Ah, shepherds of Israel who have been feeding yourselves! Should not shepherds feed the sheep? You eat the fat, you clothe yourselves with the wool, you slaughter the fat ones, but you do not feed the sheep. The weak you have not strengthened, the sick you have not healed, the injured you have not bound up, the strayed you have not brought back, the lost you have not sought, and with force and harshness you have ruled them."

Jeremiah 5 30-31 God rebuked false prophets through Jeremiah saying *"An astonishing and horrible thing Has been committed in the land: The prophets prophesy falsely, the priests rule by their own power; And My people love to have it so. But what will you do in the end?* **Matt 23** stated "For they preach, but do not practice. They tie up heavy burdens, hard to bear, and lay them on people's shoulders, but they themselves are not willing to move them with their finger … So you also outwardly appear righteous to others, but within you are full of hypocrisy and lawlessness." **Jude 12: 13** "These are hidden reefs at your love feasts, as they feast with you without fear, shepherds feeding themselves; waterless clouds, swept along by winds; fruitless trees in late autumn, twice dead, uprooted; wild waves of the sea, casting up the foam of their own shame; wandering stars, for whom the gloom of utter darkness has been reserved forever." *1 John 4.1* "Dear friends, do not believe every spirit, but test the spirits to see whether they are from God, because many false prophets have gone out into the world." *James 4:7* "Therefore submit to God. Resist the devil and he will flee from you. For these false teachers, hypocrites and false prophets possess "a form" of godliness, denying the power thereof. From such people or persons do not be afraid to turn away".

OVER COME

You overcome these types of "spiritual manipulations" by equaling works with faith and utilizing the kingdom tools of "Power and Authority" that Jesus left for you to use! We are the head and not the tail. We are above and not beneath. We don't have to fear these forces, they should be fearing us! *1 Peter 2:9* "But ye are a chosen generation, a royal priesthood, a holy nation, a peculiar people; that ye should shew forth the praises of him who hath called you out of darkness into his marvelous light". Your most vital tools are.

1. Wisdom/ Discernment
2. Knowledge of Scriptures. Reading & Understanding of God's Word
3. Earnest Prayer
4. Courage to Speak boldly and even walk away
5. Bind the Strong-Hold of the Enemy

Ephesians 1:18 "I pray that the eyes of your understanding may be enlightened in order that you may know the hope to which he has

called you, the riches of his glorious inheritance in his holy people".
1 Peter 2-9 "*But you are a chosen people, a royal priesthood, a holy nation, God's special possession, that you may declare the praises of him who called you out of darkness into his wonderful light*". **1 John 4 4-** "*Greater is he that is in you, than he that is in the world.*" **Romans 8**

Inevitably later on the Peter the disciple of Jesus went on to reiterate Christ Non-Tolerance for *Deceptions of False Teachers (2 Peter 10-21)* " For when they speak great swelling words of emptiness, they allure through the lusts of the flesh, through lewdness, the ones who have actually escaped from those who live in error. While they promise them liberty, they themselves are slaves of corruption; for by whom a person is overcome, by him also he is brought into bondage. For if, after they have escaped the pollutions of the world through the knowledge of the Lord and Savior Jesus Christ, they are again entangled in them and overcome, *the latter end is worse for them than the beginning*. For it would have been better for them not to have known the way of righteousness, than having known it, to turn from the holy commandment delivered to them. But it has happened to them according to the true proverb: "A dog returns to his own vomit," and, "a sow, having washed, to her wallowing in the mire."

A false prophet is a person who spreads false teachings or messages while claiming to speak the Word of God. In the Bible, false prophets also spoke on behalf of false gods. False prophets functioned in their prophetic role illegitimately or for the purpose of deception or high material gain. The Bible denounces false prophets for leading people astray. The Pharisees and scribes were religious hypocrites who did not practice what they preached. They were proud show-offs who enjoyed the praise and recognition of people more than honoring, obeying, and pleasing the Lord. Rather than managing their spiritual responsibilities with integrity, they abused, oppressed, and neglected God's people. Jesus went on to explain the grave consequences of being a false prophet: "Every tree that does not bear good fruit is cut down and thrown into the fire. Thus, by their fruit you will recognize them. Not everyone who says to me, 'Lord, Lord,' will enter the kingdom of heaven, but only the one who does the will of my Father who is in heaven. Many will say to me on that day, 'Lord, Lord, did we not prophesy in your name and in your name drive out demons and, in your name, perform many miracles?' Then I will tell them plainly, 'I never knew you. Away from me, you evildoers!'" *(Matthew 7:19–23).*

HUMILITY DISCLAIMER

Every Christian, in one way or another, has fallen short of the impeccable standard set forth by the Bible. No Christian has ever achieved perfect emulation of Christ's life. However, numerous Christians are earnestly striving to lead a "Christ-Centered-life", increasingly relying on the Holy Spirit for conviction, transformation, and Holy

Ghost filled empowerment. Many followers of Christ have led lives untarnished by scandal. Despite this, it's important to note that no Christian has attained perfection. However, making a mistake or failing to achieve perfection in this life does not equate to hypocrisy. The relevance of this topic is not that we gather stones for the Scribes and Pharisees because their flaws and the error of their ways are on public display. The crucial relevance of this topic is to understand why it is detrimental to acquire, utilize and exercise discernment when following the lead of all who allege they are for Christ. Many stand fronting in the name of Jesus, secretly in their heart of hearts deny him, denounce him, don't believe He is the risen Messiah or are confused themselves. Dr. Tracy F. Munsil along with Cultural Research Center at Arizona Christian University in a profound research poll found that *"Basic Biblical Beliefs Lacking Among Most Pastors in All U.S. Denominations, All Church Roles"*. showed that just 37% of Christian pastors have a biblical worldview of the Gospel, with the predominant worldview among pastors (62%) being syncretism. Un-mistakenly syncretism is a hybrid mixture of disparate worldview elements blended into a customized philosophy of life. Religious syncretism is the combination of two or more religious belief systems cross-bread into a single system, or the incorporation of foreign religious tradition of beliefs from unrelated traditions added to God's Word. It is the practice of combining different beliefs and various theological theories and ideologies. It boils down to "Carnal

Conformity and Witchcraft" sensual devices utilized to please man opposed to God! Sadly, because most pastors teach what they believe, many churches are becoming contemporary centers of syncretism and secular thought," without many on the parishioners are believers even having a clue especially if they are deceived, easy to manipulate or absent of God's word! The study went on to highlight that ...

Although 41% of senior and lead pastors have a biblical worldview (the highest among all pastoral positions), *unexpectedly substantial proportions hold beliefs that are in conflict with the Bible on a range of teachings.*

Explicitly, the report found that one-third or more of senior pastors believe:

- ➢ Sexual relations between two unmarried people who believe they love each other is morally acceptable.
- ➢ Determining moral truth is up to each individual; there are no moral absolutes that apply to everyone, all the time.
- ➢ The Holy Spirit is not a living entity, but is a symbol of God's power, presence, or purity.
- ➢ Having faith matters more than which faith you have.
- ➢ Reincarnation is a real possibility.
- ➢ A person who is generally good, or does enough good things for others, can earn a place in Heaven.

> ➤ The Bible is ambiguous in its teaching about abortion, enabling you to make a strong argument either for or against abortion based on biblical principles.

Just to name a few! *1 Timothy 4:1* "Now the Spirit expressly says that in latter times some will depart from the faith, giving heed to deceiving spirits and doctrines of demons". *Matthew 7:13-14* wide is the gate and broad is the way! that leads to destruction, and there are many who go in by it. Because narrow is the gate and difficult is the way which leads to life, and there are few who find it. *Matthew 10:16* Behold, I send you out as sheep in the midst of wolves be ye therefore wise as serpents, and harmless as doves. *1 John 4* Beloved, do not believe every spirit, but test the spirits, whether they are of God; because many false prophets have gone out into the world. By this you know the Spirit of God. Every spirit that confesses that Jesus Christ has come in the flesh is of God, and every spirit that does not confess that Jesus Christ has come in the flesh is not of God. And this is the spirit of the Antichrist, which you have heard was coming, and is now already in the world. You are of God, little children, and have overcome them, because He who is in you is greater than he who is in the world. They are of the world. Therefore they speak as of the world, and the world hears them. We are of God. He who knows God hears us; he who is not of God does not hear us. By this we know the spirit of truth and the spirit of error." *James 1:5:* "If any of you lacks wisdom, you should ask

God, who gives generously to all without finding fault, and it will be given to you." ***Philippians 1:9-10*** "And it is my prayer that your love may abound more and more, with knowledge and all discernment, so that you may approve what is excellent, and so be pure and blameless for the day of Christ." ***Ephesians 1:18.*** I pray that the eyes of your heart may be enlightened in order that you may know the hope to which he has called you, the riches of his glorious inheritance in his holy people.

The Lamb of God, Promised Messiah

Matthew 13:24

289

TUSSLING WITH THE
DEMON OF DISTRACTIONS

The word "tussle" defined by American Heritage Dictionary is "a rough or vigorous struggle; a scuffle", " conflict", or "to struggle roughly". In the twentieth century the "World Ruler of Wickedness of This Age" has commissioned a new destructive, devious demon that the saints of God has to Tussle with. That by all measure is the "Demon of Distraction" they won't teach you about the "Demon of Distraction" in church, for over 70 percent of pastors have found themselves tussling with the wicked force itself, heavily distracted by the demon of distractions along with the cares of "This World" and are not cognoscente of it. Surely Jesus Christ didn't give up his life for believers to miss the mark of heaven being distracted from the call of God by the "Hell Phone" or "Social Media Entrapment", God forbid. Let's delve into it. **Proverbs 16:3** clearly states that believers ought to "Commit thy works unto the LORD, and thy thoughts shall be established". **Proverbs 16:3** "For we are his workmanship, created in Christ Jesus unto good works, which God hath before ordained that we should walk in them". ***Ephesians 2:10***

Christians are in a spiritual battle against the forces of the evil one. The apostle Paul, in his letter to the Ephesians, describes the battle, as a fight that requires spiritual armor and prayer. He urges Christians to be strong in the Lord and to put on the full armor of God, which includes the belt of truth, the breastplate of righteousness, the gospel shoes of peace, the shield of faith, the helmet of salvation, and the sword of the Spirit, which is the word of God. In addition, Paul emphasized the importance of utilizing prayer in fighting the enemy. He strongly encouraged Christians to pray, at all times, and for all the saints. ***It is important to reiterate that the fight (the invisible war) is not solely against God's people, but against spiritual forces of evil that deliberately wage war against your mind, rob you of your peace but most importantly, distract you from Jesus Christ in order to purposely and intentionally keep you from fulfilling the "Will of God".*** Christians are called to love their enemies and to pray for those who persecute them (the Flesh). However, let us not be ignorant to satan's devices. When it comes to unseen forces of wickedness sent from hell to deliberately distract you from a relationship with Jesus Christ or the "Will of God" according to His father, you have a demon to fight. This battle will require some intricate prayer, restless nights and foot work. For we know that faith without works is dead *James 2:14-26.* Henceforth, the work must be, honest, sincere and Holy Ghost Spirit filled for anything else is "Hocus Pocus" in the eyes of God and mockery WILL FAIL YOU. See *Acts 19 11-17.*

Miracles Glorify Christ Acts 19 11-17

"Now God worked unusual miracles by the hands of Paul, so that even handkerchiefs or aprons were brought from his body to the sick, and the diseases left them and the evil spirits went out of them. Then some of the itinerant Jewish exorcists took it upon themselves to call the name of the Lord Jesus over those who had evil spirits, saying, "We exorcise you by the Jesus whom Paul preaches." Also there were seven sons of Sceva, a Jewish chief priest, who did so. And the evil spirit answered and said, "Jesus I know, and Paul I know; but who are you?"

Then the man in whom the evil spirit was leaped on them, overpowered them, and prevailed against them, so that they fled out of that house naked and wounded.

The ultimate goal of this *tussle* is to be ***More Than a Conquer through Christ***, ***to be set free from sin*** and ***not be a slave to it***, fight is to ***bring glory to God and to advance His kingdom on earth.*** Let's examine some ways the "Demon of Distraction" seeks to hinder us from the call of Jesus Christ and the Will of God.

Sowing doubt and fear:

➢ Whispering insecurities about your abilities, worthiness, and the validity of your calling.

➢ Exaggerating potential challenges and obstacles, that make your path seem insurmountable.

➢ Fueling anxiety about the risks and sacrifices involved in pursuing your call.

➢ Allowing fear to paralyze your faith.

Promoting procrastination and distraction:

➢ Tempting you to delay taking action, prioritize other tasks, or get lost in irrelevant pursuits.

➢ Encouraging apathy and inactivity, laziness & listlessness making your call seem less urgent and important.

➢ Offering unhealthy, seductive distractions like entertainment, comfort, or unhealthy coping mechanisms.

Distorting your Self-perception:

➢ Twisting your interpretation of events to make your calling seem less fulfilling or meaningful.

➢ Magnifying past failures or setbacks to reinforce negative self-beliefs and foster low self-esteem.

➢ Social comparison complex, leading you to compare yourself to others and their seemingly more successful paths.

Inciting inner conflict of Self-esteem and self-sabotage:

➢ Negative Self Talk and Criticism. This negative self-deprecating inner voice can be seriously damaging to psychological well-being, leading to demotivation and a sense of worthlessness.

➢ Triggering internal struggles and unresolved issues, diverting your energy from your calling. undermining your own progress, self-worth and capabilities to achieve dreams.

➢ Fostering unhealthy relationships and dependencies on unrealistic and sometimes untruthful styles of life that you may derail self of progress and you're calling.

➢ Encouraging a sense of fairy-tale entitlement or impatience that can lead to impulsive decisions

Demon of Distraction use of social media

➢ ***Endless Scroll, Diminished Focus:*** Social media platforms are designed for endless nothingness consumption. The demon of distraction encourages individuals to swipe, scroll, and click continually without pause. "*Addictive Social Media Algorithms*" are designed to keep us hooked, feeding us an endless stream of content that easily consumes hours of our day. This constant scrolling leaves little to no space for introspection, prayer, or reflection on deeper matters of the soul, Our Savior or the Call of God. This constant engagement limits our attention spans, making it harder and harder to focus on deeper reflections, prayer, meditations, relationships spiritual and social or scripture study.

➢ ***Envy and Comparison:*** The demon of distraction deliberately targets your mind carefully curating and flaunting online personas fueling envy and comparison complex, leading us to question our own worth and faith journey. We may find ourselves comparing our spiritual progress to others' outward displays, neglecting our own unique path with God. The Comparison Trap of social media often presents a curated version of reality, filled with perfect lives, excessive amounts of expendable cash, exotic vacations, and seemingly effortless achievements. This can trigger feelings of inadequacy, low self-esteem, envy, and dissatisfaction, leading us to focus on what we lack instead of appreciating our own blessings.

➢ ***Information Overload, Spiritual Drowning:*** The constant influx of news, opinions, and debates on social media can be overwhelming. The never-ending influx of good and bad bulletins of social media feeds, diverse opinions, and contentious debates on social media can become mind-boggling. This information overload can distract us from focusing on the more important things of life, including but not limited to our faith, spiritual growth and relationship with God. Information overload is a dangerous silent nuclear weapon that can drown out the quiet voice of Jesus Christ within, leaving us feeling confused, anxious, unfulfilled according to our purpose and unable to discern God's guidance in our lives.

> ***Instant Gratification, Delayed Growth:*** The demon of distractions uses social media platforms to thrive on instant gratification, rewarding quick interactions and passing approval. Shallow Interactions, Likes and comments offer a "quick dopamine hit", but often lack genuine connection and depth. This can lead to feeling isolated and unfulfilled, despite being surrounded by "virtual friends." Inevitably instant gratification often triggers temporary pleasure, but it is important to note it can also result in increased stress and unnecessary anxiety. The dopamine rush associated with instant gratification can provide momentary relief, but in the long run it distracts us from longer-term, more meaningful Spiritual goals such as reading the word, praying, meditating or spending meaningful time with God. This can make it harder to commit to long-term spiritual practices

like fellowship prayer, meditation, or serving others, which require patience and dedication.

➤ *Isolation in a Connected World:* The demon of distractions seeks to isolate you because an idol mind is the investable the devil's playground. Ironically, the constant "connection" to social media can lead to isolation from real-life communities and meaningful interactions. This lack of connection can weaken our spiritual support system, making it harder to find encouragement and accountability on our faith journey through means of fellowship.

➤ *Algorithm-Fueled Addiction:* Social media algorithms often curates continuous echo chambers of spiritually harmful behaviors. The demon of distractions reinforces unhealthy existing beliefs as well as developing new ones. The venomous "algorithm stupefy" primarily exposes us to information that confirms our biases, attractions or desires by way of perfected time-sapping notifications and dm's. Every ping, buzz, and pop-up pulls us away from our faith, praying, fasting, reading Gods word , fellowship and draws us closer to his demonic trap of distractions. Fragmenting our attention and hindering focused prayer, study, or service. This detrimentally limits our exposure to diverse perspectives and hinder our spiritual growth, which often requires challenging our assumptions and embracing new understandings.

➤ *Deceitful Spiritual Hypnosis, through "Flattering Inspirational Content".* The demon of distraction knows your deepest inner most desires. He cleverly uses "Spiritual Hypnosis" through intriguing social media content to stagnate your spiritual growth. While "inspirational" content on social media can be uplifting, it can also be a misleading and deceitful entrapment trap specifically designed to help you spiritually bypass an authentic faith walk, relationship, stewardship of biblical literacy and understanding by diverting your attention to diluted "happy go lucky" slogans, sayings and verbalisms that have nothing to do with Gods Word, commandments, faith or instructions.

This overtime, may impose severe identity crisis in the Lord. The pressure to curate a perfect online persona, while not offending anyone can lead to faith confusion about who we truly are and where our spiritual commitment lies. Detrimentally, this can overshadow our spiritual identity as children of God, worthy of love and acceptance regardless of online validation.

Remember, social media can be a valuable tool for connecting, sharing, and learning. However, it's crucial to be mindful of its potential pitfalls and utilize it strategically to support, not hinder, your spiritual growth, walk with Christ and the Will of God. By setting boundaries, prioritizing mindful engagement, and seeking real-life connection, you can reclaim your focus and ensure the demon of distractions does not hinder your journey towards Jesus' call. Your path must be filled with discernment, meaningful connection, and the unwavering guidance of Jesus' presence in your life!

However, we are not powerless! Here are some ways to tussle with that ugly demon of distraction:

1. *Set boundaries:* Limit your time on social media and designate specific times for checking it.

2. *Be mindful:* Pay attention to how social media makes continuous attempts to seduce , attract , or charm you. If it brings to much negativity or dissatisfaction, or stirs up un healthy sexual attractions, emotions or habits, take a break.

3. *Cultivate real connections*: Prioritize face-to-face interactions and meaningful conversations over online engagement.

4. *Seek deeper purpose:* Remember your spiritual goals and values. Use social media to connect with like-minded individuals and share your faith, not just consume content or make time go by meaninglessly.

5. ***Focus on the present:*** Practice mindfulness activities, habits to break free from the endless scroll and be fully present in the moment.

6. ***Find peace in silence:*** Disconnect from the noise and embrace quiet time for prayer, fasting reflection, and listening to God's voice.

Remember, God's call and His Will resonates deeper than any notification or trend. By reclaiming control over your social media usage and prioritizing your spiritual journey, you can silence the "Demon of Distraction" and find true fulfillment in serving Him. To avoid being distracted from the call of Jesus Christ, it is important to stay focused on God's Word and to pray for guidance and strength. As it says in ***James 4:7*** "Submit yourselves therefore to God. Resist the devil, and he will flee from you" . By staying close to God and resisting the devil's temptations, we can stay on the path that God has set for us.

Ways the demon of Distraction can use Video Platforms to hinder us from heeding to Jesus' call:

Lethal Algorithm Abyss: YouTube's recommendation algorithms is like aggressive quicksand, pulling us deeper and deeper into a personalized whirlpool of content. From humorous skits to captivating documentaries, it's easy to spend countless hours lost in an endless loop of nothingness, forgetting the quiet call of prayer or reflection that beckons in our hearts. The social media platform algorithms are masters of keeping you glued to your screen. One click on a vlog, and suddenly you're lost in a world of reaction videos, celebrity gossip, and funny cat compilations. Time melts away, and your initial intention of seeking God and growing closer to Jesus Christ gets buried under an avalanche of irrelevant content leaving us feeling drained and further from our spiritual goals.

Procrastination Paradise: Famous video platforms like YouTube can become a haven for procrastination and nothingness, a place where minutes melt into hours as we tell ourselves "just one more video" before diving into deeper spiritual practices. These platforms reward us with unhealthy mental dopamine hits for every click, like, subscribe and watch. This can chip away at our time and motivation, leaving us feeling complacent forgetting about our spiritual goals and growth. This constant stimulation can hijack our attention and make it harder to focus on activities that require sustained effort, like prayer, meditation, or scripture study.

Unintellectual Noise: The demon of distraction knows that these social media video platforms offer a smorgasbord of opinions and voices, some more grounded than others. Their recommendation engine can create echo chambers, where we are only exposed to content that reinforces our existing likes, interest, desires and sometime beliefs. This can lead to closed-mindedness, ignorance and a disconnect from Gods word and ultimately His truth, hindering our spiritual growth and understanding. The demon of distraction can tempt us to get swept away in the noise, questioning our own faith and beliefs without proper discernment. This can lead to confusion and doubt, hindering our spiritual growth and connection with God.

Idol Contrast Trap: While social media often focuses on curated images, it shines an unrealistic sometimes deceitful spotlight on captivating lifestyles and adventures. Witnessing others seemingly living their best lives can trigger feelings of inadequacy and dissatisfaction, making it harder to appreciate the unique path Jesus has laid out for us.

False Idols and Empty Fulfillment: The demon can use Social Media Video Platforms to present "quick fixes" or shortcuts to spiritual fulfillment. From motivational talks to self-help gurus, we might be tempted to seek comfort and guidance in these short cut, fleeting trends rather than turning to prayer, God's Word or the enduring wisdom of our faith.

The Procrastination Euphoria: We often turn to Social Media Video Platforms to escape boredom or challenging situations. This can become a trap, where we procrastinate on our spiritual commitments, replacing meaningful activities with unprofitable mindless entertainment.

The Spiritual Superficiality Snare: Social Media Video Platforms like YouTube and Snapchat offer a plethora of content on spirituality, from quick prayer hacks to motivational sermons. These videos can create the illusion of instant spiritual progress without the hard work of introspection, prayer, and service. This can lead to neglecting the deeper aspects of faith and relying solely on external validation. While some of it can be valuable, it can also create a sense of spiritual quick-fixism, allowing us neglect the deeper work faith such as praying, fasting, fellowship, reading Gods Word and service.

The Disconnection Dilemma: While social media video platforms can connect us to spiritual communities, it can also replace real-life interaction with virtual connection. This lack of face-to-face interaction can weaken our sense of community and belonging, making it harder to stay motivated on our faith journey.

MY IDENTITY IN CHRIST

1. I am chosen by God. **Eph 1:4**

2. I am adopted by God. **Eph 1:5**

3. I am a child of God and His family. **1 John 3:1**

4. I am forgiven by God for all of my sins. **1 John 1:9**

5. I am reconciled to God, in harmony with Him. **Rom 5:10**

6. I am seen by God as holy, blameless, above reproach. **Col, 1:21, 22**

7. I am sealed with God's Holy Spirit. **Eph 1:13**

8. I am called to accomplish God's purpose. **Rom 8:28, 30**

9. I'm a full citizen amongst God's people. **Eph 2:19**

10. I am justified the clear right in God's sight. **Rom 5:1**

11. I am sanctified, set apart by God's spirit. **1 Cor 6:11**

12. I am redeemed, purchased with Christ's Blood. **Eph 1:7**

13. I am cleansed by Christ Blood of my sin. **1 John 1:7**

14. I am an heir of God and joint heir with Christ. **Rom 8:16, 17**

15. I am complete in Christ. **Col 2: 10**

16. I am an ambassador for Christ. **2 Cor 5:20**

17. I am being conformed form to the character of Christ. **Rom 8:29**

The Lamb of God, Promised Messiah

1 John 3:1

THE GREAT COMMISSION

The Great Commission: "Therefore go and make disciples of all nations, baptizing them in the name of the Father and of the Son and of the Holy Spirit, and teaching them to obey everything I have commanded you. And surely, I am with you always, to the very end of the age." Jesus gave this command to the apostles shortly before He ascended into heaven, and it essentially outlines what Jesus expected the apostles and those who followed them to do in His absence.

WHAT IS THE GREAT COMMISSION?
Matthew 28:19-20

➢ Jesus' last command to His disciples before He ascended into Heaven.

➢ Sending out all His disciples, including us, to share the Gospel.

➢ The Commission includes Jesus' promise to be with us, "to the end of the world" *(Matthew 28:20).*

- ➢ Makes it clear that the Gospel is for everyone.
- ➢ Everybody needs to hear about Jesus; it's our job to tell them.

WHY DID JESUS GIVE US THE GREAT COMMISSION? John 14:12 and 15:26-27,Romans 10:13-17

- ➢ Jesus wants everybody to come to know Him and receive His Salvation.
- ➢ Jesus wants us, His disciples, to share in His work, because we are part of His Kingdom, God's children, and share in the eternal reward with Him.

We learn to love both Jesus and His people more as we share the Gospel with other people, fulfilling the two greatest commandments (Mark 12:29-31)

HOW CAN WE FOLLOW THE GREAT COMMISSION? Acts 17:16-31, 1 Corinthians 2:1-5, Colossians 4:2-6, 1 Peter 3:14-16

- ➢ Pray for God's guidance, that He will reveal His plans for how He wants us to be part of the work of His Kingdom.
- ➢ Pray for the people who don't yet know Jesus.
- ➢ Show an example of how wonderful it is to follow Jesus in our lives.

Be ready and willing to answer questions and tell people about Jesus when they ask us what it is that makes us so different this means we have to read the Bible a lot and Study to show ourselves approved!

HOW CAN WE WORK WITH OTHER DISCIPLES IN CARRYING OUT THE GREAT COMMISSION? Romans 12:3-16, 1 Corinthians 12:4-14, 1 Timothy 2:1-6

> ➢ Not everyone has the same role to play, even though we all have the same purpose in sharing the Gospel of Christ.
> ➢ We can always give and show support to those who work as full-time missionaries, pastors, and evangelists in that way, we are sharing in their work.

Jesus instructs His disciples (and by extension, all believers) to actively go out into the world. It's a call to action, not passivity. The heart of Jesus' command is not merely about increasing church attendance or gathering followers; it's about transforming lives so that none miss the opportunity to serve in the kingdom or miss out on God's plan of salvation. Discipleship involves teaching, mentoring, and nurturing spiritual growth. Jesus accentuates a "Global Scope" of reaching the unsaved and the lost. His love and salvation are not limited to a specific ethnicity, culture, or geographical location. It includes everyone, from every background and nation. Every believer is called to participate in making disciples. We are not passive recipients but active participants in God's redemptive plan. Making disciples involves sharing the good news of Jesus Christ. It's about introducing people to Him, leading them to faith, and helping them grow in their relationship with Him. Jesus' ministry was marked by compassion. We, too, should approach people with love, empathy, and a desire to see them transformed by God's grace. The church is not merely a building; it's a community of believers. Its purpose is to equip and empower disciples to fulfill the Great Commission. The church exists not only for its members but for the sake of those outside its walls as well. Its intent was a hub for reaching the spiritually lost and sick. Missions, evangelism, and outreach are integral to the church's identity. It sends out workers to make disciples in various contexts. Beyond the scope of its architectural landscape as His ambassadors, we ought to never forget that we (His Believers) are the church, the church without walls. For those that never see the inside of a church building ought to find Christ within us! Jesus' command to make disciples of all nations is a call to action for every believer (regardless of race, class, creed, or sex). It's about sharing God's love and the principal teachings of Jesus Christ, leading people to Jesus and the Gift of salvation, nurturing their spiritual growth cultivating a journey with God.

Matthew 28:16-20:

This is the most widely known and cited passage on the Great Commission. It depicts Jesus appearing to his disciples after his resurrection and giving them their marching orders:

" *Then the eleven disciples went to Galilee, to the mountain where Jesus had told them to go. When they saw him, they worshiped him, but some doubted. Then Jesus came to them and said, 'All authority in heaven and on earth has been given to me. Therefore go and make disciples of all nations, baptizing them in the name of the Father and of the Son and of the Holy Spirit, and teaching them to obey everything I have commanded you. And surely I am with you always, to the very end of the age."*

Jesus giving the Great Commission to his disciples

Mark 16:15-18:

Mark's Gospel offers a slightly different perspective on the Great Commission, emphasizing the urgency and cruciality of the mission:

"Then he said to them, 'Go into all the world and preach the gospel to all creation. Whoever believes and is baptized will be saved, but whoever does not believe will be condemned. And these signs will accompany those who believe: In my name they will cast out demons; they will speak in new tongues; they will take up serpents; and if they drink any deadly poison, it will not harm them; they will lay hands on the sick, and they will heal."

Luke 24:44-49:

Luke's account focuses on Jesus' explanation of the Great Commission in light of the Old Testament prophecies, highlighting the role of the Holy Spirit:

"Then he said to them, 'This is what I told you while I was still with you: Everything must be fulfilled that is written about me in the Law of Moses, the Prophets and the Psalms.' Then he opened their minds so they could understand the Scriptures. He told them, 'This is what is written: The Messiah must suffer and rise from the dead on the third day, and repentance for the forgiveness of sins must be proclaimed in his name to all nations, beginning from Jerusalem. You are witnesses of these things. I am going to send you what my Father has promised, the Holy Spirit, but stay in the city until you have been clothed with power from on high."

John 20:19-23:

John's Gospel emphasizes the connection between the Great Commission and the gift of the Holy Spirit, portraying Jesus breathing the Holy Spirit onto his disciples and entrusting them with his own authority.

"On the evening of that first day of the week, the doors of the room where the disciples were meeting were locked, for fear of the Jews. Jesus came and stood among them and said, 'Peace be with you!' Then he showed them his hands and his side. When the disciples saw the Lord, they were overjoyed. Jesus said to them again, 'Peace be with you! As the Father has sent me, I am sending you.' And with that he breathed on them and said, 'Receive the Holy Spirit. If you forgive anyone their sins, they are forgiven; if you do not forgive them, they are not forgiven.'"

Acts 1:8:

The book of Acts, which chronicles the early spread of Christianity, opens with Jesus' final words to his disciples before his ascension:

"But you will receive power when the Holy Spirit comes on you; and you will be my witnesses in Jerusalem, and in all Judea and Samaria, and to the ends of the earth." Throughout the book of Acts, we see how the apostles began to fulfill the Great Commission, as outlined in Acts 1:8. First, Jerusalem is evangelized (Acts 1-7); then the Spirit expands the church through Judea and Samaria (Acts 8-12); finally, the gospel reaches into "the ends of the earth" (Acts 13 -28). Today, we continue to act as ambassadors for Christ, and "we plead on Christ's behalf: 'Be reconciled to God'" (2Corinthians 5:20,).

Jesus gave believers their mission —to make disciples —as they live under His authority and as His representatives on earth. This mission will continue to the end of the age. Christians have the assurance that God is with us, no matter what happens, even "to the very end of the age" (Matthew 28:20).

As Jesus' time on earth neared its end, He often told His disciples of what was to come, including what would happen at the end of the age. The "end of the age" or "the end of the world" means the end of this present era and the commencement of the next release of Gods matchless power. At the end of the church age, the end-times events will occur, God will judge the wicked, and Christ will return again to establish His kingdom (Matthew24). Jesus had told His disciples that He would be killed but would rise again (Matthew 16:21). He intentionally gave them specific ways to recognize that the end was near (Matthew 24:4-14). Although Jesus did not give the disciples all the details of the end of the age, knowing they would not fully understand, His warnings came with assurances that would sustain them. Each time He warned them or gave them a command, He also gave them hope. For example, when He forewarned His followers that they would have trouble in this world, He also assured them, saying, "Take heart". I have overcome the world" (John 16:33). Jesus' warnings and commands to His own are never found apart from His assurances. Before Jesus ascended into heaven, He instructed His disciples, "All authority in heaven and on earth has been given to me. Therefore go and make disciples of all nations, baptizing them in the name of the Father and of the Son and of the Holy Spirit, and teaching them to obey everything I have commanded you. And surely I am with you always, to the very end of the age" (***Matthew 28:19–20).*** This promise that He would be with His disciples even to the end of the age still holds true for believers today. We are not yet to the end of the age.

In His promise to be with His disciples always, even to the end of the age, Jesus did not mean He would physically be with them. God is with us always through

His Spirit. Before Jesus ascended into heaven, He promised His disciples that He would send the Advocate, the Holy Spirit, to them (John 14:26). Since Pentecost, the Holy Spirit indwells all believers from the moment they are saved. He guards and guarantees our salvation (Ephesians 1:13; 4:30), leads us into righteousness (Galatians 5:16–18), reminds us of what is true (John 14:26), and gives us godly wisdom (1 Corinthians 2:10-11). Through the Holy Spirit, we have assurance that God is in control and that He is with us always, even to the end of the age.

Just as God promised Joshua that He would never leave him or forsake him (Deuteronomy 31:6), so Jesus told His disciples, "I am with you always, even to the end of the age" . This promise sustains us as we seek to make disciples and live as God's representatives on earth, no matter what trials or difficulties come our way. We have received a precious gift: "the faith that was once for all entrusted to God's holy people" (Jude 1:3). Jesus' words in the Great Commission reveal the heart of God, who desires "all people to be saved and to come to a knowledge of the truth" (1 Timothy 2:4). The Great Commission compels us to share the good news until everyone has heard. Like the servants in Jesus' parable, we are to be about the business of the kingdom, making disciples of all nations: "He called his ten servants, and delivered them ten pounds, and said unto them, Occupy till I come" (Luke 19:13).

HIS UNMATCHED
ADORATION FOR WOMEN

Jesus praise and adored woman for their faith (*Mark 7: 24 – 30*) and use women in their homes as well as their household task as examples in His parables. Women in the parables of Jesus. Women played a pivotal role not only in the church but also in his kingdom ministries notwithstanding personal ministries to Christ. Gotquestions.org describes Jesus' ministry towards women as "Jesus shattered prejudices and elevated the status of women to unprecedented heights. That value equalization continued with His apostles. Peter warned husbands that, unless they treated their wives with respect, recognizing that women are co-heirs with them in all God promised, their prayers would be hindered (*1 Peter 3:7*). Paul wrote, "*There is neither Jew nor Gentile, neither slave nor free, nor is there male and female, for you are all one in Christ Jesus*" (Galatians 3:28). The apostles did not learn the value of women from their culture. They learned it from their Master, Jesus. And Jesus treated women with the same love and respect with which He treated men. Jesus' elevation of women began before He was even born. In God's divine plan, He had chosen a woman to begin His process of redeeming mankind. God sent His angel Gabriel to a young woman in the town of Nazareth with the good news that she would be the mother of God's Son (Luke 1:26-38). Gabriel's first words to Mary were, "Greetings, you who are highly favored! The Lord is with you." God first entrusted a woman with the most important message the world has ever received: the long-awaited Messiah was on His way. When Jesus was only eight days old, the Holy Spirit revealed His identity to a woman, Anna (Luke 2:36-38). So before Jesus was even old enough to declare anyone's value, God the Father was already at work revealing His heart to His faithful daughters. When Jesus began His earthly ministry, women flocked to hear Him teach, and some even supported Him financially (Matthew 27:55; Mark 15:41; Luke 8:2-3). What was it about this Teacher that drew both men and women? Jesus was completely without prejudice. He loved every human being regardless of race, ethnicity, occupation, background, or gender. He treated them equally and included several women among His closest friends (Luke 10:38-39; 24:10; John 11:5). The fact that women are called by name in the Bible is significant. In a culture where women could not own property or testify in court, a woman's opinion or her presence at an event was not even worth mentioning. Jesus broke down more cultural barriers when He took a detour through Samaria. There, He had an encounter with an immoral [dishonorable] woman (John 4:4-26). The fact that she was a Samaritan was enough to bar her from any conversation with a self-respecting Jew, to make matters worse in the disciples' eyes, she was a woman. As they watched, their Master transformed that woman and through her impacted an entire city with His message of hope and redemption. Another time, the woman caught in the act of adultery was paraded before Jesus by Jewish leaders hoping to entrap Him (John 8:2-11). They demanded that Jesus give His opinion on the punishment she should receive for her adultery. They considered this an easy win since the law required the death penalty (Leviticus 20:10; Deuteronomy 22:22). If Jesus took the woman's side, He was negating the law. If He took her accusers' side, He was negating all He had ever taught about forgiveness (Mark 2:15-17). Either way, they figured, they had Jesus cornered. Jesus turned the tables on them and dealt with their self-righteousness, forcing them to inspect their own lives first: "Let him who is without sin cast the first stone," He said (John 8:7). Again, in this case, Jesus used the example of a woman to teach an important lesson about equality in God's eyes. We are all sinners, men and women. None of us have the right to pass final judgment on another while hiding our own similar actions (Romans 2:1-3).

The New Testament shatters those social norms by including the names of many women and the specific roles they played in furthering God's kingdom.

➢ Mary the mother of Jesus
➢ The Samaritan woman at the well
➢ The woman caught in the act of adultery
➢ Mary Magdalene whom was freed of seven devils
➢ Mary of Bethany the humble hostess
➢ Martha Bethany the "distressed sister" of Lazarus
➢ The hemorrhaged woman with the issue of blood
➢ Anna participated in the circumcision of Jesus
➢ Jairius daughter resurrected by Jesus
➢ Women of infirmity bent over 18 years Mark 7
➢ Pontius is pilot's wife who dreamt of Jesus
➢ Anna a faithful Prophetess Luke 2:38
➢ Susanna the faithful servant Luke 24 8:

Jesus demonstrated only the highest regard for women, in both his life and teaching. He recognized the intrinsic equality of men and women, and continually showed the worth and dignity of women as persons. Jesus valued their fellowship, prayers, service, financial support, testimony and witness. He honored women, taught women, and ministered to women in thoughtful ways. As a result, women responded warmly to Jesus's ministry. Jesus Christ's communication, interactions with and ministering to women were undeniably unprecedented for His era. Being brought up, and nurtured by a woman from infant to young man He openly recognized the intrinsic quality of women, and without thought continually exemplified with the upmost respect and adoration the worth and dignity of women as viable persons of the Kingdon of God. He honored women, taught women, and ministered to women in thoughtful yet impactful ways. As a result, women responded warmly to Jesus's ministering, teachings and even His rebuke which He often handed down sternly in love. One of the most notable examples of Jesus's respect and adoration for women was His interaction with the Samaritan woman at the well (John 4:7-26). He addressed her directly in public, which was unusual for a Jewish man to do at that time, Jews and Samaritans were not tight during that time. This interaction showed that Jesus saw women as genuine persons in need of Spiritual nurturing, not simply as the objects of male desire because of the records of her past. Another significant example is the story of the woman caught in adultery (John 8:1-11). The Pharisees brought a woman who had been caught in the act of adultery to be condemned publicly at the hands of the law. They told Jesus that the punishment for someone like her should be stoning, as prescribed by Mosaic Law. However, Jesus responded by saying, "Let him without sin, cast the first stone!". When the accusers heard this, they slipped away one by one, leaving Jesus alone with the woman. Jesus asked the woman if anyone had condemned her and she answered no. Jesus said that he too did not condemn her and told her to go and sin no more. This story illustrates Jesus's compassion and forgiveness, as well as his revolutionary approach to dealing with women who fell from grace. Jesus was also supported by women during His active ministry years. Women like Mary Magdalene, Joanna, the wife of Chuza, and Susanna followed Him, studied while observing His Teachings and provided financial support towards His ministry. Many women were healed by Jesus and showed their gratefulness by, serving Him and financially supporting his ministry. They were not only beneficiaries of Jesus's teachings but also active participants and supporters of his ministerial kingdom work. Jesus Christ's interactions with women were characterized by love, respect, and adoration. He treated women as equitable children of God, valued their contributions, and showed them compassion and forgiveness. He most certainly never condoned violence towards women. With all power in His hands, He could have easily Co-signed the adulterous woman's stoning, yet He chose the path of forgiveness and repentance. Inevitably He chose the high road of Love and compassion. Jesus never stoned any woman. He ransomed them with His shed Blood. According to NBC News, stoning is still legal in Afghanistan, Iran, certain sections of Nigeria, Pakistan, Sudan, and the United Arab Emirates. While Stoning is a "*relatively rare*" means of capital punishing to those who commit adultery, homosexuality, prostitution and various other sexual offences under Islamic Law. It is still prevalent today and is considered a form of community or street justice. Jesus interactions with women were revolutionary for His time, then and now and continue to serve as a model for how women should be treated today in the church, the world, relationships and marriages. His teachings and actions demonstrate that women are an integral part of divine creation with individual worth. Below is a list of women from the Bible who God Blessed with Spiritual Gifts of the Kingdom from the Old and New Testament.

Women Gifted with Spiritual Gifts

➢ ***Miriam:*** The sister of Moses and Aaron, she was a prophetess and a leader in Israel. Miriam is described as a prophetess and a leader in Israel. The Talmud names her as one of the seven *(Exodus 15:20).*

➢ ***Deborah:*** A prophetess and a judge of Israel, known as a profound woman of wisdom and faith she led the people in a time of oppression *(Judges 4:4).* Prophetess and Judge: "Now Deborah, a prophetess, the wife of Lappidoth, was judging Israel at that time. She used to sit under the palm tree of Deborah between Ramah and Bethel in the hill country of Ephraim; and the sons of Israel came up to her for judgment." *(Judges 4:4-5)*

1. ***Military Leader:*** "Now Deborah sent and summoned Barak the son of Abinoam from Kedesh-naphtali, and said to him, 'Behold, the Lord, the God of Israel, has commanded, 'Go and march to Mount Tabor, and take with you ten thousand men from the sons of Naphtali and from the sons of Zebulun.'" *(Judges 4:6)*

2. ***Deborah Spiritual Guide:*** "Then Barak said to her, 'If you will go with me, then I will go; but if you will not go with me, I will not go.' She said, 'I will surely go with you; nevertheless, the honor shall not be yours on the journey that you are about to take, for the Lord will sell Sisera into the hands of a woman.'" *(Judges 4:8-10)*

3. **Songstress:** "Then Deborah and Barak the son of Abinoam sang on that day, saying, 'That the leaders led in Israel, That the people volunteered, Bless the Lord! Hear, O kings; give ear, O rulers! I to the Lord, I will sing, I will sing praise to the Lord, the God of Israel.'" **(Judges 5:1-3)**

➢ **Huldah:** A prophetess during the reign of King Josiah, she confirmed the authenticity of the Book of the Law **(2 Kings 22:14; 2 Chronicles 34:22).**

1. **Prophetess Huldah**: "So Hilkiah the priest, Ahikam, Achbor, Shaphan, and Asaiah went to Huldah the prophetess, the wife of Shallum the son of Tikvah, the son of Harhas, keeper of the wardrobe. She dwelt in Jerusalem in the Second Quarter. And they spoke with her." (**2 Kings 22:14**)

2. **Confirmation of the Book of Law**: "Then she said to them, 'Thus says the Lord God of Israel, 'Tell the man who sent you to Me, Thus says the Lord: Behold, I will bring calamity on this place and on its inhabitants all the words of the book which the king of Judah has read because they have forsaken Me and burned incense to other gods, that they might provoke Me to anger with all the works of their hands. Therefore My wrath shall be aroused against this place and shall not be quenched." **(2 Kings 22:15-17)**

3. ***Huldah Prophesied Peace for King Josiah***: "But as for the king of Judah, who sent you to inquire of the Lord, in this manner you shall speak to him, 'Thus says the Lord God of Israel: Concerning the words which you have heard because your heart was tender, and you humbled yourself before the Lord when you heard what I spoke against this place and against its inhabitants, that they would become a desolation and a curse, and you tore your clothes and wept before Me, I also have heard you,' says the Lord. 'Surely, therefore, I will gather you to your fathers, and you shall be gathered to your grave in peace; and your eyes shall not see all the calamity which I will bring on this place.'" (2 Kings 22:18-20)1

➢ ***Anna:*** A prophetess who recognized Jesus as the Messiah when he was presented at the Temple ***(Luke 2:36-38).***

1. ***Prophetess:*** "There was also a prophet, Anna, the daughter of Penuel, of the tribe of Asher. She was very old; she had lived with her husband seven years after her marriage, and then was a widow until she was eighty-four." ***(Luke 2:36-37)***

2. ***Devotion to God***: "She never left the temple but worshiped night and day, fasting and praying." ***(Luke 2:37)***

3. ***Recognition of the Messiah***: "Coming up to them at that very moment, she gave thanks to God and spoke about the child to all who were looking forward to the redemption of Jerusalem." ***(Luke 2:38)***

➢ ***The Four Daughters of Philip***: Mentioned in the book of Acts, these women had the gift of prophecy ***(Acts 21:8-9)***.

➢ ***Lydia:*** A worshiper of God, her heart was opened by the Lord to pay attention to what was said by Paul, leading to her and her household's baptism ***(Acts 16:14-15)***.

1. ***Businesswoman and Worshiper of God:*** "A woman named Lydia, from the city of Thyatira, a seller of purple fabrics, a worshiper of God, was listening; and the Lord opened her heart to respond to the things spoken by Paul." ***(Acts 16:14)***

2. ***First European Convert and Host to Early Church***: "When she and her household were baptized, she urged us, saying, 'If you have judged me to be faithful to the Lord, come into my house and stay.' And she prevailed upon us." ***(Acts 16:15)***

➤ **_Apphia:_** she hosted believers in her home. As a member of Philemon's household, she was been directly involved in the decision concerning Onesimus. **_(Philem.2)_**

➤ **_Damaris_**: she responded to the gospel. She was able to follow Paul's conversation with the leading men and understand the gospel She became one of the new converts to Christianity in the city of Athens **_(Acts 17:34)_**

➤ **_Dorcus:_** she reached out to the poor and needy. Dorcas was known for her acts of kindness and charity, particularly in making garments for the widows in her community. Her skill in sewing and her compassionate heart made her an invaluable member of the early church. She was always doing good and helping the poor. **_(Acts 9:36-42, Prov 31:20)_**

1. **_Disciple of Christ and Charitable Works:_** "In Joppa there was a disciple named Tabitha (in Greek her name is Dorcas); she was always doing good and helping the poor." **_(Acts 9:36)_**

2. **_Resurrection:_** "Peter sent them all out of the room; then he got down on his knees and prayed. Turning toward the dead woman, he said, 'Tabitha, get up.' She opened her eyes, and seeing Peter she sat up." **_(Acts 9:40_**)

➢ ***Mary Magdeline:*** Devoted Follower of Jesus Christ. Mary Magdalene was a dedicated follower of Jesus. She had been freed by him from possession by seven devils, had followed him as a disciple, ministering to him from her means ***(Luke 8:2-3),*** and had been with Mary, the Mother of Jesus and the other women when Jesus was crucified ***(Mark 15:40-41)***. All four gospels attest that she witnessed Jesus' crucifixion and burial. She was the first person to whom Jesus appeared after the resurrection. Mary Magdalene, out of her own wealth, helped care for Jesus and the needs of his disciples. She was deeply devoted to Jesus and followed him from town to town. Not only did she provide emotional support, but she also contributed financially to Jesus' ministry. ***(Luke 8:2-3) Mark 15:40-41).***

➢ ***Mary of Nazareth:*** Submission to God's Will, When the angel Gabriel announced that she was chosen by God to give birth to the Messiah, Mary submitted herself to God's will, saying, "Behold, I am the servant of the Lord; let it be to me according to your word" ***(Luke 1:38)***. This response reflects a prayerful submission to God's plan.

1. ***Magnificat:*** After the Annunciation, Mary spoke the words of a beautiful prayer known as the 'Magnificat', expressing her wonder at what had happened. This prayer reflects her deep faith and gratitude to God ***(Luke 1:46-55).***

2. ***At the Foot of the Cross***: Mary was present at the crucifixion of Jesus *(John 19:25)*. Though the Bible does not record her prayers, her presence at this momentous event signifies her continued faith and support, which can be seen as a form of prayerful solidarity.

3. ***In the Early Church***: After Jesus' ascension, Mary was part of the early Christian community that "devoted themselves to prayer" *(Acts 1:14)*. This suggests that she continued to pray, likely for the ministry .

➢ ***Phoebe***: Paul commends Phoebe, who is referred to as a sister, a servant of the church in Cenchrea. She is believed to have been a deaconess. Phoebe delivered Paul's letter to the Christians in Rome, traveling from where Paul was staying in Corinth.

Paul describes Phoebe as a benefactor of many people, including himself. He asks the Romans to receive her in the Lord in a way worthy of his people and to give her any help she may need *(Romans 16:1–21)*.

➢ ***Priscilla:***, She, along with her husband Aquila, played a crucial role in the early Christian church they traveled throughout the country doing evangelism and missions. She also taught and learned Apollos *(Acts 18:1-3, 18-19, 26) (Romans 16:3-4) (1 Corinthians 16:19) (2 Timothy 4:19)*

1. ***Tentmakers and Missionaries***: Priscilla and Aquila were tentmakers by profession, which allowed them to earn funds for daily living and travel to teach people about God. They used their business resources to help further the gospel.

2. ***Travel and Evangelism***: Priscilla and Aquila traveled extensively for evangelism and missions. They had gone to Corinth from Rome when Emperor Claudius ordered all Jews to leave the city. They met Paul in Corinth, formed a lifetime friendship, and worked together on their mission.

3. ***Teaching Apollos***: When they arrived at Ephesus, they encountered a Jew named Apollos who was trying to share the gospel but needed more teaching to correctly preach God's word.

➢ ***Women of wealth:*** they supported Jesus work cheerfully; their generosity was a blessing to kingdom business. *(Mark 15:40, 16:1) (Luke 8 3, 23 :55, 24: 10) (Heb 6:10)*

➢ ***Older Women:*** they were to teach younger woman about godly character and home responsibilities *(Titus 2 3-5).*

Within Gods Holy Word, we find numerous examples of women who were endowed with spiritual gifts from God, contributing significantly to the edification of His Kingdom. These women were not only respected and adored by Jesus, but they were also taught by Him, and many of them contributed cheerfully, both financially and spiritually, to His ministry.

One of the most prominent examples is Mary Magdalene, who was one of Jesus' most devoted followers. She was present at the crucifixion and was the first to witness the resurrection, demonstrating her spiritual strength and commitment. Another example is Phoebe, a deaconess in the church at Cenchreae, who was commended by Paul for her service to the church.

There's also Priscilla, who, along with her husband Aquila, was instrumental in teaching Apollos, an eloquent and passionate preacher, the way of God more accurately. Lydia, a seller of purple goods, was another faithful woman who offered hospitality to Paul and his companions after she and her household were baptized.

These women, and many others, played crucial roles in the early church, breaking down gender barriers and serving God with their unique spiritual gifts. Their stories serve as a testament to the fact that in serving Christ, there is no specific gender role. As (**_Galatians 3:28_**) states, "_There is neither Jew nor Greek, there is neither slave nor free, there is no male and female, for you are all one in Christ Jesus._"

These examples underscore the Bible's affirmation of women's spiritual gifts and their significant contributions to the Kingdom of God. They were cherished, respected, and taught by Jesus Himself, and their cheerful contributions, both financial and spiritual, were integral to His ministry. Serving God or Christ, as these women exemplify, transcends gender roles. It is a universal calling, open to all who are willing to receive and use their spiritual gifts for the edification of the Kingdom of God.

> ➢ The first miracle went to a _woman._ (John 2:1-11)
> ➢ The first news of incarnation went to a _woman._ (Luke 1:35)
> ➢ The first Samaritan convert was a _woman._ (John 4:39-42)
> ➢ The first person clearly told by Jesus that he was the Messiah was a _woman._ (John 4:26)
> ➢ The first news of the resurrection when to a _woman._ (Luke 24:1-12)
> ➢ _Women_ were commissioned to tell the news of the resurrection to the disciples. (Matthew 28:10)

Jesus Miracles Among Women	
Miracle	**Reference**
Healing Peter's mother-in-law	(Matt. 8; 15; Mark 1; 30, 31; Luke 4; 38, 39)
Raising Jairus" daughter from the dead	(Matt. 9; 18, 23 -25)
Healing the Canaanite woman's daughter	(Matt. 9; 20 – 22, Mark 5; – 34: Luke 8; 43 – 48)
Raising the widow of Nain's son from the dead	(Matt. 15; 21 – 28; Mark 7; 24 – 30)
Healing the woman of 18-year infirmity bent over	(Luke 7; 11 – 15)
Turning water into wine at the wedding of Cana at the request of Jesus' mother	(John 2: 1-11)

JESUS MINISTRY TO WOMAN

- ➢ <u>Mary</u> *Luke 2: 51, 52* she nurtured Jesus as he grew onto his manhood.
- ➢ <u>Susanna</u> *Luke 8: 1 – 23* she supported the ministry of Jesus with her loving personality and resources.
- ➢ <u>Mary of Bethany</u> *Luke 10 : 39* she elicited Jesus as he shared spiritual truth.
- ➢ <u>The Samaritan woman</u> *John 4: 28 – 30* she heard Jesus share the gospel accepted his grace, then began to share her testimony with others.
- ➢ <u>Mother-in-law Peter</u> *Mark 1: 29 – 31* she was hospitable to Jesus and his disciples as she served them
- ➢ <u>The Widow with two mites</u> *Mark: 12: 41 – 44* she was generous and her support to the kingdom though she had little
- ➢ <u>Mary of Bethany</u> *Matt; 27 – 55, John 1925, 20: 16* she prepared the body of Jesus's burial
- ➢ <u>Mary Magdalene</u> *Matt: 27, 55 John 19; 25, 20: 16* she did not desert Jesus when he was rejected, she was the first of proclaimed the resurrection.

Women Healed by Jesus		
Women	Her faith	Jesus' response
Peter's mother & law (Matt. Eight; 14, 15: Luke 4: 38, 39).	None stated , although her family's fate such was demonstrated	*He saw, touch, and healed her fever.*
All women who were sick (Matt. 8; 16, 17, Mark; 32 – 34)	The people came in with faith	*He cast out the spirits and healed all who were sick*
The women with the issue of blood (Matt. Nine; 20 - 22, Mark 5; 25-34; Luke 8; 43 – 48).*	The mother expressed her faith by her persistence. She worshiped Jesus	*He felt her touch, saw her, and healed her.*
The Canaanite women's daughter (Matt. 15; 21 – 28; Mark 7: 24 - 30)	The mother expressed her faith by her persistence. She worshiped Jesus	*He heard answered her request and healed her daughter.*
The woman of infirmity parentheses Luke 13; 11 – 13)	Her faith was not stated	*He saw, called, and healed her.*

"Women were last to leave the place of Jesus' crucifixion and first at the empty tomb (*Matthew 27:61; 28:1*) indicating that the transforming power of Jesus had given the women courage and boldness to follow Him openly. In a marvelous display of the women's faith and God's approval, those women became the world's first witnesses of the resurrection (*Matthew 28:8*).

In all His interactions with women, Jesus treated them with dignity, compassion, and respect. In so doing, He countered the prevailing notions of the day concerning women and their place in society. When Jesus calls a man or a woman to follow Him, He transforms them into new creatures (*2 Corinthians 5:17*). Old prejudices and stereotypes no longer define us. Christians are united by one Spirit *(Ephesians 4:5)*, and we are to view each other as brothers and sisters in the family of God. God never pretends that men and women are the same, but Jesus' life indicated that He valued both equally. Both sexes make unique contributions to the family the church and the kingdom of God, both should work together for the advancement of all and fulfilling the Great Commission."

The Lamb of God, Promised Messiah

Luke 24:1-12

JESUS PAID IT ALL

When Jesus had received the sour wine, He said, "It is finished." And bowing His head, He yielded up His spirit. Of the last documented sayings of Christ on the cross, none is more important or more profound than, "It is finished." Found only in the Gospel of John, the Greek word translated "it is finished" is tetelestai, an accounting term that means "paid in full." When Jesus uttered those words, He was declaring the debt owed to His Father was wiped away completely and forever. Not that Jesus wiped away any debt that He owed to the Father; rather, Jesus eliminated the debt owed by mankind the debt of sin. Just prior to His arrest by the Romans, Jesus prayed His last public prayer, asking the Father to glorify Him, just as Jesus had glorified the Father on earth, having "finished the work you have given me to do" (John 17:4). The work Jesus was sent to do was to "seek and save that which is lost" (Luke 19:10), to provide atonement for the sins of all who would ever believe in Him (Romans 3:23-25), and to reconcile sinful

337

men to a holy God. "All this is from God, who reconciled us to himself through Christ and gave us the ministry of reconciliation: that God was reconciling the world to himself in Christ, not counting men's sins against them. And he has committed to us the message of reconciliation" (2 Corinthians 5:18-19). None other but God in the flesh could accomplish such a task. Also completed was the fulfillment of all Old Testament prophecies, symbols, and foreshadowing's of the coming Messiah. From Genesis to Malachi, there are over 300 specific prophecies detailing the coming of the Anointed One, all fulfilled by Jesus. From the "seed" who would crush the serpent's head (Genesis 3:15), to the Suffering Servant of Isaiah 53, to the prediction of the "messenger" of the Lord (John the Baptist) who would "prepare the way" for the Messiah, all prophecies of Jesus' life, ministry, and death were fulfilled and finished at the cross. Although the redemption of mankind is the most important finished task, many other things were finished at the cross. The sufferings Jesus endured while on the earth, and especially in His last hours, were at last over. God's will for Jesus was accomplished in His perfect obedience to the Father (John 5:30; 6:38). Most importantly, the power of sin and satan was finished. No longer would mankind have to suffer the "flaming arrows of the evil one" (Ephesians 6:16). By raising the "shield of faith" in the One who completed the work of redemption and salvation, we can, by faith, live as new creations in Christ. Jesus' finished work on the cross was the beginning of new life for all who were once "dead in trespasses and sins" but who are now made "alive with Christ" (Ephesians 2:1, 5)*Isaiah 53: Jesus Paid it All* This entire chapter prophesies about a suffering servant who will bear the sins of many. It directly speak of his substitutionary sacrifice:

"Surely he has borne our griefs and carried our sorrows; yet we esteemed him stricken, smitten by God, and afflicted. But he was pierced for our transgressions, he was crushed for our iniquities; the punishment that brought us peace was upon him, and by his wounds we are healed." Romans 5:6-8 Christ died for us while we were still sinners, demonstrating God's great love for the world. "For one will hardly die for a righteous person; though perhaps for a good person someone might dare to die. But God demonstrates his own love for us in this: While we were still sinners, Christ died for us." 1 Corin15:3-4 "For I delivered to you first of all that which I also received: that Christ died for our sins according to the Scriptures, and that He was buried, and that He rose again the third day according to the Scriptures, Galatians 3:13 "Christ has redeemed us from the curse of the law, having become a curse for us (for it is written, "Cursed is everyone who hangs on a tree"), Paul emphasizes that Christ redeemed us from the curse of the law by taking our place on the cross. Jesus redeemed us from the curse of the law by becoming a curse for us. (Hebrews 2:14-15) "Inasmuch then as the children have partaken of flesh and blood, He Himself likewise shared in the same, that through death He might destroy him who had the power of death, that is, the devil, and release those who through fear of death were all their lifetime subject to bondage". This passage explains that Jesus, by taking on our human flesh, was able to defeat death and liberate those who were in bondage to the fear of death." Since therefore the children share in flesh and blood, he himself likewise partook of the same nature, that through death he might destroy the one who has the power of death, that is, the devil, and might set free all those who, through fear of death, were subject to lifelong slavery." The phrase "Jesus paid it all" isn't found explicitly in the Bible, but the concept of Jesus' sacrifice for our sins is woven throughout Scripture. Here are some key verses that speak to this idea:

Old Testament

Isaiah 53:5-6: *"But he was pierced for our transgressions, he was crushed for our iniquities; the punishment that brought us peace was upon him, and by his wounds we are healed. All we like sheep have gone astray; we have all turned to our own way; and the Lord has laid on him the iniquity of us all."* Isaiah 53 includes a lengthy prophecy about the Messiah including the statement that "He took our infirmities" (Isaiah 53:4) or "he himself bore our sicknesses". Matthew alludes to this verse when speaking of Jesus Christ's healing ministry: "When evening had come, they brought to Him many who were demon-possessed. And He cast out the spirits with a word, and healed all who were sick, that it might be fulfilled which was spoken by Isaiah the prophet, saying:

'He Himself took our infirmities And bore our sicknesses'" (Matthew 8:16–17). After Jesus explained the righteousness needed for people to enter His kingdom (Matthew 5-7), He began healing people. He healed a leper (Matthew 8:1-4). He healed the servant of a centurion (Matthew 8:5–13). He healed Peter's mother-in-law (Matthew 8:14–15). He healed many who were demon-possessed (Matthew 8:16). Matthew explains that in healing these infirmities Jesus fulfilled Isaiah's prophecy that "He Himself took our infirmities and carried away our diseases" (Matthew 8:17). There were many evidences that Jesus was the Messiah. John the Baptist testified to His identity when he baptized Jesus (Matthew 3:15). At Jesus' baptism the Holy Spirit showed that He was upon Jesus (Matthew 3:16). Also at Jesus' baptism, the Father audibly proclaimed that Jesus was His Son and in Him the Father was well pleased (Matthew 3:17). While Jesus Himself claimed to be God (e.g., John 8:56–58), He also acknowledged that a matter should be affirmed by two or three witnesses. He offered even more than that to affirm His deity and His role as Messiah: John the Baptist, the Father, and Scripture (John 5:33–39). But Jesus also pointed people to His works as testimony of Him. He even explained that the works He did were a greater testimony than that of John (John 5:36). Those works included fulfilling Isaiah's prophecy that He Himself took our infirmities.

The works Jesus did were signs pointing people to His identity as the prophesied Messiah who would take away sins. The apostle John explains that there were many more signs that Jesus performed than were recorded in John's Gospel. The signs that John recorded were written down so that people would believe in Jesus, that He is the Christ, the son of God and that believing they might have life in His name (John 20:30-31). Isaiah and Matthew recognized that the Messiah would bear the sicknesses and griefs of the people. The Messiah would come to heal and to give life. Jesus came fulfilling those promises, even to the extent of giving His own life to pay for the sins of all humanity. As Paul would later explain, we have been saved by grace through faith in Jesus (Ephesians 2:8-9). God's gracious gift was Jesus, and by Jesus' death He graciously paid for sin. That grace is applied to us by faith (belief). Not only did Jesus carry away our physical griefs and sicknesses and we will see the results of that someday in glory but He also carried away our spiritual griefs and sicknesses. The greatest sickness of all sin is gone. Christ has redeemed us from sin and removed our condemnation. "He Himself took our infirmities and carried away our diseases."

NEW TESTAMENT ON JESUS' SACRIFICE:

John 3:16: "For God so loved the world that he gave his one and only Son, that whoever believes in him shall not perish but have eternal life."

Romans 5:8: "But God demonstrates his own love for us in this: While we were still sinners, Christ died for us."

Galatians 3:13: "Christ redeemed us from the curse of the law by becoming a curse for us, for it is written, "Cursed is everyone who hangs on a tree.""

Colossians 1:14: "In him we have redemption through his blood, the forgiveness of sins, in accordance with the riches of God's grace."

Hebrews 2:9: "But we see Jesus, who was made a little lower than the angels, for the suffering of death crowned with glory and honor, because by the grace of God he tasted death for everyone."

1 Peter 2:24: "He himself bore our sins in his body on the tree, so that we might die to sins and live to righteousness; for by his wounds you have been healed."

CRITICAL ASPECTS OF JESUS' SACRIFICE

Substitutionary atonement: Jesus took our place on the cross, bearing the penalty for our sins.

Divine love: The sacrifice was motivated by God's immense love for humanity.

Forgiveness of sins: Through Jesus' death, we are forgiven our transgressions and reconciled to God.

Redemption from the curse: Jesus liberates us from the spiritual condemnation and separation from God due to sin.

Reconciliation with God: Jesus' sacrifice bridges the gap between humanity and God, allowing us to have a relationship with Him.

"Indeed Jesus paid it all", the overarching message of Scripture proclaims the complete and sufficient sacrifice of Jesus for the forgiveness of our sins and our reconciliation with God.

Isaiah 53 provides one of the most beautiful and powerful descriptions of the Messiah in all of Scripture. One important description is how Jesus the Messiah has "surely borne our griefs" (*Isaiah 53:4*). The fact that He has surely borne our griefs is central to Jesus' work as the promised Messiah.

The Messiah is the "arm" of the Lord who has been revealed (Isaiah 53:1) but who was rejected by many. This Messiah grew up like any young thing does like a suckling or a root (Isaiah 53: 2). There was nothing abnormal or majestic about His human appearance (Isaiah 53:2). In fact, He was even despised by men and forsaken. He was a man of sorrows and acquainted with grief people hid their faces from Him, He was greatly despised, and people did not recognize or esteem Him (Isaiah 53:3). These verses explain how Jesus has surely borne our griefs (Isaiah 53:4). It was bad enough that He carried our sorrows, but, as Isaiah puts it, even as He was bearing our griefs and sorrows, we did not esteem or care for Him. The next verse explains specifically how Jesus has surely borne our griefs. Isaiah tells us that Jesus the Messiah (or the Christ) was pierced for our transgressions and crushed for our iniquities (Isaiah 53:5). He was afflicted not because of any deficiency of His own, but He took on our transgressions and iniquities and paid the price that you and I owed to God. Romans 6:23 says that the wages of sin is death. Paul explains there that the consequence of Adam's sin and our own sin because we are descended from Adam is death (Romans 5:12). Specifically, the penalty was eternal separation from God. This is the death promised in Genesis 2:17. God added physical death as a penalty and as a way to keep humanity from living eternally on earth in that condemned state (Genesis 3:19, 22). Since Adam and Eve's fall, humanity has lived in that lost state being dead in sin, separated from God because of sin (Ephesians 2:1–3). But even as God pronounced judgment on humanity after the fall, He promised that there would be redemption, accomplished by one specific Person (Genesis 3:15; Isaiah 53). It is in this way that Jesus has surely borne our griefs. Paul explains that, while we were still sinners and totally helpless, Christ died for us (Romans 5:8). None of us had any merit before God. We have all sinned and fallen short of His glory (Romans 3:23). We have all gone astray like wayward sheep, and we have all gone our own way (Isaiah 53:6). Yet in His amazing love, God allowed the eternal penalty for our sins to be paid by Jesus. The Lord caused all our iniquity to fall upon Him. This is how Jesus has surely borne our griefs (Isaiah 53:4).Jesus paid the price of our redemption willingly, going like a lamb to the slaughter (Isaiah 53:7). In doing so, He fulfilled promises

God had made to Israel that He would forgive their sin (Isaiah 53:8). Jesus fulfilled this prophecy, as He was buried in a rich man's grave (Isaiah 53:9; cf. Matthew 28:57-60). Jesus was the offering for all our guilt (Isaiah 53:10), but He did not remain dead. Rather, He arose and will prosper—and Isaiah predicted that, too (Isaiah 53:10).Just as Jesus arose from the dead to show that He had conquered death, so it is for all who believe in Him they are given eternal life (John 3:16; 6:47). In this world, believers have new life (Ephesians 2:8-9) and new purpose and joy in life (Ephesians 2:10). While many in Jesus' day did not believe in or receive Him, as Isaiah foretold (Isaiah 53:1, 3), we all have the opportunity to believe in Him for eternal life (John 20:30-31). All who have believed in Him are born again as children of God (1 John 5:13), no longer guilty of sin and separated from Him. Because Jesus has surely borne our griefs (Isaiah 53:4), if we have believed in Him, we have peace with God (Romans 5:1).

Death Sacrifice and Atonement

Romans 5:8: "But God demonstrates his own love for us in this: While we were still sinners, Christ died for us."

1 Peter 2:24: "He himself bore our sins in his body on the tree, so that we might die to sins and live to righteousness; for by his wounds you have been healed."

Hebrews 2:14: "Since the children have flesh and blood, he also shared in their humanity so that through death he might destroy the one who has the power of death, that is, the devil, and set free those who all their lives were held in slavery by their fear of death."

Isaiah 53:5-6: "But he was pierced for our transgressions, he was crushed for our iniquities; the punishment that brought us peace was upon him, and by his wounds we are healed. All we like sheep have gone astray; we have all turned to our own way; and the Lord has laid on him the iniquity of us all."

Redemption and Forgiveness of Sins

John 3:16: "For God so loved the world that he gave his one and only Son, that whoever believes in him shall not perish but have eternal life."

Colossians 1:14: "In whom we have redemption through his blood, the forgiveness of sins."

Galatians 3:13: "Christ redeemed us from the curse of the law by becoming a curse for us, for it is written, 'Cursed is everyone who is hung on a tree.'"

Ephesians 1:7: "In him we have redemption through his blood, the forgiveness of sins, according to the riches of his grace."

Justification and Salvation

Romans 3:24: "and are justified by his grace as a gift, through the redemption that is in Christ Jesus."

Titus 2:14: "who gave himself for us to redeem us from all lawlessness and to purify for himself a people for his own possession, zealous for good works."

John 19:30: "When Jesus had received the sour wine, he said, 'It is finished.' And bowing his head, he breathed his last."

Because He was not just a mere man, Jesus did not come into existence at a specific point in time. He has always existed as the Son of God (John 1:1–5; 8:58). He chose to leave heaven and enter this world in the form of a human baby (Luke 1:35; Philippians 2:5–8). And, although His mother was human, His Father was God. Jesus Christ was fully God and fully man living this earthly life so that He could become the intermediary between sinful mankind and a holy Creator (1 Timothy 2:5). He suffered as we do, yet He never sinned (Hebrews 4:15). He always did what pleased His Father (John 8:29; 14:31). And when the time came, He offered Himself as the final sacrifice for our sins (John 10:18; 2 Corinthians 5:21).

Jesus was arrested and put on trial because He claimed to be God (John 5:18; 10:33). They crucified Him as it had been prophesied in Psalm 22 and Isaiah 53 (Luke 22:37). As He hung on the cross, Jesus became every sin that humanity has invented (2 Corinthians 5:21; 1 John 2:2). He paid in full the price; we owe God so that we could be considered righteous and forgiven. When He cried out, "It is finished!" (John 19:30), He was not referring to His earthly life, because He had already told His followers that God would raise Him from the dead in three days (Mark 9:31; 10:33-34). He meant that the plan to redeem fallen man, which He and the Father had known from the beginning, had now been completed (1 Peter 1:18-20; Acts 2:23; Ephesians 1:4). Jesus really did die physically and stayed dead for the better part of three days.

Jesus was buried in a borrowed tomb, because He would not be needing it for long (Matthew 27:59-60). The tomb was secured by Roman officials with a seal and a heavy boulder, making it nearly impossible to open. Then guards were assigned to keep watch for fear the disciples would try to steal the body and pretend He had risen as He had promised (Matthew 27:62-66). Everyone was familiar with Jesus' prediction, even though no one understood exactly what it meant (Mark 9:31-32). The guards were an extra precaution requested by the Jewish religious leaders in an effort to silence forever the new teachings Jesus of Nazareth had introduced into their culture. They figured that, once the Leader was dead and gone, the fervor of His followers would die down and things could go back to the way they had been.

Things would have settled down if Jesus had stayed in the tomb. If Jesus had not risen from the dead, He would have been no different from any other zealous reformer. In fact, Paul writes in 1 Corinthians 15:14 that, "if Christ has not been raised, our preaching is useless and so is your faith." Then in 1 Corinthians 17-19 he writes, "And if Christ has not been raised, your faith is futile; you are still in your sins. Then those also who have fallen asleep in Christ are lost. If only for this life we have hope in Christ, we are of all people most to be pitied."

But Jesus did not stay dead. On the third day, just as He had said, He walked out of that tomb (Matthew 28:2-10; Mark 16:4-7; Luke 24:1-8; John 20:1-8, 19). An angel knocked the guards out, kicked the stone out of the way, and sat on it, waiting for Jesus' friends to show up (Matthew 28:2; John 20:1, 11-12). For the next forty days, Jesus appeared to over five hundred people (1 Corinthians 15:3-7), demonstrating that He was indeed fully, physically alive (Luke 24:36-42). He then ascended back into heaven in the sight of His disciples (Luke 24:51; Acts 1:9-11).

Jesus is very much alive and is now seated at the right hand of the Father (Hebrews 1:3). He "ever lives" to make intercession for His people (Hebrews 7:25) and has promised that He will come again (John 14:3; Revelation 22:2). He endured separation from God (Matthew 27:46) so that we don't have to and conquered death so that we can, too (1 Corinthians 15:55). He has set Himself apart from every other religious leader because there is no grave with His name on it. There is no tomb with a body in it. Only the Son of God could die for the sins of the world and then rise from the dead. Because of His resurrection, all who place their trust in Him can have hope of a similar resurrection. Jesus is not dead, and because He lives, we can live in eternity with Him (John 3:16–18; 14:19).

His suffering, rejection, and wounds were not in vain. Instead, they carried immense significance for our salvation. Let's break it down

> ➤ ***Despised and Rejected:*** Jesus, the Suffering Servant, was despised and rejected by His Own. Despite His divinity, He willingly embraced our human experience, sharing in our sorrows and grief.
> ➤ ***Bearing Our Burdens:*** Jesus bore our griefs and carried our sorrows. His sacrifice on the cross was not only physical but also spiritual, taking upon Himself the weight of our sins.
> ➤ ***Wounded and Bruised:*** His wounds were not accidental; they were purposeful. Through His suffering, we find healing. His stripes represent our restoration and reconciliation with God.
> ➤ ***Our Waywardness:*** Like lost sheep, we had strayed from God's path. But Jesus, the Good Shepherd, took our iniquity upon Himself, bridging the gap between us and God.

Jesus paid it all! His sacrifice covers our sins, offers peace, and brings healing. May we embrace this truth and find redemption through His unmatched love and grace. Jesus' sacrifice on the cross was a gift of love, a demonstration of ultimate selflessness, and a path to redemption and salvation for all who believe in Him.

SEEK THE LORD WHILE HE MAY BE FOUND

In Isaiah 53, the prophet describes the ordeal of the Messiah who would bear His people's iniquity and suffer on their behalf (Isaiah 53 4-6). In the next chapter, Isaiah predicts the coming glory of Jerusalem and the restoration of God's people, who would know the "everlasting kindness" and compassion of God (Isaiah 54:8). Then, in Isaiah 55, the prophet extends God's invitation to partake freely of the promised blessings and experience God's "everlasting covenant" . This promise of restoration, forgiveness, and blessing would have been especially encouraging to the future generation of battered and bruised Jews returning from their exile in Babylon.

Through Isaiah, God compassionately called the surviving remnant of Israel to spiritual renewal. As part of that renewal, they would have to thoroughly abandon their sinful lifestyles and return to Him to receive the forgiveness the Messiah made possible (Isaiah 53). They would have to "seek the LORD while he may be found; call on him while he is near" (Isaiah 55:6).

Now was not the time for Israel to drag its feet. There would be a window of opportunity and no room for delay. With the instruction to "seek the Lord while He may be found," Isaiah stressed the urgency and seriousness of God's summons. The prophet Amos communicated the same sense of urgency, repeatedly issuing the Lord's appeal to "seek me and live" (Amos 5:4-7, 14-15). Dedicating our lives to the pursuit of God is a matter of life and death. If we procrastinate, the opportunity to respond to His invitation may run out.

This theme of exigency recurs in the Parable of the Great Banquet (Luke 14:12-24) and the Parable of the Wedding Feast (Matthew 22:1-14). Just as Isaiah called the remnant to come to the Lord's table to eat and drink (Isaiah 55:1-2), Jesus urged His primarily Jewish audience to "eat at the feast in the kingdom of God" (Luke 14:15). Through the parables, Jesus explained that the invited guests rejected the Master's offer, and thus the door of opportunity was closed to them. Since those invited refused to come, everyone in "the streets and alleys of the town, the poor, the crippled, the blind and the lame" were invited to come and dine (Luke 14:21).

Proverbs 1:20-33 illustrates how God's patience with fools those who refuse to listen to the voice of Wisdom eventually runs out: "I called you so often, but you wouldn't come. I reached out to you, but you paid no attention. You ignored my advice and rejected the correction I offered. So I will laugh when you are in trouble! I will mock you when disaster overtakes you, when calamity overtakes you like a storm, when disaster engulfs you like a cyclone, and anguish and distress overwhelm you. When they cry for help, I will not answer. Though they anxiously search for me, they will not find me" (Proverbs 1:24–28).

When we hear the voice of the Lord calling us to seek Him, inviting us to fellowship at His table, we must respond immediately while there is still time. "For God says, 'At just the right time, I heard you. On the day of salvation, I helped you.' Indeed, the 'right time' is now. Today is the day of salvation" (2 Corinthians 6:2). We are not promised tomorrow (Proverbs 27:1; Luke 12:16–21). As the psalmist urged, "Therefore let all the faithful pray to you while you may be found" (Psalm 32:6). Jesus taught us to stay focused and seek God's kingdom before and above all else (Matthew 6:33–34).

Seek the Lord while He may be found means to take up our cross and become His disciple (Mark 8:34) at this very moment, today. The command is accompanied by another command and a promise: "Let the wicked forsake their ways and the unrighteous their thoughts. Let them turn to the Lord, and he will have mercy on them, and to our God, for he will freely pardon" (Isaiah 55:7). We must repent of our sin and return to the Lord right now because there will come a day when our time is up. Scripture tells us to get ready, for the day of the Lord's return will come suddenly, "like a thief in the night" (1 Thessalonians 5:2; see also 2 Peter 3:10).

While we still have time, before it's too late, we must seek the Lord. God graciously promises to be found:

"You will seek the LORD your God and you will find him, if you search after him with all your heart and with all your soul" (Deuteronomy 4:29). Over and over throughout the Bible, God calls His people to repent, return to Him, and seek the Lord while He may be found (Deuteronomy 30:2–3; Leviticus 26:40–42; 2 Chronicles 15:4; Jeremiah 29:13–14).

Jesus said, "Then I will tell them plainly, 'I never knew you. Away from me, you evildoers!" (Matthew 7:23). It seems strange to hear our all-knowing Lord say there's something or someone He doesn't know. Jesus refers not to an intellectual knowledge here but to a relational knowledge. To understand a verse, always start with the context. Jesus is wrapping up His Sermon on the Mount with a final warning about true faith. Jesus predicts that false Christian prophets will be coming as wolves in sheep's clothing (Matthew 7:15). They may use all the right "God talk" and even make impressive displays of power, but they will not belong to the Lord.

"Not everyone who says to me, 'Lord, Lord,' will enter the kingdom of heaven, but only the one who does the will of my Father who is in heaven. Many will say to me on that day, 'Lord, Lord, did we not prophesy in your name and in your name drive out demons and, in your name, perform many miracles?' Then I will tell them plainly, 'I never knew you. Away from me, you evildoers!'" (Matthew 7:21–23). In Jesus' words on Judgment Day, we see several important truths: it's not a verbal claim that one follows Jesus, that saves (Matthew 7:21). Trifling Christianity cannot save. Also, it's not a demonstration of spiritual insight or power that saves. A person can seem like a Christian in the eyes of other people, yet still be an "evildoer" in God's sight and sent away from His presence. Only those who do the Father's will and who are known of God will enter heaven. So, what is the Father's will? Some men came to Jesus once with a question about what God required of them: "They asked him, 'What must we do, to do the works God requires?' Jesus answered, 'The work of God is this: to believe in the one he has sent" (John 6:28-29). God wants us to have faith in His Son: "This is his command: to believe in the name of his Son, Jesus Christ" (1 John 3:23). Those who are born again by faith in Christ will produce good works to the glory of God (Ephesians 2:10).

When Jesus said, "I never knew you," to the artificial disciples, He meant that, He never recognized them as His true disciples or His friends. He never had anything in common with them nor approved of them. They were no relations of His (Mark 3:34-35). Christ did not dwell in their hearts (Ephesians 3:17), nor did they have His mind (1 Corinthians 2:16). In all these ways and more, Jesus never knew them. Note that Jesus is not breaking off the relationship here, there was never a relationship to break off. Despite their high-sounding words and flamboyant displays of religious fervor, they had no intimacy with Christ. *It turns out that what matters isn't so much that we know God on some level, but that God knows us.* As Paul explained, "Whoever loves God is known by God" (1 Corinthians 8:3; also see Galatians 4:9). The Lord "tends His flock like a shepherd" (Isaiah 40:11), and He knows who are His sheep (John 10:14).

Those somber words, "I never knew you: depart from me, ye that work iniquity" in Matthew 7:23 (KJV) show that Jesus is indeed omniscient. He did not "know" them in the sense He would if they were His followers, but He knew their hearts! they were full of iniquity! Isaiah's condemnation of hypocrisy fits this group well: "These people come near to me with their mouth and honor me with their lips, but their hearts are far from me" (Isaiah 29:13). The evildoers whom Jesus does not know that are fake Christians, false teachers, and nominal adherents of religion.

Those who are bid depart from the presence of the Lord will not partake of the blessings of the kingdom: "Outside are the dogs, those who practice magic arts, the sexually immoral, the murderers, the idolaters and everyone who loves and practices falsehood" (Revelation 22:15). They will be cast "into the darkness, where there will be weeping and gnashing of teeth" (Matthew 8:12). Those fake Christians whom Jesus says He never knew *will not* produce the fruit of the Spirit (Galatians 5:22-23); rather, they will produce the opposite, the works of the flesh (Galatians 5:19-21). Jesus warns that one day He will tell a group of religious practitioners [certain

Church Folks], "I never knew you." God takes no delight in sending people to hell (2 Peter 3:9). But those who are told to depart have rejected God's eternal purpose and plan for their lives (Luke 7:30). They have rejected the light of the gospel (2 Corinthians 4:4), choosing the darkness instead, because their deeds were evil (John 3:19). At the judgment, they try to justify themselves as worthy of heaven on the basis of their works (prophecies, exorcisms, miracles, etc.), but no one will be justified by his own works (Galatians 2:16). While claiming to do all these good works in Christ's name, they failed to do the only work of God, that counts: "to have faith in the one he sent" (John 6:29). And so Jesus, the Righteous Judge, condemns them to eternal separation from Him.

John 3:16

John 3:16, "*For God so loved the world that He gave His only begotten Son, that whoever believes in Him should not perish but have everlasting life.*"

John 3:16 tells us of the love God has for us and the extent of that love is so great that He sacrificed His only Son on our behalf. ***John 3:16*** teaches us that anyone who believes in Jesus Christ, God's Son, will be saved. *John 3:16* gives us the glorious hope of eternal life in heaven through the love of God and death of Jesus Christ.

There is no more powerful way to deliver the message of redemption, reconciliation and salvation than to let ***John 3:16*** speak for itself.

THE PLAN OF SALVATION

Salvation is deliverance. The Bible makes it abundantly clear, however, that there is only one plan of salvation.

The most important thing to understand about the plan of salvation is that it is God's plan, not Man's plan. Man's plan of salvation would be observing religious rituals or obeying certain commands or achieving certain levels of spiritual enlightenment. But none of these things are part of God's plan of salvation.

GOD'S PLAN OF SALVATION – THE WHY

In God's plan of salvation, first we must understand why we need to be saved. Simply put, we need to be saved because we have sinned. The Bible declares that everyone has sinned (Ecclesiastes 7:20; Romans 3:23; 1 John 1:8). Sin is rebellion against God. We all choose to actively do things that are wrong. Sin harms others, damages us, and, most importantly, dishonors God. The Bible also teaches that, because God is holy and just, He cannot allow sin to go unpunished. The punishment for sin is death (Romans 6:23) and eternal separation from God (Revelation 20:11–15). Without God's plan of salvation, eternal death is the destiny of every human being.

GOD'S PLAN OF SALVATION – THE WHAT

In God's plan of salvation, God Himself is the only one who can provide for our salvation. We are utterly unable to save ourselves because of our sin and its consequences. God became a human being in the Person of Jesus Christ (John 1:1, 14). Jesus lived a sinless life (2 Corinthians 5:21; Hebrews 4:15; 1 John 3:5) and offered Himself as a perfect sacrifice on our behalf (1 Corinthians 15:3; Colossians 1:22; Hebrews 10:10). Since Jesus is God, His death was of infinite and eternal value. The death of Jesus Christ on the cross fully paid for the sins of the entire world (1 John 2:2). His resurrection from the dead demonstrated that His sacrifice was indeed sufficient and that salvation is now available.

GOD'S PLAN OF SALVATION – THE HOW

In Acts 16:31, a man asked the apostle Paul how to be saved. Paul's response was, "Believe in the Lord Jesus Christ and you will be saved." The way to follow God's plan of salvation is to believe. That is the only requirement (John 3:16; Ephesians 2:8-9). God has provided for our salvation through Jesus Christ. All we must do is receive it, by faith, fully trusting in Jesus alone as Savior (John 14:6; Acts 4:12). That is God's plan of salvation.

God's plan of salvation – Will you receive it?

If you are ready to follow God's plan of salvation, place your faith in Jesus as your Savior and commit to Gods Will. Change your mind from embracing sin and rejecting God to rejecting sin and embracing God through Jesus

Christ. Fully trust in the sacrifice of Jesus as the perfect and complete payment for your sins. If you do this, God's Word promises that you will be saved, your sins will be forgiven, and you will spend eternity in heaven. There is no more important decision. Place your faith in Jesus Christ as your Savior today!

CHRIST KINGDOM AUTHORITY

The Heavenly Father gave full authority to his Son Jesus Christ. The Son is entrusted with authority equal to his Father. In return, the Son always does the will of his Father, and exercises his authority in complete harmony and unity with the Father. There is no inconsistency here. Although the two may have equal authority, one may defer to the other without any loss of authority. The authority of Jesus Christ is given to Him by the Father. It was always given, never borrowed, never withdrawn. The Son is commended with authority equal to his Father. He keeps that trust by exercising his authority always in deference to his Father. It was ever so; and so it shall ever be. *Ephesians 1:11* states, "*God works all things according to the counsel of his will*".

Sovereignty is authority. Where God's sovereignty is most manifested is through His Son Jesus Christ. How is this so? Jesus has dominion over all things because He paid the penalty for sin and rose to life in victorious power.

JESUS SOVEREIGN AUTHORITY

- ➤ *Matthew 28:18:* "Then Jesus came to them and said, 'All authority in heaven and on earth has been given to me."

- ➤ *John 17:2:* "You have given him authority over all flesh, so that he can give eternal life to all those you have given him."

- ➤ *Colossians 1:15-17:* "He is the image of the invisible God, the firstborn of all creation. For by him all things were created, in heaven and on earth, visible and invisible, whether thrones or dominions or rulers or authorities all things were created through him and for him. And he is before all things, and in him all things hold together."

JESUS DEMONSTRATED AUTHORITY

Jesus' authority was never borrowed or withdrawn. It was always given to Him by the Father, and He exercises it in deference to the Father. His life, death, and resurrection demonstrate divine authority over sin and death. He is the King of kings and Lord of lords (Revelation 19:16). As believers, we participate in His mission, knowing that the sovereign God empowers us to fulfill it.

- ➤ **Mark 4:39:** "Then he stood up and rebuked the wind and said to the waves, 'Quiet! Be still!' And the wind ceased, and there was a great calm."
- ➤ **John 11:43-44:** "When he had said this, he cried out with a loud voice, 'Lazarus, come out!' The man who had died came out, wrapped in linen with his face wrapped in a cloth. Jesus said, 'Untie him, and let him go.'"
- ➤ **Matthew 8:32:** "And behold, demons came out of the man and entered the pigs, and the herd, numbering about two thousand, ran violently down the steep bank into the sea, and perished in the waters."

DECREED AUTHORITY

Jesus Himself proclaimed the kingdom of God during His earthly ministry. His words and deeds demonstrated His authority. Although all authority had been given to Him, beyond empty words, He outwardly emulated the life he sought in His believers. Jesus cared for people practically, addressing their real needs. Living out His devout humility also serving His own disciples. "**Philippians 2:9-11**" Therefore God exalted him to the highest place and gave him the name that is above every name, that at the name of Jesus every knee should bow, in heaven and on earth and under the earth, and every tongue confess that Jesus Christ is Lord, to the glory of God the Father." Jesus' authority is both declarative and applied. His proclamation as the Son of God resonates throughout the ages of history, His holy spirit filled believers continue to operate in His authority as they declare His truth of Gods word in humility while serving others. 🫱 🕊️

- ➢ Mark 2:5-7: "When Jesus saw their faith, he said to the paralytic, 'Son, your sins are forgiven.' Now some experts in the law were sitting there, reasoning in their hearts, 'Why does this fellow talk like that? He's blaspheming! Who can forgive sins but God alone?"
- ➢ John 5:17-18: "But Jesus answered them, 'My Father is working until now, and I am working.' For this reason, the Jews sought all the more to kill him, because he not only broke the Sabbath, but also called God his own Father, making himself equal with God."
- ➢ John 10:30: "I and the Father are one."

JESUS DISCIPLESHIP AND AUTHORITY

Jesus delegated authority to His disciples, and this authority extends to us today. As His followers, we operate in His name, knowing that His authority empowers us to fulfill His mission.

- ➢ **Matthew 10:1:** "He called his twelve disciples to him and gave them authority to drive out unclean spirits and to heal every disease and every sickness."

➢ **Luke 9:1:** "Then Jesus summoned the twelve and gave them power and authority over all demons and to cure diseases, and he sent them out to proclaim the kingdom of God and to heal."

➢ **John 14:12:** "Truly, truly, I say to you, whoever believes in me will do the works I have done, and he will do even greater works than these, because I go to the Father."

In the beginning was the Word, and the Word was with God, and the Word was God. He was in the beginning with God. All things were made through Him, and without Him nothing was made that was made. In Him was life, and the life was the light of men. And the light shines in the darkness, and the darkness did not comprehend it. (John 1:1-5) He so loved the world that He gave His only Son, Jesus Christ (John 3:16). Jesus, the Word who was with God and was God (John 1:1), came to earth, taking the very nature of a servant and being made in human likeness (Philippians 2:7). He taught us to love the Lord our God with all our heart, soul, and mind, and to love our neighbors as ourselves (Matthew 22:37-39). Yet, we all have sinned and fall short of the glory of God (Romans 3:23). But God demonstrates His own love for us in this: while we were still sinners, Christ died for us (Romans 5:8). Through His death and resurrection, we have been justified by faith and have peace with God (Romans 5:1). Now, there is no condemnation for those who are in Christ Jesus (Romans 8:1), for if anyone is in Christ, he is a new creation (2

Corinthians 5:17). We are to set our minds on things above, not on earthly things (Colossians 3:2), and to trust in the Lord with all our heart and lean not on our own understanding (Proverbs 3:5). Therefore, if anyone is in Christ, he is a new creation; old things have passed away; behold, all things have become new"(2 Corinthians 5:17) For whom the Son sets free is free indeed (John 8:36) For we know that in all things God works for the good of those who love Him (Romans 8:28), and He has promised that He will never leave us nor forsake us (Hebrews 13:5). Therefore, we can approach God's throne of grace with confidence, so that we may receive mercy and find grace to help us in our time of need (Hebrews 4:16). His invitation is personal, intimate and heartfelt. Just as we receive invitations to special occasions, Jesus invites us to embrace a relationship with Him. He offers Himself to lost, sinner and sick. Surely, He is married to the backslider. Jesus promises not to turn away those who seek Him. His invitation echoes through time: "Ask, seek, knock" (Matthew 7:7-8). He invites us to not unto "religion" but "Relationship". In a world of social media and thousands of friends, we can't invest deeply in everyone. But with Jesus, it's different.

We can spend time with Him, learn from Him, and experience His love and grace. He invites us to partner with Him in His eternal redemptive plan of redemption and salvation. Jesus invites us into a relationship because He knows our deepest needs, desires and struggles. He longs for intimacy with us, and offers Himself as the answer and the antidote. Accepting His invitation transforms our lives taking back which was lost and stolen through the storms of life.

*God is inviting you into a
relationship with Him today!*

The Salvation Prayer!

Father, it is written in Your Word that if I confess with my mouth that Jesus is Lord and believe in my heart that You have raised Him from the dead, I shall be saved.

Father, I confess that Jesus is my Lord. I make Him my Lord and Savior right now. I believe in my heart and confess with my mouth that You raised Jesus from the dead. I renounce my past life with satan and close the door to any of his devices. I thank You for forgiving all my sins through the cost of shed blood. Jesus is my Lord, and I am a new creation. Old things have passed away; now all things become new in Jesus' name. Amen.

" Therefore, if anyone is in Christ, he is a new creation; old things have passed away; behold, all things have become new"*2 Corinthians 5:17*

For God so loved the world that He gave His only begotten Son, that whoever believes in Him should not perish but have everlasting life.

John 3.16

John 11:43-44

PRAYER OF A SECOND WIND

"He was in the world, and the world was made through Him, and the world did not know Him. He came to His own, and His own did not receive Him. But as many as received Him, to them He gave the right to become children of God, to those who believe in His name: who were born, not of blood, nor of the will of the flesh, nor of the will of man, but of God.(John 1: 10-13) And the Word became flesh and dwelt among us, and we beheld His glory, the glory as of the only begotten of the Father, full of grace and truth. John bore witness of Him and cried out, saying, "This was He of whom I said, 'He who comes after me is preferred before me, for He was before me." And of His fullness we have all received, and grace for grace. For the law was given through Moses, but grace and truth came through Jesus Christ. No one has seen God at any time. The only begotten Son, who is in the bosom of the Father, He has declared Him"

In *John 1,* the disciple John affirms Jesus Christ as the Son of God. He emphasizes that while the Law was given through Moses, grace and truth came through Jesus Christ. John describes Jesus as the Word that became flesh and dwelt among us, full of grace and truth. He asserts that Jesus, despite being in the world and being the one through whom the world was made, was not recognized by the world. He further states that Jesus came to His own, but His own did not receive Him. However, those who did receive Him were given the right to become children of God. This birth into God's family is not of blood, nor of the will of the flesh, nor of the will of man, but of God. John bore witness of Jesus, declaring that Jesus, who came after him, is preferred before him because He was before him. John also proclaims that from Jesus' fullness, we have all received grace upon grace. Lastly, John confirms that no one has seen God at any time, but the only begotten Son, who is in the bosom of the Father, has declared Him. This passage thus serves as a powerful testament to Jesus Christ's divinity, supremacy, His authority and His role as deliverer of grace and truth.

FROM THE BEGINNING

> ➤ In the beginning was the Word (Jesus), and the Word was with God, and the Word was God *(John 1:1).*

➢ Through Him, all things were made; without Him, nothing was made that has been made *(John 1:3)*.

➢ In Him was life, and that life was the light of all mankind. The light shines in the darkness, and the darkness has not overcome it *(John 1:4-5)*.

GOD'S LOVE AND SALVATION

➢ For God so loved the world that He gave His one and only Son, Jesus Christ *(John 3:16)*.

➢ The Word became flesh and made His dwelling among us *(John 1:14)*.

➢ I am the way, the truth, and the life, no man cometh unto the Father, but by me. *(John 4:6)*.

➢ For all have sinned and fallen short of the glory of God *(Romans 3:23)*.

➢ But God demonstrates His own love for us in this: While we were still sinners, Christ died for us *(Romans 5:8)*.

SPIRITUAL RENOVATION AND NEW LIFE THROUGH JESUS

➢ Therefore, since we have been justified through faith, we have peace with God through our Lord Jesus Christ *(Romans 5:1)*.

➢ Therefore, there is now no condemnation for those who are in Christ Jesus *(Romans 8:1)*.

➤ Therefore, if anyone is in Christ, the new creation has come: The old has gone, the new is here! (*2 Corinthians 5:17*).

➤ Trust in the LORD with all your heart and lean not on your own understanding (*Proverbs 3:5*).

FREEDOM AND HOPE IN CHRIST JESUS

➤ It is for freedom that Christ has set us free (*Galatians 5:1*).

➤ And we know that in all things God works for the good of those who love Him, who have been called according to His purpose (*Romans 8:28*).

➤ Let us then approach God's throne of grace with confidence, so that we may receive mercy and find grace to help us in our time of need (*Hebrews 4:16*).

RECONCILIATION TO CHRIST IS A PERSONAL JOURNEY THAT INVOLVES SEVERAL KEY STEPS:

➤ *Acknowledgment of Self-Sin (Not your Neighbor Sin*): Recognize and admitting that you have sinned and fallen short of God's glory.

➤ *Repentance*: Feel genuine remorse for your sins, and make a conscious decision to "*repent*" and "*turn*" away from your sinful ways.

➤ *Full Faith and Belief in Jesus Christ*: Have faith in Jesus Christ, acknowledging that He died on the cross for our sins and was resurrected.

- ➤ *Acceptance of Salvation*: Accept the gift of salvation offered through Jesus Christ.
- ➤ *Obedience to Gods Will and Not our Own*: Strive to live according to God's commandments and teachings.

TO BE RECONCILED TO CHRIST

Jesus offers reconciliation, not just forgiveness, by bridging the gap between a sinful humanity and sinless God. Jesus Christ sacrifice at Calvery serves as the definitive payment for our sins, paving the way for salvation through full faith and belief. Reconciliation, however, extends beyond a mere pardon. It signifies an unfathomable transfiguration and restoration of unity to God our father through the Son Jesus Christ. The Gospel embodies this message despite man's repeated sinful transgressions, Jesus though His priceless sacrifice of shed blood and death provides an acceptable path back to God through belief, emulation, repentance and adherence to His teachings. By embracing this path, we unlock the door to restored salvation and spiritual wholeness.

TIME FOR EFFECTUAL PRAYER PRAYER OF SURRENDER, REPENTANCE & RECONCILIATION

Our Father, only wise God, which art in the heavens, hallowed be the name. We bow in complete surrender to you. Acknowledging that your Will be done on earth as it is in heaven. Today we draw near to your throne of grace, we wash our hands and purify our hearts. Your word says that if your people, who are called by Your name, will humble themselves and pray and seek Your face and turn from their wicked ways, then you will hear from heaven, you will forgive their sin and heal their land. Whoever conceals their sins does not prosper, but the one who confesses and renounces them, they find mercy. Therefor we willfully repent of our sins with Godly Sorrow before you, understanding that the "Kingdom of Heaven is at hand. Have mercy on us "O God, of Our Salvation" according to Your lovingkindness; and your tender mercies, blot out our transgressions although we are not worthy, we ask that you wash us thoroughly from our iniquity, and cleanse us from our sins committed before you. We were brought forth in iniquity, in sin, our mothers conceived us. Father God hide Your face from our sins, blot out all our iniquities. May our names be written in the Lambs book of life, for life! For surely the heavens rejoice over the 1 who repents opposed to the 99 who don't. We produce good fruit in keeping with our repentance. We repent willfully that we will not perish.

Weeping may endure for a night but joy cometh in the morning, through your grace and mercy. Though he slay me, yet, will I trust in your plan for my life. You know the way in which I should take and when you have tried me , I am coming fourth as pure Gold. Forgive me my trespasses, as I forgive those who trespass against me.

Your anger be for a moment but your love for a lifetime. You love this world so much you gave your only begotten Son that who so ever believeth on Him shall not parish but have everlasting life. If Christ be lifted up, He'll draw all men unto Him! He who forgave my sins and healed all of my diseases. Lead us from temptation and deliver us from evil. If God be for us that's better than the whole world against us. Surely Jesus is the way , the truth and the life. No one gets to the Father except through the Son! Rejected and despised for 'many". Jesus Paid it all ! to Him all I Owe. Thank You for taking up the cross meant for me. Wounded for our transgressions, bruised for our iniquities; The chastisement of our peace was upon Him. By His stripes we are healed. The Lamb of God committed no violence, nor was any deceit in His mouth. He bore our sins and paid a debt we could never afford to pay! You already proved who you are when you poured your soul out unto death, making intercession for the transgressors. For to this end Christ died and lived again, that He might be Lord both of the dead and of the living. Surely your living was not in vain, If we stay steadfast, may we find eternal gain. Greater is He that is in me, than he that is in this world. Jesus Christ is the "resurrection" and the "life". He who believes in the only true 'Son of God" though he dies, he lives. New Birth to a living Hope, hallelujah! We believe that Jesus died and rose again, the place where he lay is empty, He rose again just like he said. I know my redeemer liveth and will stand upon a hill one day as the heavens rejoice. Father God, thank you for hearing and answering our prayer believing that it is already done! Thank you, Jesus, for interceding for me and taking your precious prayers before your father, I thank you for giving me the victory this day! I lift up the name of Jesus, I give you all the glory, all the honor and all the praise. I thank you now for my , healing, my deliverance and my salvation. I shout the victory now. For whom the son sets free is free indeed. Broad is the way and narrow is the gate that leadeth to destruction, only few will find it. No condemnation for those who are in Christ foreal and not for fake! When the kindness and the love of God our Savior toward man appeared, not by works of righteousness which we have done, but according to His mercy He saved us, through the washing of regeneration and renewing of the Holy Spirit, whom He poured out on us abundantly through Jesus Christ our Savior, that having been justified by His grace we should become heirs according to the hope of eternal life. This is love, not that we loved God, but that he loved us first and sent his Son as an atoning sacrifice for our sins. God reconciled us to himself through Christ and gave us the ministry of reconciliation. Praise your name that anointing be upon me! Crucified with Christ bearing His marks in my own flesh. I boldly confess I shall live and not die. I will live to do the works of my Father, according to His Will and not my own. To heal the broken hearted, to preach the gospel to the poor, to preach deliverance to the captives, and recovering sight to those who are blind. I will live to set at liberty them that are bruised and to tell the goodness of the Lord in the land of the living. For when the Holy Ghost fall upon me I shall have power. I will live Lord to shout and claim the victory of the cross and overall satanic forces of my life. Thank You Jesus for all you have done for me. I will never forget the price you paid for a sinner like me at "Calvary's Cross"!

Father, I thank You for saving me from `the vicious wrath of death and everlasting punishment. If when I was Your enemy, I was reconciled to You through the death of Your Son, much more, having been reconciled, I shall be saved by His life, death and resurrection as it is prophesized. I also rejoice in You through my Lord Jesus Christ, through whom I have now received reconciliation. I shall rejoice in You and be glad in the name of Jesus.

I accept your plan of salvation for my life! Father, it is written in Your Word that if I confess with my mouth that Jesus is Lord and believe in my heart that You have raised Him from the dead, I shall be saved. Father, I confess that Jesus is my Lord. I make Him my Lord and Savior right now. I believe in my heart and confess with my mouth that You raised Jesus from the dead. I renounce my past life with satan and close the door to any of his devices. I thank You for forgiving all my sins through the cost of shed blood. Jesus is my Lord, and I am a new creation. Old things have passed away; now all things become new in Jesus' name.

I seal this prayer in the name and by the blood of the Promised Risen Messiah, that it can't be un-done. In Jesus Mighty and Majestic name! Amen.

Romans 5:9-11

FALLING IN LOVE WITH JESUS! WAS THE BEST THING IVE EVER DONE

F alling in Love with Jesus has unequivocally been the best thing I ever did. Undeniably there is no other man, profit, god, Archbishop, disciple, teacher or chief priests that has ever accomplished the astonishing things that Jesus Christ has accomplished during his short life within his ministry on earth. He rebuked with a stern hand but loved with a soft heart. That no one will be deprived of the gift of "eternal life". Indeed, there are so many accomplishments I cannot possibly list them all here. Many will argue that He, in an unconventional, nonconformist way built His own "Kingdom Movement" on earth in the unprecedented way he delivered the "*Good News of The Gospel*". He revolutionized a "Spiritual Kingdom Movement" on earth that opened a door to salvation, otherwise closed to the lost, sick and sinners. A faithful Lord to the faithless. In every aspect of his life, he was victorious and the sword of victory is what he brought from heaven. The cruciality of His shed Blood as an atonement was legal and mandatory in satisfying the will of God. His sacrificial death on the cross reconciled us to God opening the door to eternal life, that those who believes shall by no means be cast out *John 3 16.* His shed blood satisfied a death that no amount of money on earth could do, that the Redeemed of God may declare it. With all deliberate intension He build his squad of disciples from scratch. Not interested in credentials he didn't seek out or call the qualified, He charismatically qualified all whom He chose. They were every day men , and when called before the Sanhedrin some were classified as "unschooled men". One can only imagine how it must have angered the chief priest, elders, and leaders of the synagogues when he brazenly bi-passed all of their scholarly knowledge, wisdom, credentials and accolades unapologetically employing fishermen and tax collectors. A few of which didn't even have employment statuses documented. Yes indeed, He did it His way while enforcing it Gods way. His distinctive, authoritative doctrines often challenged the status quo and established religious and social traditions of His time. He confronted hypocrisy and rebuked religious hypocrites outrightly. He advocated for the cast out, marginalized, lost and the sinners. Boldly He emphasized Compassion, Mercey, Love, Repentance and Gods Will, opposed to fruitless, unprofitable ritualistic religious practices that served as satisfying man's ego opposed to satisfying the "Emphatical Will of God". His authority was conjoined parallel to his victory and He indeed was victorious like no other. Jesus Christ was victorious over, *sin, death, satan, sickness and disease, over nature, heaven & earth, over injustice and oppression, temptation, death, hell the grave and abyss. Consequently, He was also victorious over thirst & famine, persecution, over hypocrisy, over demons, over false prophesy, over the tomb and even entrapment.* While other Prophets may have been virtuous, upright men of valor, no other man, prophet , priest has accomplished such achievements. Not Moses, Mohammed, not Buddha, not Ghandi or Confucius not one of them. They all lay in their graves while Jesus Boldy defeated death just like he said He would. Teaching, inspiring, warning and uplifting Jesus was the ultimate "Supreme Teacher" who offered a free education to all who so desired. His out-door religious institutions did not require fees or high price tuitions. His only pre-requisite was "ears to hear" and a "willing heart". He taught un-paralleled heavenly wisdom where ever He saw fit. He taught in the fields, on the mountains, in the synagogues, in the dessert wherever the Holy Spirit led Him. He didn't just sit by waiting for the seats of the synagogues to fill up, rather He bought the true gospel of the synagogue to the streets. While the cost of discipleship is rather costly on earth its benefits of entering into eternal like is priceless. As a woman and "Ambassador for Christ", I feel comfortable, safe, loved, respected and adorned entering into His gates with thanks giving and His courts with praise. Throughout His Life and ministerial call, He persistently showed women unmerited, respect, adoration and love breaking down societal barriers that often oppressed and ostracized locking up their bestowed spiritual gifts into a box. Rather He taught them or they willing appeared for teachings. He healed them when they were sick, He rebuke them when they were wrong but ministered to them when they were lost. He did not condone capital punishment measures of stoning for sinful women rather a stern rebuke and a second chance reminding us that He without sin should cast ye the first stone. His weapons of choice were "non-violent weapons of rebuke", ministry, insight to Gods commandments, compassion and love . Surely Jesus had much opportunity to stone all of the sinful women He encountered however utilizing mercy, grace and compassion, He healed them and delivered them from their demons. Stoning is a form of capital punishment that is still used in various parts of the world today. According to NBC News and Wikipedia.org, stoning is still legal in Afghanistan, Iran, sections of Nigeria, Pakistan, Sudan, and the United Arab Emirates among other various nations. While Stoning is a _relatively rare_ means of capital punishing to those who commit adultery under Islamic Law. It is still prevalent today and is considered a form of community or street justice. In retrospect Jesus didn't oppress the women, he loved on them and taught them as well as men, that that their salvation may not be robbed by the devil. Jesus wants everybody to come to know Him and receive His Salvation, male and female. Not everyone has the same role to play, even though we all have the same purpose in sharing the Gospel of Christ. The Gift of salvation is afforded to all who believe irregardless to sex, race or origin. Though He is with us to the end of the world. He has been faithful through the ages. In retrospect, that's why the relationship you cultivate with Jesus Christ will cement the foundation for every other relationship you establish on earth. Indeed, I reiterate " Falling in Love with Jesus is the best thing, I ever done!

WORKS CITED

Radmacher, E. D. (1978). **NKJV Study Bible**, *Full Color Edition: A Complete and Reliable Guide to Studying God's Word* (3rd ed.). Thomas Nelson. https://www.thomasnelsonbibles.com/product/nkjv-study-bible-full-color/.

Hudson, C. D. (Ed.). (2011). **The KJV Study** *Bible: Red Letter Edition.* Barbour Publishing. https://www.barbourbooks.com/bibles/king-james-version.

Nelson, Thomas. "**The Woman's Study Bible**, NKJV: Receiving Gods truth for Balance, Hope and Transformation." *Thomas Nelson*, n.d., https://www.thomasnelsonbibles.com/product/nkjv-womans-study-bible/. Accessed 4 February 2023.

Bible Study Tools. "New King James Version NKJV: About the New King James Version." *Bible Study Tools*, n.d., https://www.biblestudytools.com/nkjv/. Accessed 4 February 2023.

OpenBible.info. "Topical Bible: 77 Bible Verses about Sinew." *OpenBible.info*, n.d., www.openbible.info/topics/sinew. Accessed 4 February 2023.

Bible Gateway. "Verse of the Day." *Bible Gateway*, n.d.,
    https://www.biblegateway.com/. Accessed 4 February 2023.

King James Bible Online. "Matthew 28:19: "Go ye therefore, and
    teach all nations, baptizing them in the name of the Father,
    and of the Son, and of the Holy Ghost"." *King James*
    version, n.d.,
    https://www.kingjamesbibleonline.org/Matthew-28-19/.
    Accessed 4 February 2023.

King James Bible Online. "Isaiah 25:8: "He will swallow up death
    in victory; and the Lord GOD will wipe away tears from off
    all faces." *King James version*, n.d.,
    https://www.kingjamesbibleonline.org/Isaiah-25-8/.
    Accessed 4 February 2023.

King James Bible Online. "Hebrews 4:15." *King James version*,
    n.d., https://www.kingjamesbibleonline.org/Hebrews-4-15/.
    Accessed 4 February 2023.

King James Bible Online. "John 12:31 - 12:33: Now viewing
    scripture range from the book of John chapter 12:31 through
    chapter 12:33." *King James version*, n.d.,
    https://www.kingjamesbibleonline.org/John-12-31_12-33/.
    Accessed 4 February 2023.

King James Bible Online. "Matthew 8:2 - 8:3: Now viewing
    scripture range from the book of Matthew chapter 8:2
    through chapter 8:3. *King James Bible Online,* n.d.,
    https://www.kingjamesbibleonline.org/Matthew-8-2_8-3/.
    Accessed 4 February 2023.

King James Bible Online. "Matthew 9:2 - 9:8: Now viewing
    scripture range from the book of Matthew chapter 9:2
    through chapter 9:8." *King James Bible Online*, n.d.,

https://www.kingjamesbibleonline.org/Matthew-9-2_9-8/. Accessed 4 February 2023.

King James Bible Online. "Mark 4:35 - 4:41: Now viewing scripture range from the book of Mark chapter 4:35 through chapter 4:41." *King James Bible Online,* n.d., https://www.kingjamesbibleonline.org/Mark-4-35_4-41/. Accessed 4 February 2023.

King James Bible Online. "Matthew 28:18: "And Jesus came and spake unto them, saying, All power is given unto me in heaven and in earth"." King James Version, n.d., https://www.kingjamesbibleonline.org/Matthew-28-18/. Accessed 4 February 2023.

King James Bible Online. "John 11:1 - 11:44: Now viewing scripture range from the book of John chapter 11:1 through chapter 11:44." *King James Bible Online,* n.d., https://www.kingjamesbibleonline.org/John-11-1_11-44/. Accessed 4 February 2023.

King James Bible Online. "Matthew 5:3 - 5:12: Now viewing scripture range from the book of Matthew chapter 5:3 through chapter 5:12." *King James Bible Online,* n.d., https://www.kingjamesbibleonline.org/Matthew-5-3_5-12/. Accessed 4 February 2023.

King James Bible Online. "Hebrews 2:18: "For in that he himself hath suffered being tempted, he is able to succour them that are tempted"." *King James Bible Online,* n.d., https://www.kingjamesbibleonline.org/Hebrews-2-18/. Accessed 4 February 2023.

King James Bible Online. "Matthew 28:5 - 28:7: Now viewing scripture range from the book of Matthew chapter 28:5 through chapter 28:7." *King James Bible Online,* n.d.,

387

https://www.kingjamesbibleonline.org/Matthew-28-5_28-7/. Accessed 4 February 2023.

King James Bible Online. "Ephesians 4:9: "Now that he ascended, what is it but that he also descended first into the lower parts of the earth?"." *King James Bible Online*, n.d., https://www.kingjamesbibleonline.org/Ephesians-4-9/. Accessed 4 February 2023.

King James Bible Online. "1 Corinthians 15:55: "O death, where is thy sting? O grave, where is thy victory?"." *King James Bible Online*, n.d., https://www.kingjamesbibleonline.org/1-Corinthians-15-55/. Accessed 4 February 2023.

King James Bible Online. "Revelation 20:1 - 20:3: Now viewing scripture range from the book of Revelation chapter 20:1 through chapter 20:3." *King James Bible Online*, n.d., https://www.kingjamesbibleonline.org/Revelation-20-1_20-3/._Accessed 4 February 2023.

King James Bible Online. "Matthew 15:32 – 28: Now viewing scripture range from the book of Matthew chapter 15:32 through chapter 28." *King James Bible Online*, n.d., https://www.kingjamesbibleonline.org/Matthew-15-32_39/. Accessed 4 February 2023.

King James Bible Online. "John 7:39: "(But this spake he of the Spirit, which they that believe on him should receive: for the Holy Ghost was not yet given; because that Jesus was not yet glorified.)"." *King James Bible Online*, n.d., https://www.kingjamesbibleonline.org/John-7-39/. Accessed 4 February 2023.

King James Bible Online. "Matthew 5:10 - 5:12: Now viewing scripture range from the book of Matthew chapter 5:10

through chapter 5:12." *King James Bible Online*, n.d., https://www.kingjamesbibleonline.org/Matthew-5-10_5-12/. Accessed 4 February 2023.

King James Bible Online. "Matthew 15:7 - 15:9: Now viewing scripture range from the book of Matthew chapter 15:7 through chapter 15:9." *King James Bible Online*, n.d., https://www.kingjamesbibleonline.org/Matthew-15-7_15-9/. Accessed 4 February 2023.

King James Bible Online. "Matthew 12:22 - 12:28: Now viewing scripture range from the book of Matthew chapter 12:22 through chapter 12:28." *King James Bible Online*, n.d., https://www.kingjamesbibleonline.org/Matthew-12-22_12-28/. Accessed 4 February 2023.

King James Bible Online. "Jeremiah 23:16." *King James Bible Online*, n.d., https://www.kingjamesbibleonline.org/Jeremiah-23-16/. Accessed 4 February 2023.

King James Bible Online. "2 Timothy 4:3 - 4:4: Now viewing scripture range from the book of 2 Timothy chapter 4:3 through chapter 4:4." *James Bible Online*, n.d., https://www.kingjamesbibleonline.org/2-Timothy-4-3_4-4/. Accessed 4 February 2023.

Storms, Sam. "10 things you should know about the christus victor theory of the atonement." *Sam Storms*, n.d., www.samstorms.org/enjoying-god-blog/post/10-things-you-should-know-about-the-christus-victor-theory-of-the-atonement. Accessed 4 February 2023.

Gane, Roy. "Altar Call: Part V: Jesus Isn't Finished with Me Yet." *SDAnet's At Issue*, n.d., www.sdanet.org/atissue/books/altar/altar5-finish.htm. Accessed 4 February 2023.

Howard, Molly. "Weekly Devotional: Jesus Paid It All." *Grand Canyon University*, 16 July 2021, https://www.gcu.edu/blog/spiritual-life/weekly-devotional-jesus-paid-it-all. Accessed 4 February 2023.

Wikipedia. "Capital punishment in Judaism" https://en.wikipedia.org/wiki/Capital_punishment_in_Judaism, 12 December 2023, n.d.,

BibleGateway "Galatians 3:13-15: GOD'S WORD Translation." *Bible Gateway*, n.d., https://www.biblegateway.com/passage/?search=Galatians%203:13-15&version=GW. Accessed 4 February 2023.

C.S. Lewis Institute "Matthew 28:19-20: UNDERSTANDING THE GREAT COMMISSION: Jesus last command" n.d., https://www.cslewisinstitute.org/resources/understanding-the-great-commission/ 1 September, 2020

OPES DEI "Matthew 22 :34-30 "Commentary on the Gospel: The Great Commandment" n.d., https://opusdei.org/en/gospel/commentary-on-the-gospel-the-great-commandment/ Accessed 28 December 2023.

Jesus Film Project – A Crue Ministry "John 13:15" "Commentary on the Gospel: Jesus Washing the Disciples' Feet: Accessed 17 2022 https://www.jesusfilm.org/blog/jesus-washing-the-disciples-feet/

Bibletools.org Resurrection of Just and Unjust "John 5:29" "Commentary on Resurrection of Just and Unjust" Accessed 14 April 2024 https://www.bibletools.org/index.cfm/fuseaction/Topical.show/RTD/cgg/ID/20864/Resurrection-Just-Unjust.htm

A. C. University "Basic Biblical Beliefs Lacking Among Most
        Pastors in All U.S. Denominations, All Church Roles"
        Accessed 30 August 2022
        https://www.arizonachristian.edu/2022/08/30/basic-
        biblical-beliefs-lacking-among-most-pastors-in-all-u-s-
        denominations/

McLelland, Kristi " Women and Jesus" : What can we learn from
        what the Bible says about Jesus and women?
        https://www.gotquestions.org/Jesus-and-women.html
        gotquestions.org, n.d. Accessed 12 February 2023

Gotquestions.org " What can we learn from what the Bible says
        about Jesus and women? https://www.gotquestions.org/it-
        is-finished.html gotquestions.org, n.d. Accessed 16 February
        2023

Gotquestions.org "What does John 3:16 mean?"
        https://www.gotquestions.org/John-3-16.html
        gotquestions.org, n.d. Accessed 23 April 2023